DEBATES ON EARLY CHILDHOOD POLICIES AND PRACTICES

Globally, early years policies and documents have set out aspirational outcomes and benefits for children, their families and the wider society. These policies have emphasised the place of early childhood provision within the wider global agenda, by tackling inequality and disadvantage early on in children's lives. However, these strategies have also raised further debates regarding the way they have informed and shaped curricula frameworks and pedagogical approaches.

The international team of contributors to this book argues that if these issues are not explicitly acknowledged, understood, critiqued and negotiated, emerging policies and documents may potentially lead to the disadvantaging, marginalising and even pathologising of certain childhoods.

Divided into two parts, the volume demonstrates the dialectic nature of both policy and practice. The chapters in this wide-ranging text:

- explore and articulate the philosophical premises and values that underpin current early childhood policy, curricula and pedagogies;
- explicitly acknowledge and articulate some of the potential conflicts and challenges they present;
- provide examples of divergent and creative pedagogical thinking;
- highlight opportunities for enabling pedagogical cultures and encounters.

Debates on Early Childhood Policies and Practices is aimed at a wide readership including academics and researchers in early years education, policy makers, undergraduate and postgraduate students, practitioners and early childhood professionals.

Theodora Papatheodorou, PhD and MBPsS, is an early childhood educator and researcher.

DEBATES ON EARLY CHILDHOOD POLICIES AND PRACTICES

Global snapshots of pedagogical thinking and encounters

Edited by Theodora Papatheodorou

Routledge
Taylor & Francis Group

LONDON AND NEW YORK

First published 2012
by Routledge
2 Park Square, Milton Park, Abingdon, Oxon OX14 4RN

Simultaneously published in the USA and Canada
by Routledge
711 Third Avenue, New York, NY 10017

Routledge is an imprint of the Taylor & Francis Group, an informa business

British Library Cataloguing in Publication Data
A catalogue record for this book is available from the British Library

Library of Congress Cataloging in Publication Data
Debates on early childhood policies and practices : global snapshots of pedagogical
thinking and encounters / [edited by] Theodora Papatheodorou.
p. cm.
Includes bibliographical references and index.
1. Early childhood education–Cross-cultural studies. 2. Child
development–Cross-cultural studies. I. Papatheodorou, Theodora, 1953–
LB1139.23.D43 2012
372.21–dc23
2011048330

ISBN: 978-0-415-69100-0 (hbk)
ISBN: 978-0-415-69101-7 (pbk)
ISBN: 978-0-203-15795-4 (ebk)

Typeset in Bembo by Keystroke, Station Road, Codsall, Wolverhampton

MIX
Paper from
responsible sources
FSC www.fsc.org FSC® C013604

Printed and bound by CPI Group (UK) Ltd, Croydon, CR0 4YY

CONTENTS

FIGURES

TABLES

CONTRIBUTORS

Evelyn Angiwan, Professor of Early Childhood at Benguet State University, the Philippines, has been an early childhood practitioner since 1983. She holds a Master of Arts in Education from the University of Baguio, and a PhD in Educational Management from the University of the Cordilleras in the Philippines. She pioneered and served as teacher and directress at the United Church of Christ in the Philippines (UCCP) Integrated Preschool for 17 years and as teacher and coordinator at the Early Childhood Development Centre at Benguet State University for three years. She developed an early childhood curricular programme for teacher education in 2000. Currently, she is teaching on major early childhood disciplines. She is also a speaker and facilitator at national and local training events.

Carol Aubrey is Emeritus Professor of Early Childhood at the University of Warwick and Visiting Professor at Birmingham City University, UK. She trained as a primary school teacher and educational psychologist and spent a number of years in primary teacher education, focusing on the early years, first at University College Cardiff and then at the University of Durham. Her research interests lie in the areas of childhood policy and services, and early learning and development, especially early mathematics development and inclusion/special education needs.

Gill Boag-Munroe, PhD, currently works in the Department of Education at the University of Oxford, UK, teaching on the MSc in Learning and Teaching. She was part of the team which conducted the National Evaluation of the Early Learning Parenting Partnerships. She is also the Reviews Editor for the *International Journal of Mentoring and Coaching* (European Mentoring and Coaching Council).

Sue Callan is currently Associate Lecturer in the Faculty of Education and Language Studies at the Open University, UK. She has a research interest in critical reflective practice, and regularly contributes to publications focusing on the developing professionalism of the early years workforce. She has worked in further and higher education since 1990 specialising in community-based practice, in particular working with mature students in both personal tutor and mentor roles.

Keryn Davis is an early years professional development facilitator at CORE Education Ltd in Christchurch, New Zealand. Her interests include collaborative practitioner research and change, teaching and learning in the early years and assessment. She has worked collaboratively with practitioners, primary advisors and academics promoting cross-sector relationships and understandings for the past ten years. Currently, her work is split between facilitating Ministry of Education-funded professional development and research.

Florence Dinneen, PhD, former Head of the Department of Reflective Pedagogy and Early Childhood Studies at Mary Immaculate College, University of Limerick, Ireland, now works as a freelance consultant in early childhood care and education. She has recently completed a review of early childhood curricula with an international dimension and combines her interest in curricula with her ongoing research into professionalism in the field of early childhood care and education. Her specific curricular focus is on relational pedagogy.

Hasina Banu Ebrahim is Associate Professor of Early Childhood Education (ECE – birth to nine) at the University of the Free State, South Africa. Her interest lies in deepening knowledge and practice for ECE, teacher education and research from local realities. She is interested in alternative perspectives for enhancing practice, strengthening research capacities and informing policy. She is Deputy President of the South African Research Association for ECE.

Rozalina Engels-Kritidis, PhD, is Chief Assistant Professor at the Faculty of Primary and Preschool Education, Sofia University 'St Kliment Ohridski', Bulgaria. She teaches several academic disciplines, especially the basis and theory of pre-school education, and language acquisition and speech development in the early years. She is co-author of the Friends pre-school educational programme, approved by the Bulgarian Ministry of Education. Her scientific interests include allegory interpretation by pre-schoolers and the education of migrant children.

Jan Georgeson is Research Fellow in Early Education Development at Plymouth University, UK. She taught in the early years sector from 1984, mainly working with children with special educational needs. In 2006, she completed her doctorate in educational disadvantage and special educational needs, researching organisational structure and pedagogy and interaction in day nurseries and pre-school playgroups. Since then, she has worked on several research projects on disability and children's voice, and supporting parents as educators of very young children. She has particular interest in practitioners taking vocational pathways into work in early years settings, and from 2006 has been involved with training early years professionals.

Athina Kammenou has studied Psychology and Educational Sciences at the University of Geneva, Switzerland, and obtained a postgraduate degree in Special Education. She has taught in the Faculty of Kindergarten Teachers in the canton of Geneva. She is currently a laboratory assistant at the Department of Preschool Education of the Technological Educational Institute (TEI) of Athens, Greece. She is responsible for creating and implementing individualised programmes for the integration of children with special needs.

Chul Woo Lee, from Seoul in South Korea, is a graduate of Benguet State University, the Philippines. He holds a PhD in Educational Management. His thesis on current early childhood practices in Benguet served as a benchmark for the establishment of his early childcare centre in Manila.

Shu-Ying Liu is Associate Professor of Early Childhood Education at the National Hsinchu University of Education, Taiwan. She also teaches at Macau University, and previously in the UK, USA and Portugal. She has led projects writing hand-books for creative dance in early childhood and elementary education for Taiwanese teachers, and edited and translated several English dance books into Chinese. She has a PhD from Roehampton University, UK, and an MFA from UCLA, USA.

Percyveranda A. Lubrica holds a PhD in Educational Management from Benguet State University, the Philippines. She served as Dean of the College of Teacher Education for nine and a half years. She spearheaded the institutionalisation of the Early Childhood Education Centre as a pre-school laboratory of the university and the development of an early childhood curricular programme. She taught diverse learners in Maryland, USA, for an academic year. She is a national speaker and lecturer in the field of education and she is actively involved in generating research to improve educational policies and practices.

Janet Moyles is Professor Emeritus at Anglia Ruskin University, UK, and a play/early years consultant. She has worked as an early years teacher and head and has written and edited widely. Her books include *Just Playing?* (OUP, 1989), *The Excellence of Play* (OUP, 2009) and *Effective Leadership and Management in the Early Years* (OUP, 2007). She has directed several research projects including 'Jills of All Trades?' (ATL, 1996), 'Too Busy to Play?' (Esmée Fairbairn Trust/University of Leicester, 1997–2000), 'SPEEL (Study of Pedagogical Effectiveness in Early Learning)' (DfES, 2002) and 'Recreating the Reception Year' (ATL, 2003). Her PhD was in the area of play, learning and practitioner roles.

Pamela Oberhuemer was based for many years at the State Institute of Early Childhood Research in Munich, Germany, and currently works as a freelance researcher and journal editor. Her research foregrounds cross-national perspectives relating to early childhood education and care systems, curricular frameworks, and initial and continuing professional development. Her most recent book (with Inge

Schreyer and Michelle Neuman) on the 27 European Union countries is *Professionals in Early Childhood Education and Care Systems: European Profiles and Perspectives* (Verlag Barbara Budrich, 2010).

Elin Eriksen Ødegaard, PhD, is Associate Professor at the Centre of Educational Research at Bergen University College, Norway, where she is leading the project 'Kindergarten as an Arena for Cultural Formation', founded by the Norwegian Research Council. The subjects of her published books and articles include narrative inquiry, children's play and meaning making, teacher professionalism, history and politics. She is also head of the Norwegian branch of OMEP, the World Organisation for Early Childhood Education.

Monica Odinko is Senior Research Fellow in the Institute of Education at the University of Ibadan, Nigeria. She holds two PhDs on educational evaluation of early childhood-related matters: one from the University of Ibadan (2002) and the other from the University of Edinburgh, Scotland (2007). She obtained an MEd in Guidance and Counselling and a BEd in Pre-Primary and Primary Education/ Language and Arts from the University of Ibadan. Her research interests include: evaluation of pre-school teaching and learning activities; comparative study of basic education; material provisions and learning resources and their use in teaching and learning; and instructional modes at the basic level of education.

Theodora Papatheodorou, PhD and MBPsS, is an early childhood educator and researcher. She trained as pre-school teacher and worked initially as nursery teacher and then in higher education. Her teaching and research are in the areas of pre-school curriculum and pedagogy, educational and social inclusion, behaviour problems, multicultural pedagogy and bilingualism. She is the author of *Behaviour Problems in the Early Years* (Routledge, 2005) and co-editor (with Janet Moyles) of *Learning Together in the Early Years: Exploring Relational Pedagogy* (Routledge, 2009) and *Cross-Cultural Perspectives on Early Childhood* (Sage, 2012); and co-author (with Paulette Luff and Janet Gill) of *Child Observation for Learning and Research* (Pearson, 2011).

Sally Peters, PhD, is Associate Professor at the University of Waikato, Hamilton, New Zealand with a background in early childhood education and a particular interest in children's development from 0 to 8 years. She has been involved in a range of research projects, including several Teaching and Learning Research Initiative (TLRI) projects, on which she worked collaboratively with ECE and/or school teachers.

Michael Reed is Senior Lecturer in the Institute of Education at the University of Worcester, UK. He teaches on undergraduate and postgraduate courses. His most recent research has focused upon developing communities of professional practice and how tutors can most effectively research student learning as active participants in the process. He is an experienced author and has developed a number of edited texts for Sage Publications.

Peter Rule, PhD, is Senior Lecturer in the Centre for Adult Education at the University of KwaZulu-Natal in Pietermaritzburg, South Africa. His research interests include dialogue and learning, case study methodology and emancipatory action research. He has experience of working with NGOs in KwaZulu-Natal in the fields of adult literacy, disability, gender and early childhood development.

Sharon Smith is course leader for the Sector Endorsed Foundation Degree in Early Years (SEFDEY) and Foundation Degree Learning Support at South Worcestershire College and a part-time Lecturer at the University of Worcester, UK. She has a Master's degree in Education and her research interests include working with mature students to deliver higher education in further education institutions. Her background is in classroom practice and special educational needs. She has been a member of the University of Worcester SEFDEY partnership team for six years, with a special interest in developing virtual learning environments.

Anita Soni, DEd Psy, is an educational psychologist with specialism in early years. She works part time as Senior Lecturer at Coventry University, UK, and Academic Tutor at the University of Birmingham, UK, and independently with primary schools and children's centres in the West Midlands. She has a particular interest in the personal, social and emotional development of children, the key person approach and the use of group supervision with those working with children and families.

Manabu Sumida is Associate Professor of Science Education in the Faculty of Education at Ehime University, Japan. He earned his PhD in Science Education from Hiroshima University, Japan. His research areas are culture studies in science education and science education for the early childhood years. He has been a committee member of the Trends in International Mathematics and Science Study (TIMSS) in 2003, the TIMSS 1999 Video Study and the OECD Programme for International Student Assessement (PISA) in 2006. He received the Young Students' Award from the Japan Society for Science Education in 1996 and the Best Paper Presentation in 2007 and 2008. He received the Young Scholars' Award from the Society of Japan Science Teaching in 1999. He is Director of the Japan Society for Science Education.

FOREWORD

Janet Moyles

Lilian Katz (2012: 220), one of the most influential and widely acknowledged international early childhood experts, argues, 'Today, no one with serious educational and social policy-making responsibility for a community or even a country all around the world, would argue against the proposition that the experiences of the early years of life have a powerful influence on later ones.' Governments throughout the world have apparently taken this on board with varying degrees of intervention via the imposition of policies intending to lead practices through such elements as statutory curricula and advice on pedagogical strategies for early childhood leaders and practitioners. Research frequently adds another dimension to these aspects which occasionally influences policy makers or practitioners but, arguably, insufficient attention is paid in many countries to research findings. The Organisation for Economic Co-operation and Development (OECD) report *Starting Strong II* (2006), for example, recommended governments internationally to give sustained support to research on key policy goals.

The economic and political climates in many countries also 'lead' policy decisions putting sometimes inadvertent but significant pressures on practitioners to practise in ways which are often against their individual and collective philosophies and values of early childhood education; setting, for example, children's rights and perceived need to play and/or a curriculum based on child development against one focusing mainly on assessed teaching outcomes. As Woodhead (2006: 33) warns us: 'It is salutary to remember that "early childhood" is . . . a culturally constructed concept, and [we should] ask how theories, research and policies about early childhood connect to the young children they purport to describe, explain, protect and promote through laws and services . . .'

So teachers and other conscientious practitioners involved in the education and care of young children often find themselves in a quandary as to how they are intended to practise as professionals in the early childhood field to the benefit of children and society in general. The reasons for this, as we have seen, are complex but stem from the perceived and actual demands made upon them not only by governments and policy makers and the daily challenges of dealing with young children, but also by parents, multi-professional colleagues and the wider communities that practitioners serve. But how far do policies drive practice and how far are practices and practitioners, in themselves, initiators of policy? This timely and invaluable book offers some insights into these challenges and processes examining, in a range of international contexts, how introduced policy and guidance have been received and interpreted in different countries from different perspectives.

The questions and issues identified by contributors in this broad-ranging book *Debates on Early Childhood Practices and Policies* offer inspirational ideas and examples to readers contemplating their own country's policy/practice interface. Readers can learn much from reflecting on how other countries and policy makers deal with early childhood education curriculum and pedagogy in a variety of very differing contexts. From the challenges faced in Germany and Norway (Chapters 1 and 2) – traditional means of making transitions and the children's influences on curriculum respectively – to the way in which curriculum, pedagogy and policy in a particular setting may inhibit family involvement in the English context or reach out to families and communities in South Africa (Chapters 15 and 16) or the complex influence of the environment (Chapter 17), this collection covers many original policy/practice dilemmas and issues. The range of topics in the two parts of this collection is extensive and thought-provoking: in Bulgaria (Chapter 3), the efforts to modernise its traditional strong early years foundations can be compared and contrasted to Uzbekistan (Chapter 4), where the impact of economic decline has challenged the upgrading of existing ECEC provision, significant in many countries internationally. South Africa is the context for discussion of two models – centre- and community-based settings – of reaching and making provision for poor and vulnerable children (Chapter 5), and we can learn much from the Philippines where quality and effective ECEC provision is predicated on the need for effective administration (Chapter 6).

In the Nigerian context, where the interpretation and implementation of top-down policies are fraught with difficulties and challenges due primarily to limited resources and lack of appropriate training, we see the struggles experienced by many minimally trained practitioners (Chapter 7). In England and Ireland, the term 'new professional', and its definition in terms of the roles identified in early years government initiatives, directives and regulations, shows a whole other range of potential conflicts and confrontations (Chapters 8 and 9).

In Part II, Chapter 10 questions Western and Eastern worldviews on science education in the context of a modern industrial, technological and scientifically oriented society such as Japan. Moving to Taiwan, Chapter 11 explores the links between aesthetics and culture in relation to dance and the visual arts, before the focus moves to New Zealand with a stress on children's dispositions and working theories and how these affect practitioners' pedagogy and assessment strategies (Chapter 12). Focusing on children with special needs in Greece, Chapter 13 reveals the challenges experienced by multi-professionals in the field of educational inclusion and children's well-being and the impact of policies on practice, while in Chapter 14, we return to the English context through an exploration of the promotion of emotional well-being and mental health and the potential differences which are not explicitly revealed in the English early years curriculum.

Reading the whole chapters involves readers in considering new approaches to contemplating varied early childhood concerns from differing angles. As Penn (2011: 6) suggests, 'what others see from their various perspectives . . . may help us overcome our own parochialism, in whichever country we reside'. It is difficult to overestimate the impact of the knowledge and understanding to be obtained from this incredibly important and interesting collection. Examining inspirational ideas away from one's own shores is good for all nations and this book promotes and supports out-of-the-box thinking. This searching book raises any number of fundamental issues in considering how policy and practice impact on each other, and emphasises how this interface is multidirectional. As Woodhead (2006: 34) states: 'Any close study of young children reveals the complexity of the worlds they inhabit, the very different pressures on parents, caregivers and others on whom their wellbeing depends.' This book shows just how much policy, practice, research and beliefs can fundamentally impact on children and practitioners in a range of international settings.

References

Katz, L. G. (2012) Where are we now and where should we be going?, in T. Papatheodorou and J. Moyles (eds) *Cross-Cultural Perspectives on Early Childhood*, London: Sage.

Organisation for Economic Co-operation and Development (OECD) (2006) *Starting Strong II: Early Childhood Education and Care*, Paris: OECD.

Penn, H. (2011) *Quality in Early Childhood Services: An International Perspective,* Maidenhead: Open University Press/McGraw Hill.

Woodhead, M. (2006) *Changing Perspectives on Early Childhood: Theory, Research and Policy*, Paris: United Nations Educational, Scientific and Cultural Organization (UNESCO).

ACKNOWLEDGEMENTS

This volume includes chapters based on a selection of papers on policy and practice presented at the international conference 'Early Childhood Policy, Curriculum and Pedagogy in the 21st Century: An International Debate', which was organised by the Early Childhood Research Group at Anglia Ruskin University on 25–27 March 2010. The conference was supported by the British Academy with a conference support grant (award number CSG: 55280) and hosted by Anglia Ruskin University. I would like to acknowledge and thank both institutions for their support.

I would like to express my appreciation and thanks to my colleagues and members of the Early Childhood Research Group: Anabel Corral Granados, Mallika Kanyal, Sara Knight, Pauline Loader, Paulette Luff, Janbee Shaik, Chris Such, Rebecca Webster and Hazel Wright. Their commitment, enthusiasm and hard work made the conference a positive experience for all. My gratitude goes to Professor Janet Moyles, who has consistently supported my colleagues and me before, during and after the conference and in the compilation of this volume. Thank you, Janet.

I would also like to thank Professor Tricia David for supporting the application to the British Academy, all the contributors to this volume and the anonymous and eponymous reviewers of the book proposal and individual chapters. Without their constructive feedback and support this volume would not have been possible. My thanks also go to Alison Foyle, commissioning editor at Routledge, and her team for their support and advice in preparing the manuscript.

ABBREVIATIONS

AIDS	acquired immuno-deficiency syndrome
BMA	British Medical Association
CABE	Commission for Architecture and the Built Environment
CAMHS	Child and Adolescent Mental Health Services
CBO	community-based organisation
CEDAW	Convention on the Elimination of All Forms of Discrimination against Women
CEE	Central and Eastern Europe
CDFSP	Community Development and Family Support Programme
CDP	Community Development Practitioner
CGFS	Curriculum Guidance for the Foundation Stage
CIPP	Context–Inputs–Process–Product model
CIS	Commonwealth of Independent States (in Chapter 4)
	Classroom Interaction Sheet (in Chapter 7)
	Caregiver Interaction Scale (in Chapter 9)
DAP	Developmentally Appropriate Practice
DCAP	Developmentally and Culturally/Contextually Appropriate Practice
DCSF	Department for Children, Schools and Families
DfES	Department for Education and Skills
EC	early childhood
ECCD	Early Childhood Care and Development
ECCE	early childhood care and education
ECD	early childhood development
ECE	early childhood education
ECEC	early childhood education and care
ECM	Every Child Matters
EFA	Education for All

EHWB	emotional health and well-being
ELDS	Early Learning and Development Standards
ELG	Early Learning Goals
EPPE	Effective Provision of Pre-school Education
EYPs	early years professionals
EYFS	Early Years Foundation Stage
Fd	Foundation Degree
FE	further education
FEI	further education institution
FEP	Family Education Project
FF	family facilitator
FHE	further and higher education
FRN	Federal Republic of Nigeria
FSP	Family Support Programme
HE	higher education
HEI	higher education institution
HIV	human immuno-deficiency virus
IDEIA	Individuals with Disabilities Education Improvement Act
IECCD	Integrated Early Childhood Care and Development Project
IEP	Individualized Educational Programme
IMF	International Monetary Fund
IPPA	Irish Preschool Playgroup Association
ISSA	International Step-by-Step Association
JIEs	Joint Involvement Episodes
KE.D.D.Y	Centres of Differential Diagnosis and Support [in Greek, ΚΕ.Δ.Δ.Υ: Κέντρα Διαφοροδιάγνωσης, Διάγνωσης και Υποστήριξης]
L–C	language–culture
LEA	Local Education Authority
LETCEE	Little Elephant Training Centre for Early Education
LGA	local government authority
MDGs	Millennium Development Goals
NCE	National Certificate of Education
NEELPP	National Evaluation of the Early Learning Partnership Project
NERDC	Nigerian Educational Research and Development Council
NESS	National Evaluation of Sure Start
NGO	non-governmental organisation
NHS	National Health Service
NICHD	National Institute of Child Health and Human Development
NIP	National Integrated Plan
OECD	Organisation for Economic Co-operation and Development
OFSTED	Office for Standards in Education
PBL	problem-based learning
PISA	Programme for International Student Assessment
PSED	personal, social and emotional development

PSHE	personal, social and health education
QCA	Qualifications and Curriculum Authority
SAE	standard average European
SCAA	School Curriculum and Assessment Authority
SEAL	social and emotional aspects of learning
SEFDEY	Sector Endorsed Foundation Degrees in the Early Years
TMI	Ten-Minute Interaction
UBE	Universal Basic Education
UN	United Nations
UNCRC	United Nations Convention on the Rights of the Child
UNDP	United Nations Development Programme
UNESCO	United Nations Educational, Scientific and Cultural Organization
UNICEF	United Nations International Children's Emergency Fund
W-science	Western science
W-scientific	Western scientific
WHO	World Health Organization
VLE	virtual learning environment

INTRODUCTION

Early childhood policies and practices

Theodora Papatheodorou

OVERVIEW

Since the last part of the twentieth century, we have seen the steady increase of early years provision with more governments developing policies and allocating funds for the out-of-home care and education of young children. Research findings, which demonstrate the accrued value of such provision on children, their families and the wider society, form the foundation of such policies and practices. In this chapter, I will first provide an overview of some relevant research which has been the cornerstone for promotion of early childhood provision among policy makers. I will then explore how policy has informed practice through the introduction of curriculum frameworks, children's assessment and programme evaluation. I will conclude the chapter by arguing that both policy and practice can be debated, in order to reform and transform the field on both fronts. The content of this volume demonstrates that questioning and contesting policies and practices are vital to ensure that children receive their entitlement to education and care to reach and fulfil their potential.

Key words: policy; curriculum; pedagogy; early childhood.

Introduction

Internationally, it is now well documented and accepted that early childhood provision impacts on children's education and has long-term effects in their adult lives. Additionally, the lifespan impact of early childhood provision also affects directly and indirectly the social and economic well-being of families, communities and the society in general. Belfield and Schwartz (2006), drawing from the findings of two major US studies (Early Childhood Longitudinal Survey and Schools and Staff Survey), reported that children improved their productivity in class, increased their achievement in reading and mathematics in the third and fifth grade, and showed self-control and reduced challenging behaviour. Grade retention and special educational needs placements were reduced as was the school expenditure for special education and academic support programmes. Teachers' satisfaction increased, while teacher absenteeism and turnover were reduced.

James Heckman (2000, 2006), reviewing US childhood intervention programmes (such as the Perry pre-school programme, the Syracuse Preschool programme, the Abecedarian project, the Head Start), further supported such conclusions. His findings show that children who regularly attended well-resourced pre-school provision did better in school, were less likely to drop out and completed their schooling. They were less likely to be involved with anti-social behaviour and criminal acts, and their special educational needs were addressed early. In the long term, as adults, they were in regular and better paid employment, paid taxes and contributed to society's overall economy. They were less likely to be involved in crime or to be arrested, thus reducing their dependency on welfare services. The financial returns of investment in early childhood were as high as 15–17 per cent (Heckman 2006). Similar trends have also been revealed in low- and middle-income countries (Engle *et al.* 2011).

In the UK, the Effective Provision of Pre-school Education (EPPE) project also showed that high-quality pre-school provision has positive effects on children's learning and behaviour, especially for children who experience social disadvantage and/or have special educational needs (Sylva *et al.* 2004). The researchers concluded that high-quality early childhood provision gives children a head start in their education by enabling them to reach their potential and acquire a certain level of skill and readiness necessary for entry to school. Children who fail to reach this level of skill stay behind their peers and the gap widens as they go through their schooling.

Childhood provision has wider impact, beyond education, especially on health, child and social protection (van de Gaag and Tan n.d.), particularly for children and communities which experience social and economic challenges and/or disadvantage (UNESCO 2010). Early childhood services can provide, for example, good nutrition to children, immunisation, medication and other basic health services to reduce child and maternal malnutrition, other diseases and mortality. They offer parent education programmes to increase knowledge about children's needs for physical, social, psychological and emotional development and safety and reinforce relevant skills. They articulate expectations for minimum standards of educational and health provision to promote child welfare and well-being. They raise awareness of child-rearing practices, and children's and parents' rights to demand and enable provision of social protection services. The better educated, healthy and productive the adults are, the better they are equipped to deal with issues of child upbringing and education and their own situations and challenges (UNESCO 2007).

It is argued that the compensatory and preventative nature of some early childhood services becomes the protective element in children's lives. It enables them to develop attachment and the social skills and abilities that are necessary for their motivation and educational profile and for developing and establishing positive relationships that lead to productive lives. Heckman (2000) highlights that the greater impact of pre-school education is on soft outcomes, such as social and attachment skills, that are difficult to measure and thus sometimes obscure the overall impact of pre-school.

This is a view that is further supported by the EPPE study in the UK and the Head Start impact study in the US. The EPPE study demonstrated that the greatest benefits of early childhood provision were on children's social and emotional indicators (Siraj-Blatchford *et al.* 2002), while the Head Start evaluation demonstrated that younger children (3 years old compared to 4 years old) showed greater differences in socio-emotional indicators and parental interaction at the end of Grade 1 than the children in control groups who did not participate in the Head Start programme (US Department of Health and Human Services, Administration for Children and Families 2010).

Evidence from neuroscience has also supported these arguments by confirming the importance of early stimulation on brain development (Shonkoff and Phillips 2000; Woodhead 2006). Synthesising knowledge from neuroscience about the development of the foetus and young children, Shonkoff and Phillips (2000) have drawn attention to critical periods during these ages in their report *From Neurons to Neighborhoods*. Ten years later, the National Scientific Council on the Developing Child (2010: 1) at Harvard University has concluded that 'the experiences children have early in life—and the environments in which they have them—shape their developing brain architecture and strongly affect whether they grow up to be healthy, productive members of society'.

Adopting a *biodevelopmental framework*, the National Scientific Council on the Developing Child (2011) explains how children's genes and experiences interact to create physiological adaptations or disruption in the body that influence lifelong outcomes in health, learning and development. The National Scientific Council on the Developing Child (2010: 1) asserts that 'This growing scientific evidence supports the need for society to re-examine the way it thinks about the circumstances and experiences to which young children are exposed.'

Finally, the impact and benefits of early childhood provision on women's employment and families' economic well-being cannot be underestimated. Since the last part of the twentieth century, childcare availability increased women's participation in employment and provided employment opportunities. Many women who secured child care were able to take up employment and others joined the early childhood workforce itself. Both availability of and demand for early childhood services increased women's personal financial status, and their employment in the sector contributed to the local economy (OECD 2008; Brown *et al.* 2008). Education and training opportunities, offered through engagement and employment in the early childhood sector, have also been the catalysts for women's empowerment and exercise of choice (Wright 2010).

The underlying messages of research evidence are that:

- the earlier children are exposed to rich and diverse educational experiences through high-quality early years provision the better their development and learning;
- early childhood provision increases children's educational opportunities, attainment and outcomes;
- early childhood provision is a protective element against social and economic disadvantage;
- early childhood provision enables parental employment and is a source of employment; it increases household income and reduces poverty;
- a small investment in early childhood improves educational performance, and increases earning capacity with social effects of reducing dependency on welfare and minimising the costs of criminal activity later;
- early childhood provision is a service to children, their families and communities, and the society in general.

These messages demonstrate the inter-dependence and dynamic relationship of education with health and general social and economic protection and well-being as the determinants for improving human capital (see Figure I.1). It could be argued

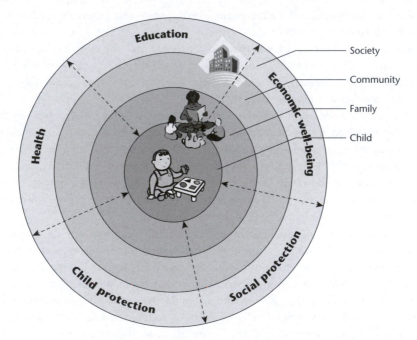

FIGURE I.1 Model of determinant influences on early childhood

◄┈┈┈► Indicates bi-directional influences from society to child development and fluid boundaries between different systems of influence (family; community; and society) and areas of provision (education; health; child protection; social protection; and economic well-being)

here that in their totality the direct and indirect impact and influences of early childhood provision contribute towards the indicators of a just and equal society articulated in the final report of the Equalities Review: *Fairness and Freedom* (Cabinet Office 2007). These are: longevity; physical security; health; education; standard of living; productive and valued activities; individual, family and social life; participation, influence and voice; identity, expression and self-respect; and legal security.

Early childhood policies and influences on practices

This evidence has become the cornerstone of international policies and commitments for early childhood provision. For example, the United Nations Convention on the Rights of the Child (UNCRC) set out universal values and aspirations for children's development, well-being, protection and participation (UNICEF 1989). More than 15 years later, the UNCRC devoted its fortieth session to discussing the implementation of child rights in early childhood, asserting that 'young children are rights holders of all rights enshrined in the Convention and that early childhood is a critical period for the realization of these rights' (UNCRC 2006: 1)

The Jomtien Declaration on Education for All affirmed that learning starts at birth (UNESCO 1990); the subsequent Dakar Framework for Action included as its first goal the expansion and improvement of early childhood care and education (UNESCO 2000). At European level, the Commission of the European Communities (2006) has also acknowledged the high returns of pre-school education for the whole lifelong learning continuum, especially for the most disadvantaged. The OECD reports *Starting Strong, Starting Strong II* and *Starting Strong III* have reiterated the importance of early childhood provision, and especially the availability of flexible services to accommodate the diverse needs of children and their families (OECD 2001, 2006, 2012).

At global level, the commitment to children's rights and their educational needs is reflected in the Millennium Development Goals (MDGs), six of which are clearly linked with the benefits accrued from early childhood provision (UNDP 2000). These MDGs are:

1. eradicate extreme poverty and hunger (MDG1);
2. achieve universal primary education (MDG2);
3. promote gender equality and empower women (MDG3);
4. reduce child mortality (MDG4);
5. improve maternal health (MDG5);
6. combat HIV/AIDS, malaria and other diseases (MDG6).

Most countries are signatories of these declarations and have committed to observe them by introducing policies and/or aligning existing ones with the values, aspirations and intended outcomes underpinning the declarations. Inevitably the economic arguments for early childhood provision and the investment made or required to be made have changed the landscape of the field of early childhood.

Indeed, by 2007, we saw the steady increase of the gross enrolment ratio of children in pre-primary (early childhood) settings, reaching 41 per cent compared with 33 per cent in 1999, especially for Sub-Saharan African countries and South and West Asia. In developed countries, although gross enrolment rates are high, disparities still exist in access and duration across and within countries (UNESCO 2010).

Governments started to invest more than ever before on early childhood services, and gradually, a series of measures have been introduced to ensure the benefits and returns of investment on early childhood provision. The introduction of early years curricula is now almost a common element in many countries and children's assessment and programme evaluation have been introduced to measure the quality of services in some countries (Oberhuemer *et al.* 2010).

In the European and Anglo-Saxon educational systems, initial pre-school curricula were much influenced (and, in many ways, are still influenced) by child development theories that informed the so-called Developmentally Appropriate Practice (DAP) (Bredekamp 1987). Child-centredness and play were recognised in curricula and practices as legitimate means of learning (Moyles 1989, 2005; Smilansky and Shefatya 1990).

Many researchers contested the notion of developmentally appropriate curricula and practices. They argued that these assume universal truths and laws about individuals' development and learning, ignoring the cultural and social influences. Thesse researchers maintained that what and how we learn is culture-bound and culture-influenced (Cannella 2005; Dahlberg *et al.* 2007). Developmentally Appropriate Practice was reviewed to encompass the cultural and contextual influences on development and learning and became Developmentally and Culturally (or Contextually) Appropriate Practice (DCAP) (Hyun 1998; NAEYC 1996).

In parallel with these theoretical perspectives, we have also seen the emergence of two other discourses; that is, the human capital and the rights of the child. The first emerged from the economic arguments for investment in early childhood. It focuses on 'the importance of skills in the modern economy and the dynamic nature of the skill acquisition processes' (Heckman 2006: 2). The human capital discourse *'provides a simple framework that is consistent with observations about skill formation and helps us predict how various policies would be likely to affect skill formation'* (Kilburn and Karoly 2008: 5; emphasis in original).

The influence of the human capital discourse is evident in terms and associated concepts which entered policy documentation and the vocabulary of practitioners, such as desirable learning outcomes and benchmarking, standards and school readiness, children at risk and early intervention, quality indicators and best practice (Cannella 2005; Moss 2008). Researchers who have argued against the assumed universalistic and static nature of DAP have also contested these terms and concepts, arguing that they imply quantifiable and measurable certainties against which individuals are measured and judged; these terms ignore the fact that quality of practice is culture- and context-bound (Cannella 1999, 2005; Dahlberg *et al.* 2007; Moss 2008). These scholars argue that the child remains the focus of assessment as an independent entity without considering cultural and contextual influences.

The rights of the child discourse derived from the UN Convention on the Rights of the Child (UNICEF 1989). It perceives young children as 'rights holders' and requires that the quality of provision is evaluated to determine the extent to which these rights are exercised (UNCRC 2006). It views them as meaning makers and active citizens with the right to participate and voice their views, wants and needs; the right to be nurtured, cared for and educated (Anderson 2000; Dahlberg 2000; Woodhead 2000); the right to be, to belong and to become (Papatheodorou 2010). These notions have gradually started to be acknowledged in policy documents and enter the vocabulary of early childhood practitioners and to be explicitly articulated in some curricula frameworks (e.g. the Norwegian curriculum discussed in Chapter 2 in this volume). The child's rights discourse has articulated ethics as the fundamental dimension of curricula frameworks and pedagogical praxis. It has placed emphasis on the soft learning outcomes and practices for a just and equal society.

Proponents of each theoretical perspective may defend it by contesting and opposing competing arguments and in this way maintain a healthy debate for exchange of ideas and influences on practices. Policy, however, is influenced by the many and often competing ideological viewpoints that prevail at any place and time. It attempts to negotiate and balance diverse ideologies, perspectives and agendas through complex interactions between all interested parties (e.g. politicians, civil servants, researchers and professional groups) (Baldock *et al.* 2009). This negotiation is not arbitrary, though. It takes place on the principles that policy must be evidence-based, to be inclusive and joined up; to be innovative and creative, and to be forward and outward looking (National Audit Office 2001).

The negotiation of multiple perspectives in policy is evident in a recent publication which reports on a comparative study conducted among the 27 countries of the European Union, and the USA and Australia (Oberhuemer *et al.* 2010). Looking at early childhood curricula, programme evaluations and children's assessments, it is evident that since the 1990s, all countries have introduced curricula frameworks and in many instances these have been reviewed and revised more than once. Many countries also have in place some kind of external and/or internal programme evaluation and some form of children's assessment.

In close examination, some interesting patterns emerge. Whilst the majority of these early childhood curricula are framed around intended learning outcomes, programme evaluation has shifted from external to internal/self-evaluation. Similarly, children's assessment has shifted from normative and standardised assessment to more open modes of assessment, including children's portfolios and learning journeys that incorporate children's views.

Oberhuemer *et al.*'s (2010) comparative publication illustrates that policy does indeed incorporate competing ideologies. Interestingly, such competing ideologies seem to create and give opportunities for the generation of new ideas and renewal of practice. Whilst, for example, articulation of intended learning outcomes in curricula may appear to 'narrow down' pedagogical practice, emerging modes of children's assessment and programme self-evaluation signpost the way to more open and flexible ways of thinking and innovative practices.

Emerging issues in policy and practice: global research snapshots

Similar issues and messages emerge from the research included in this volume which is divided into two parts. Part I is entitled 'Early childhood policies: implications for provision and practice'. It comprises nine chapters which discuss early childhood policy and its interpretation and translation into practice, and its influence on curriculum, early childhood pedagogy and training, and early childhood provision. Each chapter author addresses issues that are pertinent to the context of their own country. In their totality however, the chapters provide a thread of arguments which demonstrate the complexity of the issues raised and signpost perspectives that are critical of and informative for both policy and practice.

In Chapter 1, Pamela Oberhuemer focuses on policy initiatives in Germany and raises questions about the shift of guiding values and the tensions between traditions and transitions as a result of the implementation of policy goals into practice. In Chapter 2, Elin Eriksen Ødegaard, referring to the Norwegian policy changes and context, reminds us about the complexity of pedagogical practice. Her chapter highlights the importance of constant negotiation of policy imperatives, professional values and respect, and attention to children's interests.

Chapters 3 and 4 take us to two countries in Eastern Europe – Bulgaria and Uzbekistan – which traditionally had strong foundations in early childhood provision. The changes in the political climate in both countries during the 1990s meant significant challenges and opportunities in the field of early childhood. In Chapter 3, Rozalina Engels-Kritidis reports on efforts made to modernise and Europeanise early childhood provision and how the impact of incoming migration in Bulgaria necessitated the review of curriculum and pedagogical practice. In Chapter 4, Carol Aubrey reports on research undertaken in Uzbekistan. She discusses current efforts to upscale provision through donor support after the economic decline in the country and illustrates some of the challenges of such initiatives.

Hasina Banu Ebrahim in Chapter 5 discusses two alternative approaches for early childhood provision in South Africa; that is, centre-based and community-based provision. She illustrates the appropriateness of both models for communities with different needs and discusses the challenges which policy presents in developing the community-based provision. In Chapter 6, Percyveranda A. Lubrica, Chul Woo Lee and Evelyn Angiwan report on their research in the Philippines, highlighting the need for baseline requirements in order to improve quality and effective practice for early childhood provision. In Chapter 7, Monica Odinko takes us to the Nigerian context, where the interpretation and implementation of top-down policies are fraught with difficulties and challenges due primarily to limited resources and insufficient teacher training.

Chapter 8 refers to the English context, where Sue Callan, Michael Reed and Sharon Smith explore the term 'new professional' and its definition in terms of the roles identified in government initiatives, directives and regulation. The authors argue that such policy drives have put pressure on the design and development of policy-responsive training, whereas they argue for the development of training that has a pedagogic base and allows practitioners to question policy and challenge its assumptions. In Chapter 9, Florence Dinneen continues on the same theme with reference to the Irish context. The research reported here looks into the training of educarers, as this has been informed and shaped as a result of policy requirements. The conclusions of the research illustrate that the education of educarers cannot be rushed just because of policy imperatives. Becoming an educarer requires time and space to develop and embrace a personal meaningful pedagogy.

Part II of the volume is entitled 'Early childhood practice: enabling pedagogical cultures and encounters' and comprises eight chapters. In response to some of the dilemmas and challenges experienced in the field of early childhood, the authors of these chapters provide snapshots of divergent and creative pedagogical thinking and propose alternative enabling learning encounters. This part of the volume starts with Chapter 10 which refers to the Japanese early childhood context. Manabu Sumida makes a distinction between the worldviews of nature held in Western and Eastern societies and invites us to consider the impact of language and culture on scientific thinking. He argues for activities that are based on the Japanese language, culture, philosophy and aesthetics to facilitate and support children's Japanese ways of thinking. Linking to aesthetics and culture, in Chapter 11, Shu-Ying Liu reports on research conducted in the Taiwanese context. Drawing from Western theoretical models about visual arts and dance, but incorporating themes from the local culture, Shu-Ying Liu explores how children enhance their observational skills, increase their awareness of shape and stimulate figurative expression. In Chapter 12, Sally Peters and Keryn Davis focus on children's dispositions and working theories and explore the pedagogical and assessment challenges experienced by early years practitioners in New Zealand.

The next two chapters address some of the challenges experienced in multi-professional practice in the field of educational inclusion and children's well-being. At a time when much discussion takes place about educational inclusion, in Chapter 13, Athina Kammenou reports on some of the successes of the inclusion of children with special educational needs in mainstream kindergartens, and she high-lights some of the challenges experienced with regard to multi-professional practice in the Greek context. With reference to children's well-being, in Chapter 14, Anita Soni examines the importance of terminology and its definition for functional multi-professional practice. The author argues for a common language referring to children's mental health and well-being in order to enable practitioners to build upon their current understanding and practice.

In Chapter 15, Gill Boag-Munroe sets out to explore and understand how the early years curriculum, pedagogy, policy and the setting itself may inhibit or deter families, especially those who are 'hard-to-reach', from accessing the facilities and services. Peter Rule, in Chapter 16, takes us to the South African context to propose a model of relational pedagogy for reaching out to families and communities that are unable to access centre-based early years provision. Relational pedagogy is articulated as a model where professional, community and inter-generational learning meet to enrich individuals and communities. In Chapter 17, Jan Georgeson and Gill Boag-Munroe focus on the less-explored issue of the 'architexture' of the physical environment of early years settings. They explore how the architecture of the building and the combination of sensory, social and cultural affordances may affect how welcomed and comfortable users feel. The authors argue that this aspect of the physical environment is particularly important for hard-to-reach, uncertain and reluctant users.

Finally, the Conclusion brings together the key issues and arguments raised from the selection of chapters and it signposts a positive vision of early childhood in the twenty-first century. It highlights the importance of understanding the diversity and complexity of experience at different times and places, and over time and across places (cultural and historical dimensions of experience) and illustrates the dialectic nature of policy and practice rather than the unidirectional influence of policy on practice. A holistic approach to children's development and learning potential requires a holistic understanding of the field, responsiveness to change, and a capacity to negotiate conflicting and competing ideas and claims to inform meaningful practices.

This volume has been compiled with three aims: first, to acknowledge and inter-rogate a wide range of global and local imperatives of early childhood policies and practices; second, to stimulate and challenge thinking and debate about a wide range of issues related to early childhood policies and practices; and third, to strengthen international consciousness and give inspiration to students, researchers and policy makers around the globe. As such, it would be of interest to those working and researching in academia and in policy, and to those who practise in the field of early childhood. It would also be a useful companion for undergraduate and postgraduate students who study early childhood education; child and family studies; youth development; developmental psychology; early intervention; public policy studies; child advocacy; or social work.

Main features of the volume and clarifications

Each chapter starts with an overview of its focus and content and ends with three questions for thinking about policy and practice. Most chapters are written by researchers who are not native English speakers, and although editorial efforts have been made to 'streamline' language, some terms appear in the text as the authors have initially used them to reflect cultural variations and nuances.

Although there is variation in their definition and understanding, the terms kindergarten, nursery school or class, pre-school/pre-primary, early years setting, day care are used as interchangeable terms to refer to settings where young children receive education and care. Similarly, the terms early years practitioner, early years teacher, nursery teacher, kindergarten teacher and educarer are used to refer to those who work with young children, although in different roles and capacities. A list of various abbreviations used throughout the chapters has also been provided for easy reference for the reader.

Conclusion

In this introductory chapter, I have referred to some salient research evidence which has been instrumental in developing international and national policies in the field of early childhood. I have also discussed the influence of policy, current dominant theoretical perspectives and discourses on the development of early childhood curricula frameworks, programme evaluation and assessment practices. I have concluded that a dialogic exchange of research evidence from policy and practice signifies great benefits in both fields. The brief outlines of the chapters included in this volume support this view further.

QUESTIONS FOR THINKING ABOUT POLICY AND PRACTICE

1. What kind of research is evident in early childhood policies in your own country?
2. To what extent has research undertaken in your own country influenced early childhood policy?
3. In what ways has early childhood policy and research influenced your own practice?

References

Anderson, P. (2000) The rights of young children, in H. Penn (ed.) *Early Childhood Services*, Buckingham: Open University Press.

Baldock, P., Fitzerald, D. and Kay, J. (2009) *Understanding Early Years Policy*, 2nd edn, London: Sage.

Belfield, C. R. and Schwartz, H. (2006) *The Economic Consequences of Early Childhood Education on the School System*, Research prepared for the National Institute of Early Education Research, Rutgers University, available online at: http://nieer.org/docs/index.php?DocID=283 (accessed 7 February 2012).

Bredekamp, S. (1987) *Developmentally Appropriate Practice in Early Childhood Programmes*, Washington, DC: NAEYC.

Brown, B., Ramos, M. and Traill, S. (2008) *The Economic Impact of the Early Care and Education Industry in Los Angeles County*, Los Angeles: Insight, Centre for Community Economic Development, available online at: http://ceo.lacounty.gov/ccp/pdf/LA%20Economic%20Impact%20Report-Jan08.pdf (accessed 12 May 2010).

Cabinet Office (2007) *Fairness and Freedom: The Final Report of the Equalities Review*, London: Cabinet Office, available online at: http://webarchive.nationalarchives.gov.uk/20100807034701/http://archive.cabinetoffice.gov.uk/equalitiesreview/upload/assets/www.theequalitiesreview.org.uk/equality_review.pdf (accessed 31 August 2011).

Cannella, G. (1999) The scientific discourse of education: Predetermining the life of others – Foucault, education and children, *Contemporary Issues in Early Childhood*, 1(1): 36–44, available online at: www.wwwords.co.uk/ciec/content/pdfs/1/issue1_1.asp#3 (accessed 12 May 2010).

Cannella, G. (2005) Reconceptualizing the field (of early care and education): If 'Western' child development is a problem, then what do we do? in N. Yelland (ed.) *Critical Issues in Early Childhood Education*, Maidenhead: Open University Press

Commission of the European Communities (2006) *Communication from the Commission to the Council and the European Parliament: Efficiency and Equity in European Education and Training Systems (COM 2006, 481 Final of 8 September)*, Brussels: CEC, available online at http://ec.europa.eu/education/policies/2010/doc/comm481_en.pdf (accessed 22 March 2011).

Dahlberg, G. (2000) Everything is the beginning and everything is dangerous: Some reflections on the Reggio Emilia experience, in H. Penn (ed.) *Early Childhood Services*, Buckingham: Open University Press.

Dahlberg, G., Moss, P. and Pence, A. (2007) *Beyond Quality in Early Childhood Education and Care: Languages of Evaluation*, London: Routledge.

Engle, P. L., Fernald, L. C. H., Alderman, H., Behrman, J., O'Gara, C., Yousafzai, A., Cabral de Mello, M., Hidrobo, M., Ulkuer, N., Ertem, I., Iltus, S. and the Global Child Development Steering Group (2011) Child Development 2: Strategies for reducing inequalites and improving developmental outcomes for young children in low-income and middle-income countries, *The Lancet*, 378: 1339–1353.

Heckman, J. J. (2000) Policies to foster human capital, *Research in Economics*, 54, 3–56, available online at: http://ideallibrary.com (accessed 10 July 2011)

Heckman, J. J. (2006) Investing in disadvantaged young children is an economically efficient policy, presented at the Committee for Economic Development/The Pew Charitable Trusts/PNC Financial Services Group Forum on 'Building the Economic Case for Investments in Preschool', New York, 10 January, available online at: www.ced.org/images/library/reports/education/early_education/report_2006prek_heckman.pdf (accessed 1 September 2011).

Hyun, E. (1998) *Making Sense of Developmentally and Culturally Appropriate Practice (DCAP) in Early Childhood Education*, New York: Peter Lang

Kilburn, R. M. and Karoly, L. A. (2008) *The Economics of Early Childhood Policy. What the Dismal Science Has to Say about Investing in Children*, Santa Monica, California: RAND Corporation, available online at: http://www.rand.org/pubs/occasional_papers/2008/RAND_OP227.pdf (accessed 31 August 2011).

Moss, P. (2008) Meeting across the paradigmatic divide, in S. Farquhar and P. Fitzsimons (eds) *Philosophy of Early Childhood Education: Transforming Narratives*, Malden, MA: Blackwell

Moyles, J. (1989) *Just Playing? Role and Status of Play in Early Childhood Education*, Buckingham: Open University Press.

Moyles, J. (2005) *The Excellence of Play*, 2nd edn, Maidenhead: Open University Press & McGraw-Hill Education.

NAEYC (1996) *Developmentally Appropriate Practice in Early Childhood Programs Serving Children from Birth through Age 8*, Position Statement, available online at: www.naeyc.org/files/naeyc/file/positions/position%20statement%20Web.pdf (accessed 14 May 2010).

National Audit Office (2001) *Modern Policy Making: Ensuring Policies Deliver Value for Money*, London: National Audit Office.

National Scientific Council on the Developing Child (2010) *Early Experiences Can Alter Gene Expression and Affect Long-Term Development*, Working Paper No. 10, available online at: http://developingchild.harvard.edu/index.php/resources/reports_and_working_papers/working_papers/wp10 (accessed 31 August 2011).

National Scientific Council on the Developing Child (2011) *How Early Experiences Get into the Body: A Biodevelopmental Framework, Children's Genes and Experiences Interact to Create Physiological Adaptations or Disruptions*, available online at: http://developingchild.harvard.

edu/index.php/resources/multimedia/interactive_features/biodevelopmental-framework (accessed 31 August 2011).

Oberhuemer, P., Schreyer, I. and Neuman, M. J. (2010) *Professionals in Early Childhood Education and Care Systems: European Profiles and Systems*, Opladen and Farmington Hills, MI: Verlag Barbara Budrich.

OECD (2001) *Starting Strong. Early Childhood Education and Care*, Paris: OECD.

OECD (2006) *Starting Strong II: Early Childhood Education and Care*, Paris: OECD.

OECD (2008) *Highlights UK. Babies and Bosses: Policies towards Reconciling Work and Family Life*, available online at: www.oecd.org/dataoecd/38/60/39696404.pdf (accessed 14 May 2010).

OECD (2012) *Starting Strong III: A Quality Toolbox for Early Childhood Education and Care, Executive Summary*, available onlie at: www.oecd.org/dataoecd/6/34/49325825.pdf (accessed 27 February 2012).

Papatheodorou, T. (2010) Being, belonging and becoming: some worldviews of early childhood in contemporary curricula, *Forum on Public Policy Online*, 2 (September), available online at: http://forumonpublicpolicy.com/spring2010.vol2010/spring2010 archive/papatheodorou.pdf (accessed 23 March 2011).

Siraj-Blatchford, I., Sylva, K., Muttock, S., Gilden, R. and Bell, D. (2002) *Researching Effective Pedagogy in the Early Years*, Research Report 356, Norwich: DfES.

Shonkoff, J. P. and Phillips, D. (2000) *From Neurons to Neighborhoods: The Science of Early Child Development*, [National Research Council and Institute of Medicine, Committee on Integrating the Science of Early Childhood Development, Board on Children, Youth and Families, Commission on Behavioural and Social Sciences and Education], Washington, DC: National Academy Press

Smilansky, S. and Shefatya, L. (1990) *Facilitating Play: A Medium for Promoting Cognitive, Socio-Emotional and Academic Development in Young Children*, Gaithersburg, MD: Psychosocial and Educational Publications.

Sylva, K., Melhuish, E. C., Sammons, P., Siraj-Blatchford, I. and Taggart, B. (2004) *The Effective Provision of Pre-school Education (EPPE) Project, Technical Paper 12*, London: DfES/Institute of Education, University of London

UNCRC (2006) *Convention on the Rights of the Child, General Comment No. 7 [2005], Implementing Child Rights in Early Childhood*, fortieth session, 20 September, Geneva: UN, available online at: http://www.childrensrights.ie/files/CRC-GC7_EarlyChildhood05.pdf (accessed 31 August 2011).

UNDP (2000) *The Millennium Development Goals*, available online at: www.beta.undp.org/undp/en/home/mdgoverview.html (accessed 26 August 2011).

UNESCO (1990) *World Declaration on Education for All and Framework for Action to Meet Basic Learning Needs* (adopted by the World Conference on Education for All: Meeting Basic Learning Needs, Jomtien, Thailand, 5–9 March), Paris: UNESCO, available online at: www.unesco.org/education/pdf/JOMPIE_E.PDF (accessed 14 March 2008).

UNESCO (2000) *World Education Forum: The Dakar Framework for Action, Education for All: Meeting Our Collective Commitments* (adopted by the World Education Forum 26–28 April), Paris: UNESCO, available online at: www.unesco.org/images/0012/001211/121147e.pdf (accessed 14 March 2008).

UNESCO (2007) *EFA Global Monitoring Report 2007, Strong Foundations: Early Childhood Care and Education*, Paris: UNESCO.

UNESCO (2010) *EFA Global Monitoring Report 2010, Reaching the Marginalized*, Paris: UNESCO and Oxford University Press.

UNICEF (1989) *United Nations Convention on the Rights of the Child*, available online at: www2.ohchr.org/english/law/crc.htm (accessed 23 March 2011).

US Department of Health and Human Services, Administration for Children and Families (2010) *Head Start Impact Study, Final Report*, Washington, DC: US Department of Health and Human Services, Administration for Children and Families, available online at: www.acf.hhs.gov/programs/opre/hs/impact_study/reports/impact_study/executive_summary_final.pdf (accessed 30 August 2011).

van de Gaag, J. and Tan, J.-P. (n.d.) *The Benefits of Early Childhood Development Programs: An Economic Analysis*, Education, The World Bank, available online at: http://siteresources.worldbank.org/INTECD/Resources/Benefits.pdf (accessed 31 August 2011).

Woodhead, M. (2000) Towards a global paradigm for research into early childhood, in H. Penn (ed.) *Early Childhood Services*, Buckingham: Open University Press.

Woodhead, M. (2006) Changing perspectives on early childhood: Theory, research and policy. Background Paper prepared for the *EEA Global Monitoring Report 2007, Strong Foundations: Early Childhood Care and Education* (Ref. 2007/ED/EFA/MRT/PI/33/REV), Paris: UNESCO, available online at: http://unesdoc.unesco.org/images/0014/001474/147499e.pdf (accessed 12 May 2010).

Wright, R.H. (2010) From parent to practitioner: Alternative ways to professionalism, Paper presented at the international conference Early Childhood Policy, Curriculum and Pedagogy: An International Debate, at Anglia Ruskin University, Chelmsford, 25–27 March.

PART I

Early childhood policies: implications for provision and practice

1

BALANCING TRADITIONS AND TRANSITIONS

Early childhood policy initiatives and issues in Germany

Pamela Oberhuemer

OVERVIEW

This chapter analyses current early childhood policy initiatives in the German context and their transformational implications for the field. Over the past decade, three issues in particular have received marked policy attention. The first was a decision by all 16 federal states (*Länder*) to introduce curricular frameworks for the early childhood sector. A second round of policy initiatives focused on enhancing language and literacy skills, and particularly on the support of children with German as a second language. The third major area of policy attention has been directed towards provision for children from birth to three. Following a focus on these three issues, the chapter concludes by asking whether there have been detectable shifts in guiding philosophies and values in recent years and whether tensions are visible in the balancing of traditions with current transitions from policy goals to practical interpretations.

Key words: Germany; early childhood; policy initiatives; early education reforms.

Introduction: looking to the past to understand the present

As in most countries across Europe, the first centres for young children emerged during the onset of industrialisation as purely custodial establishments (Oberhuemer *et al.* 2010). Friedrich Froebel's (1782–1852) concept of early childhood institutions challenged the predominantly utilitarian approaches of the time. In 1840 he founded the first 'kindergarten' which combined a philosophy of social pedagogy, care and early education. In 1848, in the context of a democracy movement that culminated in a revolutionary parliament, Froebel proposed the integration of the kindergarten into the general education system: 'As education for all, and from an early age, it was seen as the prerequisite for the democratisation of society' (Urban 2010: 3). However, this radical idea was not politically viable at the time and this has been the case up to the present day (2012). In post-war *West* Germany and in today's post-1990 Federal Republic of Germany, all institutional forms of child care and education prior to compulsory schooling have been positioned within the child and youth welfare system.

Following the post-war division of Germany, the two separate nations developed distinctly differing systems of early education and care. Whereas in the eastern socialist German Democratic Republic the labour force participation of women was a declared political goal underpinned by the provision of full-day and publicly funded kindergartens (within the education sector) and day nurseries (within the health sector), in the western Federal Republic of Germany, women were encouraged to care for their young children in the home and provision levels were very low. The 1952 Youth Welfare Act in West Germany re-endorsed the so-called *subsidiarity principle* anchored in the first Youth Welfare Act of 1922. According to this principle, public authorities are only obliged to provide social services if non-governmental agencies are not in a position to do so. This principle was again re-authorised in the 1990 Social Code, Book VIII – Child and Youth Services (Child and Youth Services Act) which came into force in October 1990 in the five eastern *Länder* (federal states), and in January 1991 in the 11 western *Länder* of the newly unified Federal Republic of Germany. Federalism and subsidiarity are therefore key political principles underpinning the organisation, funding and regulation of early childhood services in Germany.

Concept of early education and care in the Child and Youth Services Act 1990/1991

In the specific section on day care institutions and family day care in the 1990/1991 Child and Youth Services Act (para. 22), it is stated that these services should support the child in developing independence and a sense of community; support and extend the upbringing and education in the family; and help parents to combine employment and childrearing. The overall approach is described as a combination of upbringing (*Erziehung*), education (*Bildung*) and care (*Betreuung*). Provision – both from a pedagogical and an organisational point of view – is to be adapted to the 'needs of children and their families'. Parents are to be included in decision-making processes about key aspects of the childcare service. Wherever possible, children with disabilities are to be included in mainstream group provision. Programmatic educational aims are formulated only at a very general level.

The 16 regional governments are responsible for developing childcare laws in alignment with the main features of federal legislation. These are prepared by the ministry with overall responsibility for youth affairs (*Oberste Landesjugendbehörde*). At the local level, the municipalities are obliged to guarantee service provision and secure funding for kindergartens (for 3- to 6-year-olds), day nurseries (for 0- to 3-year-olds) and school-age childcare (for 6- to 14-year-olds) and other age-combined forms of provision. However, public administration does not directly provide the majority of these services (at least in the western *Länder*) but co-operates with a variety of non-profit service agencies. Here, church and voluntary organisations play a pivotal role. Around two-thirds of centre-based early education/care provision across the country is run by these so-called 'free providers' (*Freie Träger der Jugendhilfe*).

The traditional dominance of the non-governmental sector has not only been maintained but has been increasing. A recent independent survey (Schreyer 2009) of the providers of centre-based services for children in 13 *Länder* registered an increase of almost 42 per cent over the last seven years. According to this study, the decrease in the numbers of public, municipality-run centres is particularly marked in the eastern part of the country; whereas in the western *Länder*, the absolute number of church-affiliated centres has decreased. However, the proportion of non-church free providers has increased significantly in both parts of the country.

In other words, responsibility is shared between the federal government, the 16 regional governments and local government bodies in partnership with a wide range of non-profit agencies.

The PISA challenge and school readiness issues

During the late 1990s, debates began to surface regarding the efficacy of traditional early childhood programmes. On a general level, these arguments related to international discourses around the concept of life-long learning, the publication of neuro-scientific research on brain development during the first years of life, and also a growing acknowledgment of a rights-based approach to early education as inscribed in the UN Convention on the Rights of the Child. On a more specific level, a number of national reports on education also emphasised the need for reform in the early childhood sector; moreover, empirical research in three of the 16 *Länder* had revealed considerable differences in quality between kindergartens across the country (Tietze 1998). These varying strands of debate all contributed towards a heightened public and policy interest in the education of young children.

However, it was the so-called 'PISA shock' which generated the necessary political pressure and led to a number of significant policy initiatives. The findings of the first round of the comparative OECD Programme for International Student Assessment (PISA) of 15-year-olds and their school achievements across 32 countries (OECD 2001) were given extensive media coverage. Not only was Germany's overall ranking level unexpectedly low, but the study also illustrated how the education system was failing to compensate for differences in social background and that migrant children in particular were disproportionately represented among the low achievers. These findings further fuelled controversial debates across the country on the goals, content, pedagogy and structural organisation of the public education system. The early childhood sector, although not part of the official education system, was included in this debate. In this sense, the policy initiatives that followed were part of a school readiness discourse and led in the first instance to the introduction of first-time curricular frameworks for work in early childhood centres.

A curriculum for the early childhood sector? Not one, but many

Up to 2002, formal curriculum guidelines for the early childhood field were neither seriously debated nor high on the policy agenda in Germany. Apart from the very general educational aims set down in both the federal-level Child and Youth Services Act 1990/1991 and in the complementary *Länder* legislation, any kind of specification regarding the pedagogical programme in post-unification Germany was low key. A major reason for this is that the voluntary and mainly church-affiliated agencies which provide the majority of services have had considerable independence in the field and traditionally have resisted regulatory initiatives.

However, as a consequence of the PISA findings, the overall political situation was such that between 2003 and 2008, all 16 regional governments decided to regulate the field more closely and to issue first-time curricular frameworks, a move which was generally supported by the major service provider organisations. Bavaria took the initiative in these developments (Fthenakis 2003), followed closely by the city-state of Berlin.

Moreover, in 2004, another historically unique step was taken. The 16 Ministers for Youth Affairs and the 16 Ministers of Education agreed to adopt a Common Framework for Early Education. Although this Common Framework is not binding, it reflects many of the general features of the varying curricular documents. Basic principles include a holistic approach towards learning; involving children in decision-making processes; intercultural pedagogy; gender-sensitive practices; specific support for at-risk children and children with (potential) disabilities; support for gifted children. 'Through their informal learning environments, early childhood centres offer a supportive framework for developing experiential learning and for promoting a probing, enquiring, questioning and challenging disposition towards learning' (A Common Framework for Early Education 2004: 18–19).

The areas of learning highlighted in the Common Framework are similar to those in many other curricula across Europe: (1) language, literacy and communication; (2) personal and social development, ethics and religion; (3) mathematics, science and (information) technology; (4) arts education/media; (5) physical development, movement, health; (6) nature and culture. Improving the transition from early childhood education to school is particularly emphasised. As in many countries, kindergartens and schools have developed in very different ways in the past in terms of educational philosophy, organisational structures and staffing requirements. One of the significant challenges for the future is therefore to strengthen co-operative strategies at all levels: the steering level; the local and institutional level; and the curricular level (Oberhuemer *et al.* 2010).

Most of the curricular documents are based on a view of children as agents of their own learning in a co-constructive process with adults and other children, and all are committed to the holistic approach of encompassing education, care and upbringing. The main differences are in the length, and whether or not the curriculum is mandatory. Whereas most are considered to be 'guidelines', in Bavaria, Berlin, Saxony and Thüringen, early childhood centres are obliged by law to include the main principles, aims and areas of learning in their own centre-specific programmes (which are individually geared to local needs). The city-state of Berlin has taken the most far-reaching steps in terms of curriculum assessment. The implementation of the Berlin Early Childhood Curriculum (Prott and Preissing 2006) is combined with prescribed evaluation procedures. An agreement with the service providers requires the implementation of specific self-assessment and (every 5 years) external assessment procedures. A specialist institute – the Berlin Institute for Quality Improvement in Early Childhood Provision – is responsible for monitoring and evaluating the overall assessment procedures. The evaluation findings are to be included in steering recommendations for regional government administration, the provider organisations and the youth offices, and thus contribute to the ongoing development and improvement of early childhood services.

I shall now move on to the second area of recent policy initiatives – language and literacy in the early years.

A sharper focus on language and literacy

Whereas language enrichment activities were traditionally part of regular early childhood programmes in Germany, it has been suggested that these were not carried out systematically enough or in an appropriately purposeful way (Fried 2009). This was one of the reasons why language and literacy were foregrounded in the early childhood curricula – in fact, the English term 'literacy' was introduced into the Bavarian curriculum since there is no equivalent in German.

Besides the generally sharper focus on language and literacy in recent years, particular emphasis has been placed on the support of children from families with a background of migration. This support, however, tends to be directed at second-language learning and not at enhancing their first-language competence. More than a quarter of children in centre-based settings in the western part of Germany come from families where at least one parent was born outside Germany, and over half of these children do not speak German in the home (Leu and Schelle 2009: 11). This situation, in combination with the PISA findings which illustrated how disadvantaged many immigrant children are within the school system, has led to a flurry of policy initiatives in this area. In a number of *Länder* it is now a requirement for children to participate in a language screening assessment prior to school entry.

However, there are considerable regional variations in the types of assessment used, and also in the kinds of focused language support measures implemented. Some start when the children are 2 years old, whereas others do not begin until the last year in kindergarten. In Bavaria, for example, no language screening test is required, but since the autumn of 2005, the language competence of children whose parents were both born outside Germany is assessed by practitioners with the help of a prescribed observation instrument; and since 2008, the language competence of *all* children is assessed towards the end of the year preceding the final year in kindergarten, also through a prescribed assessment procedure (Ulich and Mayr 2006). Beyond this, an extensive network of early childhood language co-ordinators was launched in 2008 across Bavaria with considerable government funding support. These language advisers, who undergo a targeted and evaluated course of training, work closely with early childhood centres on a regional basis. The impact of this network on the language- and literacy-related work of the centres is being assessed over time by a research team at the State Institute of Early Childhood Research in Munich.

Expanding provision for the under-threes

The Child and Youth Services Act has been modified several times since 1990/1991. The first significant amendment was in 1996, when children from the age of three up to school entry (at age six) were granted a legal entitlement to a place in a kindergarten. The concept of 'place' was not defined, and in practice, the right to access in terms of hours of attendance daily varies considerably. Nearly ten years later, the Day Care Expansion Act (*Tagesbetreuungsausbaugesetz – TAG*) which came into force in 2005, set the framework for expanding provision for the under-threes. The legislation pledged to provide 230,000 extra places in kindergartens, day nurseries and family day care by 2010, and access for 35 per cent of the age-group by 2013. The most recent amendment is the 2009 Childcare Funding Act (*Kinderförderungsgesetz – KiFöG*) which includes a legal entitlement to a place in a centre-based setting or family day care for all children aged 1 and 2 years by 2013.

At the time of the unification of the two German nations in 1990, differences in the level of provision for the under-threes were very marked. Even 12 years later, in 2002, there was little observable change, with places available for 37 per cent of under-threes in the east and only for 3 per cent in the west, with an overall provision level of around 9 per cent. However, as a result of the legislation mentioned above, this situation is changing. A more detailed breakdown is available from the official statistics. In 2007, of the 15.5 per cent of children under three years enrolled in early childhood provision, 2.1 per cent were in family day care. Regional differences, however, remained significant. Whereas the enrolment rate for under-threes in the eastern part of Germany was 41 per cent (including family day care), in the western *Länder* it totalled just 10 per cent (Statistisches Bundesamt 2008). In 2009, 17.4 per cent of under-threes across Germany were enrolled in centre-based settings and 2.8 per cent in family day care. For children aged 3 to 6 years, the respective figures were 91.2 per cent and 0.4 per cent (Federal Statistical Office 2010).

Thus, within a very short space of time, provision for the under-threes has been catapulted into the limelight, but not without problems. As a result of the government target of providing for 35 per cent of under-threes by 2013, experts have estimated that not only do 319,000 places need to be created in centre-based settings, but also 136,000 places in family day care. Beyond this, if an average staff/child ratio of 1:5 is the basis of calculation, a further 50,000 full-time jobs would be needed for the main occupational group (*Erzieherinnen*) in early childhood provision (Rauschenbach and Schilling 2009). Besides the pressing issue of expansion, questions about the quality of provision are therefore increasingly being raised. A focus on work with the under-threes has traditionally been under-represented in initial and continuing professional development courses for early childhood educators.

Balancing traditions and transitions

The implications of the three early childhood policy initiatives described above – first-time curricular requirements, specific strategies for language enrichment and assessment, unprecedented expansion of provision for the under-threes – mean that the early childhood field in Germany is in a process of considerable transition and transformation. I will therefore conclude by reflecting on whether there have been detectable shifts in guiding philosophies and values in recent years, and whether evaluations and analyses have revealed points of tension between policy goals and practical interpretations.

Shifts in guiding philosophies and values?

Although the closer regulation of the field through the introduction of framework curricula is undoubtedly a new step in the history of early childhood education in Germany, and one which is opening up possibilities of a steadier and more systematic collaboration with the school system, the commitment to an early childhood sector independent from the school sector, with its politically endorsed diversity of service agencies, has remained in place, as has the general acceptance of a holistic approach towards education, upbringing and care as codified in the Child and Youth Services Act. In this sense, transitions to new ways of regulating the early childhood field have been accommodated within existing frameworks.

The official curricula can be seen in some ways as an official endorsement of traditional philosophies, value orientations and practices such as a strong commitment to play-based learning and community networking; on the other hand, they have also resulted in shifts such as:

- a new public awareness of the importance of the early years;
- a broadening of the scope of early years learning activities;
- a sharper focus on previously neglected areas of learning such as science and technology;
- a more reflective and systematic approach towards observation and planning in early childhood settings.

In the area of language and literacy, many initiatives are under way. However, figures from the Federal Statistical Office show that more than 50 per cent of the children in the western regions who do not speak German at home are concentrated in about 7 per cent of centres (Deutsches Jugendinstitut and Dortmunder

Arbeitsstelle 2008: 162). Additional figures from a monitoring report by the Bertelsmann Foundation (Bock-Famulla and Große-Wöhrmann 2010) also show considerable differences in the enrolment rates of children from German-speaking and non–German-speaking families. In Schleswig-Holstein the difference is most marked, with 91 per cent of non-migrant children and only 60 per cent of migrant children enrolled. Similar discrepancies can be found in Bavaria (95/75 per cent), Bremen (96/75 per cent) and the city-state of Berlin (100/80 per cent). If the transition to more focused approaches towards language and literacy is to take effect, there is an obvious need for a redistribution of resources and targeted funding for work with these children and their families (Leu and Schelle 2009).

In terms of the policy thrust and legislation to expand services for the under-threes, a very significant shift has taken place in the western *Länder*. As reported earlier, support for publicly subsidised services for this age-group in the former West Germany was traditionally very low key. Centre-based settings were mainly to be found only in the larger cities such as Berlin, Frankfurt and Munich. The rapid expansion currently taking place across the western *Länder* represents a significant paradigm shift in terms of the previously ingrained attitudes at the political decision-making level. However, for a successful transition to high-quality practices, work with the under-threes needs to be more strongly represented in initial and continuing professional development and to be well resourced in terms of space and personnel (Wertfein *et al.* 2009).

Tensions between policy goals and practical interpretations?

For practitioners with an understanding of professional autonomy located within the described cultural framework of politically endorsed diversity, and who at the same time have strong socio-pedagogical (and not school-oriented) roots, a specified framework of domain-oriented curricular activities could arguably precipitate feelings of ambivalence. On the one hand, practitioners may appreciate the improved status which this kind of codification of professional practice implies, including an implicit levelling up in terms of comparisons with primary schooling. On the other hand, a prescribed framework could be interpreted as a measure which potentially undermines professional autonomy.

The findings of a questionnaire survey carried out by the State Institute of Early Childhood Research of the views of staff in the 104 early childhood centres involved in the pilot run of the Bavarian curriculum were therefore somewhat surprising. Sixty-three per cent were convinced that the curriculum should be made compulsory, and a further 30 per cent were positively inclined in this direction. Critical comments focused not so much on the curriculum document itself, but on the conditions for implementing the wide range of pedagogical activities formulated, including lack of planning and development time, group size, and the lack of professional knowledge provided in initial education/training (Berwanger *et al.* 2009). Two years after the introduction of the curriculum across Bavaria, 78 per cent of centre leaders (N = 319) were convinced that the curriculum helped to improve the pedagogical work of the centre. However, 45 per cent were concerned that there could be a danger of 'schoolification', an 11 per cent increase compared with the previous year (Lorenz and Minsel 2007). It seems that when trying to translate at least certain of the curricular requirements into practice, there could be a danger that pedagogical activities will be narrowed rather than broadened. As yet, however, there are few evaluative studies to draw on.

Conclusion

Initiated one hundred and sixty years ago, Friedrich Froebel's concept of 'Kindergarten' and early childhood education undoubtedly had significant influence both across Europe and beyond in the decades that followed. In Germany today, the widely accepted broad socio-pedagogical approach codified in the Child and Youth Services Act which views upbringing, education and care as complementary in a holistic way, was identified by the OECD review team as a strength of the German system: 'rich concepts, with deep historical roots' (OECD 2004: 41). There remains a steady undercurrent of resistance to policies perceived as narrowly defining what learning and well-being in early childhood are about. In an international context heavily influenced by school readiness discourses focusing on supposedly discrete skills and competences, this may be one of the main messages for cross-national dialogue from Germany today.

QUESTIONS FOR THINKING ABOUT POLICY AND PRACTICE

1. How are children viewed in current early childhood policy in your country?
2. Who has a voice in early childhood policy making?
3. What are the policy chances and challenges in creating more equity and equality in early childhood?

References

A Common Framework for Early Education adopted by the Standing Conference of the Ministers for Youth Affairs and the Standing Conference of the Ministers of Education and Cultural Affairs (2004), in Pestalozzi-Fröbel-Verband e.V. (ed.) *Frühe Bildung und das System der Kindertagesbetreuung in Deutschland* [in English: *Early Childhood Education and Care in Germany*, translation by Pamela Oberhuemer], Berlin: Verlag das Netz (pp. 14–21).

Berwanger, D., Lorenz, S. and Minsel, B. (2009) Sicherung von Qualität durch Evaluation und Dokumentation: Vergleich der Erprobungsergebnisse Bayern-Hessen, in F. Becker-Stoll and B. Nagel (eds) *Bildung und Erziehung in Deutschland. Pädagogik für Kinder von 0 bis 10 Jahren*, S.177–192, Berlin, Düsseldorf, Mannheim: Cornelsen Scriptor.

Bock-Famulla, K. and Große-Wöhrmann, K. (2010) *Länderreport Frühkindliche Bildungssysteme 2009. Transparenz schaffen: Governance stärken*, Gütersloh: Verlag Bertelsmann Stiftung.

Deutsches Jugendinstitut and Dortmunder Arbeitsstelle Kinder- und Jugendhilfestatistik (2008) *Zahlenspiegel 2007. Kindertagesbetreuung im Spiegel der Statistik.* Available online at: www. bmfsfj.de/Publikationen/zahlenspiegel2007/root.html (accessed 3 August 2011).

Federal Statistical Office (2010) Statistische Ämter des Bundes und der Länder, *Kindertagesbetreuung regional 2009,* Wiesbaden: Statistisches Bundesamt.

Fried, L. (2009) Education, language and professionalism: issues in the professional development of early years practitioners in Germany, *Early Years: An International Journal of Research and Development,* 29(1): 33–44.

Fthenakis, W.E. (ed.) (2003) *Elementarpädagogik nach PISA: Wie aus Kindertagesstätten Bildungseinrichtungen werden können,* Freiburg im Breisgau: Herder.

Leu, H.R. and Schelle, R. (2009) Between education and care? Critical reflections on early childhood policies in Germany, *Early Years: An International Journal of Research and Development,* 29(1): 5–18.

Lorenz, S. and Minsel, B. (2007) BayBEP – Bavarian early childhood curriculum: Findings from the second survey of centre directors, Working Document, Munich: State Institute of Early Childhood Research.

Oberhuemer, P., Schreyer, I. and Neuman, M.J. (2010) *Professionals in Early Education and Care Systems: European Profiles and Perspectives,* Opladen & Farmington Hills, MI: Barbara Budrich.

OECD (2001) *Knowledge and Skills for Life: First Findings from the OECD Programme for International Student Assessment (PISA) 2000.* Available online at: www.oecd.org/document/46/0,3343,en_32252351_32236159_33688686_1_1_1_1,00.html (accessed 3 August 2011).

OECD (2004) *Early Childhood Education and Care Policy in the Federal Republic of Germany: Country Note.* Available online at: www.oecd.org/document/50/0,3343,en_2649_33723_37591602_1_1_1_1,00.html (accessed 3 August 2011).

Prott, R. and Preissing, C. (2006) (eds) *Bridging Diversity: An Early Childhood Curriculum. Berliner Bildungsprogramm,* Berlin: Verlag das Netz.

Rauschenbach, T. and Schilling, M. (2009) Demografie und frühe Kindheit: Prognose zum Platz- und Personalbedarf in der Kindertagesbetreuung, *Zeitschrift für Pädagogik,* 55(1): 17–36.

Schreyer, I. (2009) Die Kita-Trägerlandschaft in Deutschland, in M. Hugoth and X. Roth (eds) *Handbuch für Träger von Kindertageseinrichtungen,* Kronach: Carl Link.

Statistisches Bundesamt (2008) *Kinder- und Jugendhilfestatistiken: Tageseinrichtungen für Kinder am 15.03.2008.* Available onlne at: www.destatis.de (accessed 3 August 2011).

Tietze, W. (1998) (ed.) *Wie gut sind unsere Kindergärten? Eine Untersuchung zur pädagogischen Qualität in deutschen Kindergärten,* Weinheim: Beltz.

Ulich, M. and Mayr, T. (2006) *Seldak. Sprachentwicklung und Literacy bei deutschsprachig aufwachsenden Kindern (Beobachtungsbogen und Begleitheft),* Freiburg: Herder.

Urban, M. (2010) Rethinking professionalism in early childhood: untested feasibilies and critical ecologies, *Contemporary Issues in Early Childhood,* 11(1): 1–6. Available online at: http://dx.doi.org/ 10.2304/ciec.2010.11.1.1 (accessed 3 August 2011).

Wertfein, M., Spies-Kofler, A. and Becker-Stoll, F. (2009) Quality curriculum for under-threes: the impact of structural standards, *Early Years: An International Journal of Research and Development,* 29(1): 33–44.

Website addresses

Berlin Institute for Quality Improvement in Early Childhood Provision: http://www.beki.ina-fu.org (accessed 3 August 2011).

State Institute of Early Childhood Research: www.ifp.bayern.de (accessed 3 August 2011).

2

PIRACY IN POLICY

Children influencing early childhood curriculum in Norway

Elin Eriksen Ødegaard

OVERVIEW

Norwegian society, to a large extent, has been an egalitarian one, where child centeredness has a long tradition in kindergarten practice. Due to structural and rapid changes in the sector, however, there are now a number of new discussions about the curriculum and practice. In recent policy documents and curricula frameworks we find competing claims that challenge child-centred practices and reveal a more complex picture.

In this chapter, I will reflect upon and discuss how it is possible for a two-year-old to influence the programme in his kindergarten. A case called 'Captain Andreas and his Crew' describes and suggests that a child, rich in play initiatives and talk, can provide the conditions that may influence the kindergarten programme. A participating space for children's perspectives, as often found in a play-based curriculum, and teacher practices characterised by child centredness make it possible for children to introduce play-themes, take the initiative to talk and participate in democratic practices. Such conditions have been considered a quality of the Nordic holistic approach. Individual child-centred practice, however, is not considered enough to ensure opportunities for all children to participate.

Key words: Norway; children's influence; serious playfulness; co-narrative; child-centred discourse.

Introduction

The purpose of this chapter is to elaborate, demonstrate and reflect on how small children can take part in, and shape, democratic practices. I will first introduce you to Andreas, a two-year-old boy, and Marit, his kindergarten teacher (the use of teachers' first names is usual in school settings in Norway). I first met them in a kindergarten group of nine children (one to three years old), during my field work as a researcher, some years ago. On my first day in the kindergarten, after being introduced to the staff and the children, Andreas grabbed my hand and followed me out into the hall. He stopped in front of a collection of pictures of him and his family, all nicely put together in a collage. He pointed at a picture where he was dressed with a pirate's hat on his head. I commented on the picture and, later that day, this event was written up in my field notes.

At the time, little did I know that I would find this little episode worth mentioning in my study. I did not know that Andreas was going to enlighten my understanding about how early childhood policy and curricula inform practice; neither was I aware of how a two-year-old boy would be recognised as a negotiating participant who influences practice. In fact, this episode has been the starting point of writing the case of 'Captain Andreas and his crew'; a case about children's meaning-making and teachers' practices (Ødegaard 2007a).

Later, during my visits, I noticed that Andreas often initiated play and conversations where the pirate Captain Sabertooth was the protagonist. Andreas's family had visited a theme park in Norway and there they had joined a Captain Sabertooth show. Subsequently, Andreas had also watched the cartoon movie. Spin-off products like swords, hats and pirate flags were made available to him by his parents. In the kindergarten he gathered a crew of pirates. His initiatives were initially ignored, but eventually were noticed, picked up and extended by his kindergarten teacher.

Starting from this episode, I will reflect upon and discuss how it is possible for a two-year-old boy to influence the kindergarten programme. For this, I will first provide some background information in order to contextualise the case. I will then discuss how the so-called Nordic model of early childhood practice operates by giving some examples. I will finally take in hand some complex issues which underpin official Norwegian policy documents.

On board the Norwegian ship

Since 1975, Norway has had one institution of early childhood provision, called 'barnehage' (translated from the German word 'kindergarten'). This institution is for all children under the age of compulsory schooling. The youngest children, one- to three-year-olds including children with special needs, are educated and cared for in the same educational institution that is governed by the same kindergarten act.

One of the salient characteristics of early education in Norway is the strong discourse of 'a good Norwegian childhood'. This notion of childhood places emphasis on children's free play, outdoor activities and friendship, and it offers them opportunities to explore their environment without being overprotected by adults (Kristjansson 2006; Röthle 2007; Strand 2006). This historical child-centred pedagogical discourse is also present in the Kindergarten Act 2006, which states that every child should impact on their own daily activities and that the kindergarten daily content should be organised according to children's maturity (Ministry of Education and Research 2006).

A child-centred practice has now been made more explicit in the Norwegian legislation, not in the Kindergarten Act only. Norway is the first country to protect the rights of children with the Ombudsman for Children in 1981; and since the 1990s, it is the only country where it is possible for children to divorce their parents (Kristjansson 2006). Yet, as I will illustrate later, there are competing discourses which struggle to balance children's rights and a holistic, play-based curriculum with practice which emphasises goal-oriented learning, literacy and numeracy. In Norwegian policy documents and curricula framework plans we will also find competing claims, which sketch out a complex pedagogical picture. Due to structural and rapid changes in the sector in Norway, there are a number of new discussions about curriculum issues. What is often referred to as the Nordic holistic approach has more facets and, in fact, it is now at stake.

Scary episodes happen

I will now present some empirical data from my field study in a Norwegian kindergarten. The data consisted of video-recorded mealtime conversations and video logs from everyday activities, planned as well as unplanned. An ethnographic approach was crucial in order to contextualise the co-narratives and write up a critical events case (Czarniawska 2004; Polkinghorne 1988, 1995; Webster and Mertova 2007).

In order to study children's meaning-making, I asked: *What is worth talking about for the two-year-olds?* From video recordings of 15 meals, I found 102 co-narratives which I organised into child-initiated and teacher-initiated co-narratives: 39 child-initiated co-narratives were found, initiated mostly by two boys in the group and supported by the teacher, leading to co-narrated stories (Ødegaard 2006).

'Co-narratives' in this study is a speech genre in which children and adults participate in creating episodic accounts. Co-narratives created in kindergartens often involve several participants, including younger children, and consist of children's verbal meaning-making as well as utterances, mimicry and gestures. Children between the ages of one and three years old are dependent upon verbal support by others in order to be able to participate in creating narratives (Ødegaard 2007a; Pramling and Ødegaard 2011).

The important role of extended child–teacher and teacher–child conversations in shaping children's language and early literacy development is well documented. Less explored is how narrative meaning-making also shapes the kindergarten classroom as a culture-generating forum. Studying such conversations can unfold underpinning ideas and bring dilemmas and challenges to the surface. By studying children's initiatives we can gain a closer understanding of what has relevance to them and how they create meaning in their interaction with the world around them.

From my transcripts of my data, the theme of survival and the area of tension between fear and pleasure appeared to be particularly relevant to those children who took the initiative to talk. The children used the genre of the co-narrative to bring up and examine what seemed to be challenging aspects of life. The stories had some interesting similar features; 'being afraid or being scared' was a dominant child perspective in the conversational narratives during mealtimes in this group (Ødegaard 2006).

By studying play, however, I could see that to *be* scary, to *make* scary things *happen* was also a dominant play theme. Andreas not only initiated stories about pirates during mealtime conversations, but he also initiated pirates as a play theme. During my nine-month field work in the kindergarten, I observed him dancing with imaginary swords, as well as using an imaginary telescope to watch the pirate approach. By swinging the swords, the children could explore and experience being scary by playing pirates attacking and shouting: 'Walk the plank and jump in the ocean!' By looking through the telescope they could explore and experience being afraid by withdrawing and shouting: 'The pirates are coming, heeelp!' Andreas's use of the stereotype protagonist in the pirate story was explored in a variety of ways where being scared seemed to be as prevalent as being scary.

Captain Andreas on a voyage towards influence

During my time in the kindergarten, Andreas repetitively engaged with the pirate theme which came into action in his initiatives to talk as well as in initiatives to play. Marit did not like this popular cultural anti-hero. She disliked the pirate for being an evil character in a play without literary quality. In spite of her attitude towards the pirate content, she permitted Andreas to bring his pirate spin-off products to the kindergarten and introduce them to his mates. In the beginning, the pirate play went on in the peripheries of adults' activities and location; for instance, in the bathroom or in the hallway.

A turning point in Marit's attitude occurred in the middle of a co-narrative, where Andreas told about the pirate in a playful way. Then Marit sighed: 'We have to arrange a Captain Sabertooth party soon.' She invited him to tell about what pirates eat and how they are dressed, and to contribute to the planning by being an expert on the theme. Their preparation was presented in a written plan and it was introduced to the parents the week after. Andreas had become an engaged participant in the co-construction of the planned programme in his kindergarten.

This case illustrates how a boy, repeatedly and in a shifting manner, brings the pirate to the table, floors, benches and sandpits. Andreas's serious playfulness and his repeated initiative, when it came to play activities and conversations with other children and adults, became – metaphorically speaking – his voyage towards influence. The kindergarten teacher shifted from a practice of ignoring his interest to one of inclusion of 'media-inspired' play activities and conversations, a content that was seen as highly 'gender-stereotyped'. Marit was faced with the dilemma of choosing to include Andreas's interests in the programme and, at the same time, to include content that was highly gender-stereotypical; she chose to follow up Andreas's interests.

Outlining a map of narratives

Child-centeredness was also found in teacher-initiated co-narratives (Ødegaard 2007b). To illustrate this, let me give an example. For some time, Alf Prøysen's children's story *The Billy-Goat Who Could Count to Ten* (2000) was the focus of teacher-initiated co-narratives which refer to the curriculum-based content. This is a didactic story of the billy-goat who counts the animals he meets on his way. The formulated goal was to learn the numbers from one to ten. Let us see what happens during this co-narrative process.

Nine little billy-goats were hanging in a mobile over the table. The children had coloured in drawings of the billy-goat. Andreas (two years, seven months) watched the animals and stretched out to reach them. Then Marit invited him to take part in a reconstruction of the story:

Marit: *Yes, what happened to the billy-goat?*
Andreas looked at Marit and sat down again.
Yes, Marit tried again, *What happened?*
Andreas was occupied with chewing his bread and did not respond.
Marit tried one more time: *What had he learned?*
Vidar (one year, six months), who was sitting close to Marit, rose up to reach for the billy-goats.
Then Marit changed the direction of the co-narrative: *Yes! That other billy-goat, the one who bit your finger.*
Then Andreas joined in: *Took my biscuit.*
Marit laughed: *He took your biscuit.*
Andreas continued: *My Papa . . .*
Marit came in with more details: *When you were on holiday.*
Andreas answered: *On farm.*
Marit: *Oh yes, on the farm.*
Andreas: *Yes.*
Marit laughed: *Yes.*
Andreas continued: *The cows, the pigs.*
Marit: *Were there pigs as well? Were there even more animals there?*
Andreas answered: *Yes*, and turned away.
Vidar was still occupied with the mobile on the ceiling. He pointed and uttered: *There, there.*
Marit answered: *There are the billy-goats, yes.*
Andreas turned back and reached for the billy-goats again.
Then Marit said in a humorous tone: *Watch out so he doesn't bite your finger!*

Wide horizons

In this story we can see that Marit made an effort to reconstruct Prøysen's story that was presented to the children several days before. When she said '*What had he learned?*' she referred to the fact that the billy-goat in the story had learned to count to ten. When Andreas did not respond to her initiative, she remembered the story about another billy-goat; Andreas's parents had told her about his visit to a farm where a billy-goat had tasted his finger. So she adjusted her narrative to what she remembered to be his experience.

Marit's flexible attitude appeared to serve as a key to making Andreas into a co-narrator. This process can be categorised as a pattern of communication, which Bae (2004) calls 'spacious pattern'; a pattern where the teacher opens up for children's contributions. Marit elicited his experience and added scaffold to his story; she made him use language to share an anecdote with her and the others who were listening. The overruling agenda did not seem to be the co-construction of Prøysen's curriculum-based story, but rather to seize an opportunity to empower one of the children to participate in the narrative as soon as she remembered his experience. This example illustrates a dominant feature in the teacher-initiated co-narratives. The teacher was child-centric; she was concerned with the individual child and sensitive to his intentions in participating.

These examples display how teachers in a Norwegian kindergarten classroom with a long history and tradition of child-centred approaches to play and learning adjust to unanticipated contributions from the children in the process of conversational practice. The teachers do so by supporting children's initiatives and responding to their contributions in the co-narrative practice as well as by adjusting their own planned activities accordingly. As we can see, the respect for children's perspective is a core issue.

Battles on board the Norwegian ship

When the first Framework Plan for the Content and Task of Kindergartens was introduced (Ministry of Child and Family Affairs 1996), everyone seemed to clap their hands. Finally, there was a written document that described kindergarten in a way that was recognisable and the challenges that it aroused were to a large extent known and not particularly controversial. Core ideas in this plan were expressed in the statement of 'the good childhood', where children's play was a central idea. The Framework Plan also introduced five academic subject areas, including the arts. Language, social competence and ethics were expected to be integrated in planned activities as well as in everyday practice. This socio-culturally inspired curriculum viewed the child as a participant who constructed meaning contextually. Issues such as play, humour, peer relations and interaction between child and teacher were stressed as important factors for well-being. The Framework Plan from 1996 emphasised educational processes rather than defined knowledge and plans for episodes rather than specific time frames. The plan was to a large extent informed by existing practices and issues like moral and social competence as well as the child's independent voice were predominant.

According to Alvestad and Pramling Samuelsson (1999), who compared the Swedish and Norwegian kindergarten curricula, the issue of learning in the Norwegian Framework Plan from 1996 is more related to socialisation, well-being and care, while the Swedish approach from 1998 is more socio-cognitive. They trace the reason for this difference between these two Nordic countries to later urbanisation in Norway and to the fact that Sweden had stronger connections to the continent of Europe. This indicates that so-called Nordic discourse is not a coherent discourse.

Nevertheless, to the extent that we can talk about a Nordic discourse, its position and mode of practice can be traced back to the ideas of Rousseau, Pestalozzi, Froebel and Dewey, where the teacher is the coach and facilitator and the child is seen as being able to self-organise her/his play and learning projects. According to Glenda MacNaughton (2003), such a position can be described as 'reforming society'. This approach rests on the belief that education can and should produce rational independent individuals. The self-governing child, the child that will achieve full potential by operating in an individualised curriculum linked to the individual child's interest will be an ideal.

Swords in action

The picture of this approach as *the* Nordic approach might now be an image which is about to crack. During the last few decades, the early childhood sector has expanded rapidly as a result of a public political effort to offer education to every child with a parent who so wishes. From coverage of less than 10 per cent in 1975, Norway now has full coverage. Full coverage means that 75 per cent of one- and two-year-olds and 98 per cent of three- to five-year-olds attend kindergarten. In addition, 7,200 children are users of open parent and children's kindergartens.

Such an expansion of provision has caused great public attention on quality. Fulfilment of full coverage over a short time reveals that this coverage is not automatically synonymous with quality. Consequently the debate is now about quality issues. In Norway, which has traditionally been perceived as a homogeneous and egalitarian society, we also now have debates focusing on increased educational gaps, child poverty, the indigenous Sami people, immigration and cultural diversity. The gap between the richest and poorest is widening and the number of young boys leaving compulsory schooling is increasing. Young women and men stereotypically study different subjects, and Norway has one of the most gender-segregated workforces in Europe. There is also a growing underlying anxiety about the future. What shall we live from when there is no oil left? What will we do with the fact that tests, such as the OECD Programme for International Student Assessment (PISA), show Norwegian school children not at the top of the list? This leaves the situation open to the bond between knowledge and finance.

Crossing the ocean

In the autumn of 2005, kindergartens were transferred from the Ministry of Children and Family Affairs to the Ministry of Education and Research (in Norwegian: *Kunnskapsdepartementet*). This transfer aimed at ensuring coherence and continuity in the education of children and young people along with the Norwegian Framework Plan for the Content and Task of Kindergartens (Ministry of Education and Research 2006). The plan requires that all kindergartens work with goal-oriented planning for children's development and learning. There are seven identified knowledge areas, but the approach is open with broad aims for the learning outcomes.

Yet the change from 1996 to 2006 can be seen as a step towards a stronger framing of the pedagogy. Is the holistic approach challenged? In a range of new official documents, kindergarten curricula are regarded as a crucial means and answer to societal challenges. A Danish study states that a holistic approach to early childhood education programmes has limitations when it comes to socially endangered children (Jensen 2009). This conclusion is in accordance with ideas presented in the *Official Norwegian Report* from the Ministry of Finance (2009). With the mandate to suggest a strategy for equalising the increasing gaps in society – for instance, decreasing child poverty and equalising opportunities for social mobility – the curriculum framework plan is made more concrete on learning outcomes. It is recommended that what and how children learn should be made explicit to ensure equality and better future perspectives for children at risk. In addition, these recommendations indicate new changes – an even stronger framing of the pedagogy with a focus on academic learning and outcomes.

In the white paper *Quality in Kindergarten* (Ministry of Education and Research 2008–2009), the underpinning belief is that social mobility is achieved through early intervention and the intervention implies a change towards more structure in the curriculum. The answer to societal needs seems to be a curriculum position that 'conforms to society' (MacNaughton 2003: 121). Such a curriculum position values observable behaviours, states what you want to achieve and emphasises knowledge skills such as literacy and numeracy. The role of education rests on the belief that education can and should achieve national social goals and, thus, governments define roles and purposes within education in order to ensure these goals. The teacher approaches are based on technical skills and methods.

Still, this position is not coherent in these recent official papers. In the same white paper, the concept '*danning*' is introduced. It is a concept that can be translated into the German word and continental tradition of '*bildung*' or the English expression (cultural) 'formation'. In the document it is explained as a continuing process which premises lifelong reflection. Word counts tell us that 'children's influence' is mentioned 27 times and children's participation seven times. This indicates that the teachers' approach is supposed to be child-centred.

McNaughton (2003: 183) also describes a curriculum position called 'transforming society'. This curriculum position contains ideas of justice and injustice; an attitude that she names 'ethico-political'. Such an approach to education equips children with knowledge and experience that enable them to recognise and confront injustice and resist oppression. It lays out diverse possibilities and provides inclusive educational environments to empower children with disabilities and/or at risk. In the latest Kindergarten Act (Ministry of Education and Research 2010: 1), the first paragraph ends: 'Kindergarten shall promote democracy and equality and work against all forms of discrimination.' This formulation is new, and being in the first paragraph conveys a significant message that points towards an 'ethico-political' curriculum. Still, the most predominant positions in the current Norwegian early childhood curriculum are the 'reforming' and 'conforming to society' ideas.

So what we find in these new policy documents is a bend towards a stronger framing of the curriculum and the pedagogy. In line with the political ideas of a socio-democratic welfare state, the kindergarten is seen as an instrument for building a democratic society and a means for protection against early deprivation and marginalisation of certain groups of children. At the same time, children's influence on the planned programme as well as everyday practice is still encouraged in order to enhance multicultural as well as indigenous and local cultural issues.

Conclusion: teachers on the open sea

Teachers who work in Norwegian kindergartens are given a complex mandate: to ensure children's influence on curriculum and, at the same time, to bridge gaps and solve increasing societal and cultural challenges by means of a more teacher-structured and framed programme. This mandate can be perceived as contradictory or, at least, demanding.

The current policy documents strongly indicate more complexity when it comes to kindergarten practices. Competing claims about what is in the best interest of the child and what kind of arena the kindergarten is going to be in the future expose many challenges, and the battle is about the Norwegian kindergarten's heart and soul. It can be said that the new policy documents in Norway reflect a greater interconnection to the global society and a belief that 'control works'. Such strategies seem to have taken a dominant position, but they are also contested (Fuller 2007; Dahlberg and Moss 2005).

We know that individual child-centred practice is not enough to ensure opportunities for all children to participate. To do so we will need a teacher role that can orchestrate the different voices in groups of children and attempt to include the vague initiatives and the silent voices. The teacher needs to manoeuvre between being the educational leader and letting it go in order to allow children's perspectives to be embedded in everyday practice (Ødegaard 2009).

Being with the youngest children and getting to know Andreas, it is my experience and conclusion that children can inform us in fighting policy battles. Andreas can teach us a lesson. Pirate play may bring about chaos and will often oppose and contradict teachers' agendas, but when scary things happen in the early childhood field we, as actors in the field of teacher education and research, will need some piracy in policy.

QUESTIONS FOR THINKING ABOUT POLICY AND PRACTICE

1.   What conditions would 'Captain Andreas and his Crew' experience in your practice and how might they influence it?
2.   What is the relation (weak or strong) between the frame of reference (e.g. curriculum framework and guidance) of your practice and children's influence?
3.   To what extent should it be the task of pre-school teachers to solve societal challenges?

References

Alvestad, M. and Pramling Samuelsson, I. (1999) A comparison of the national preschool curricula in Norway and Sweden, *Early Childhood Research & Practice*, 1(2), available online at: http://ecrp.uiuc.edu/v1n2/alvestad.html (accessed 4 August 2011).

Bae, B. (2004) Dialoger mellom førskolelærer og barn: En beskrivende og fortolkende studie [Dialogues between preschool teachers and children: A descriptive and interpretive study], Unpublished PhD Thesis, University of Oslo, Institute of Special Education.

Czarniawska, B. (2004) The uses of narrative in social science research, in M. B. A. Hardy (ed.) *Handbook of Data Analysis*, London: Sage Publications.

Dahlberg, G. and Moss, P. (2005) *Ethics and Politics in Early Childhood Education*, New York: RoutledgeFalmer.

Fuller, B. (2007) *Standardized Childhood: The Political and Cultural Struggle over Early Education*, Stanford, CA: Stanford University Press.

Jensen, B. (2009) A Nordic approach to early childhood education (ECE) and socially endangered children, *European Early Childhood Education Research Journal*, 17(1): 7–21.

Kristjansson, B. (2006) The making of Nordic childhoods, in J. Einarsdottir and J. T. Wagner (eds) *Nordic Childhoods and Early Education*, Greenwich, CT: Information Age Publishing (pp. 13–43).

MacNaughton, G. (2003) *Shaping Early Childhood: Learners, Curriculum and Contexts*, Maidenhead: Open University Press.

Ministry of Child and Family Affairs (1996) *Rammeplan for Barnehagens* [Framework Plan for Kindergarten], Q-0903b, Oslo: Ministry of Child and Family Affairs.

Ministry of Education and Research (2006) *Rammeplan for Barnehagens Innhold og Oppgaver* [Framework Plan for the Content and Task of Kindergarten], Oslo: Ministry of Education and Research.

Ministry of Education and Research (2008–2009) *Kvalitet i Barnehagen [Quality in Kindergarten]*, Stortingsmelding nr. 41[White paper 41], Oslo: Ministry of Education and Research.

Ministry of Education and Research (2010) Lov om Barnehager med Forandringer fra 1. August 2010. [Kindergarten Act with Changes from 1 August 2010], available online at: www.lovdata.no/all/tl-20050617-064-001.html#1 (accessed 31 August 2011).

Ministry of Finance (2009) *Fordelingsutvalget* [Official Norwegian Report NOU: 10, 2009], Oslo: Ministry of Finance.

Ødegaard, E. E. (2006) What's worth talking about? Meaning-making in toddler-initiated co-narratives in preschool, *Early Years: An International Journal of Research and Development*, 26(1): 79–92.

Ødegaard, E. E. (2007a) *Narrative Meaning-making in Preschool*, Göteborg Studies Educational Science 255, Gothenburg: Acta Universitatis Gothoburgensis.

Ødegaard, E. E. (2007b) What's on the teacher's agenda?, *International Journal of Early Childhood*, 39(2): 45–65.

Ødegaard, E. E. (2009) Children's initiatives and teachers' practices: Educational maneuvers in the Norwegian preschool classroom, in J. L. McConnell-Farmer (ed.) *The Education of Young Children: Research and Public Policy*, Louisville: KY: Linton Atlantic Books.

Polkinghorne, D. (1988) *Narrative Knowing and the Human Sciences*, Albany, NY: State University of New York Press.

Polkinghorne, D. (1995) Narrative configuration in qualitative analysis, in J. A. Hatch (ed.) *Life History and Narrative*, London: RoutledgeFalmer.

Pramling, N. and Ødegaard, E. E. (2011) Learning to narrate: Appropriating a cultural mould for sense-making and communication, in Niklas Pramling and Ingrid Pramling Samuelsson (eds) *Educational Encounters: Nordic Studies in Early Childhood Didactics*, Dortrecht, Heidelberg, London & New York: Springer.

Röthle, M. (2007) Norsk barnehagepedagogikk: Et historisk og komparativt perspektiv [Norwegian policy on early childhood: A historical and comparative perspective], in T. Moser and M. Röthle (eds) *Ny Rammeplan: Ny Barnehagepedagogikk [New Frameworkplan: New Pedagogy]*, Oslo: Universitetsforlaget.

Strand, T. (2006) The social game of early childhood education: The case of Norway, in J. Einarsdottir and J. T. Wagner (eds) *Nordic Childhoods and Early Education*, Greenwich, CT: Information Age Publishing (pp. 71–101).

Webster, L. and Mertova, P. (2007) *Using Narrative Inquiry as a Research Method: An Introduction to Using Critical Event Narrative Analysis in Research on Learning and Teaching*, London: Routledge.

3

DEVELOPMENTS IN PRE-SCHOOL EDUCATION IN BULGARIA

Achievements and challenges

Rozalina Engels-Kritidis

OVERVIEW

This chapter presents the Bulgarian modern theoretical framework for pre-school education, as it has been defined in the 1990s. It is based on the ideas of the significance and 'preciousness' of childhood, the stimulating functions of the material and intellectual surroundings, the encouragement of children's activities and the importance of pre-school education as a basic component of the educational system. The chapter also outlines the availability and demand of pre-school services, the training of pre-school teachers, the research activity undertaken in the field and issues raised from the increased emigration of Bulgarians abroad. The chapter concludes by highlighting some of the challenges faced by the sector.

Key words: Bulgaria; pre-school; education; pedagogy; situation; challenges; emigrant.

Introduction: transition, society and education

> We have always belonged to Europe – in searching for the truth for ourselves and for the others, in building our own national identity and representing Europe with dignity. The wide and dashing spirit of the Bulgarians went through the centuries, life–asserting and teaching, with one of the oldest state systems, cultures, literacy and education in Europe. A nation for which the education is weaved into its highest strivings and hopes . . .
>
> (Professor Elena Roussinova in Roussinova and Angelov 2008: 2)

In Bulgaria, during the last 20 years, economic, political and socio-cultural trans-formations have had an impact on its educational development. New models of education are now required in response to the needs and development of the society and in compliance with its evolving professional structure. Research is also needed for the optimisation of the Bulgarian education system in order to facilitate the country's effective integration into the European structures. The main goals of Bulgarian education are to educate a new generation who will be able to flourish in civil society and in the conditions of European integration by building upon the values and quality of the Bulgarian educational system (Roussinova and Angelov 2008).

Several other changes during the 1990s have also had an impact on education, for example:

- demographic developments such as the negative population growth, birth-rate reduction, population aging, population increase in the capital and large cities, reduction of kindergartens and primary schools in small towns and villages;
- reflux in the teacher profession due to low salaries and the high number of children in big cities, as well as unemployment in small towns and villages;
- export of young pedagogical personnel abroad, where they could gain expe-rience, due to the high professional competencies and skills attained in Bulgarian universities;
- tendencies of emigration among the young population.

As a result of these demographic changes, the educational goals have had to be reconsidered by acknowledging both global and specific national functional aspects of life. The current educational goals include the humanisation of society, the inte-gration process for achieving positive pedagogical practices and their constructive reconsideration in local conditions (Roussinova and Angelov 2008).

The modern theoretical framework of Bulgarian pre-school education

In response to these reviewed educational goals, two pre-school educational pro-grammes were developed during the 1990s: the *Educational Program for Children Aged 2–7 Years* (Roussinova 1993) and the *Children's Kindergarten Activities* (Vitanova 1993). The first programme was developed by the scientific group of the Department of Preschool Education of Sofia University 'St Kliment Ohridski'; the latter was developed by another scientific group. These programmes are seen as having laid the foundation of modern pre-school education in Bulgaria.

Both programmes promote the 'pedagogical situation' as the basic form of interaction, with the child being at the centre of it. Roussinova and her colleagues (1993) defined 'pedagogical situations' as interactions that take place on equal terms; involve discretion as far as the pedagogical strategy is concerned; consider differen-tiation and the individuality of the interactions; and have variety in terms of educational content. They argue that each pedagogical situation must be realised in accordance with the defined educational goals, the individual characteristics of children and the competence of the whole group, while taking into account the prospect of further development.

The *Educational Program for Children Aged 2–7 Years* has articulated its conceptual framework more explicitly and accurately. It is based on the ideas of:

• the significance and 'preciousness' of childhood taken in perspective;
• the stimulating functions of material and intellectual surroundings;
• the encouragement of children's activities;
• the importance of pre-school education as a fundamental component of the educational system;
• the synchronisation of educational activities and interaction;
• the integration of the national educational experience with universal educational practices.

The programme is designed to focus on children's developmental needs and it is structured in compliance with three formulated types of *goals of pedagogical interaction*:

1. cognitive development;
2. stimulation of individual emotional experiences;
3. dissemination of practical experience.

These goals are realised, by building one upon the other, in the three main *stages of pedagogical interaction*:

1. perception;
2. experiment;
3. expression.

One key feature of the theoretical framework of this programme is the separation of pedagogical situations into two main categories: *planned* and *spontaneous situations*. Planned situations are designed and structured by the teacher systematically, in accordance with the level of development and need of the group under their care. Spontaneous situations allow children to express their personal experiences more freely and to demonstrate their individual level of skill and potential in a group situation. The children are stimulated and supported, according to their individual needs, during the life of the pedagogical situation. The teacher's role is to find the proper approach for transforming that life situation into a pedagogical one, taking into account the moment when the child's need is manifested. Often, these spontaneous situations are initiated by the child, but they could also be provoked and stimulated by the teacher through proper material and social means (these pedagogical approaches are similar to those discussed in Chapter 2 with regard to the Norwegian context). Figure 3.1 illustrates the Bulgarian contemporary model

THE SURROUNDINGS

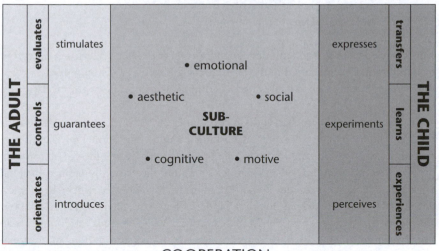

FIGURE 3.1 The Bulgarian model of pedagogical interaction in pre-school age

Source: Roussinova 1993

of pedagogical interaction in pre-school age, contained in the programme under examination.

National educational standards for early childhood education

National educational standards for early childhood education and for the preparation of children for primary school have been established by the content of Decree No. 4 for Early Childhood Education, which was issued by the Ministry of Education, Youth and Science (2000). Further additions and amendments were published in 2005. These standards are now required to be considered in the development of all future early childhood educational programmes.

The national standards for early education included the development of pre-school curricula for children 3–7 years old. The curricula define the attainable *knowledge, skills and attitudes* which children are expected to achieve. These are classified under several *educational directions*, each of which is further divided into educational kernels (subjects), that is:

- Bulgarian language and literature;
- mathematics;
- social orientation;
- natural environment orientation;
- fine arts;
- sport activity;

- music;
- constructional, technical and everyday essential activities;
- games and play culture.

The knowledge, skills and attitudes of children and the expected learning outcomes from education are specified in the curriculum for each age group separately (ages 3–4; ages 4–5; ages 5–6) as well as for the compulsory preparatory group/class (ages 6–7).

It should be noted here that work on developing the national educational standards for early childhood education and establishing a unified educational programme for pre-school ages continues. However, based on the two aforementioned educational programmes (Roussinova 1993; Vitanova 1993) and the currently defined national standards, several newer educational programmes (schemes of work) have been developed and used widely in Bulgarian kindergartens (e.g. 'Hand by Hand' in 2003; 'Molivko' in 2003; 'I am in the Kindergarten' in 2007; 'Friends' in 2008). These usually consist of the teacher's books, children's books and various educational materials (cardboards, posters, stickers, etc.), developed according to the specifics of the pedagogical work in the four pre-school age groups. They are approved by the Ministry of Education, Youth and Science for use in pre-schools.

Bulgarian pre-schools and the network of Bulgarian kindergartens

Organised public pre-school education in Bulgaria has a long history. The first kindergarten in Bulgaria was established in 1882 in Svishtov (an economically developed town at the time, located on the Danube River). The institution, founded by Bulgarian educationalist Nikola Zhivkov, was named 'Childish Wisdom'. Contemporary pre-school education in Bulgaria is regulated by the Ministry of Education, Youth and Science and takes place in kindergartens where children aged 3–7 years old are taught. Children enrol in the first grade of compulsory education at the age of seven.

In 2002, a preparatory compulsory year (at age 6) was introduced with effect from the school year 2003–2004. This was offered either in preparatory groups in kindergartens, or in preparatory classes in schools (*Bulgarian Government Gazette* 2002). Recently, further changes in the same article require that compulsory pre-school education is offered for children (at age 5) with effect from October 2010 (*Bulgarian Government Gazette* 2010).These policy requirements are expected to enhance the indispensable role of pre-school education in children's development and the formation of their personality (Ministry of Education, Youth and Science n.d.) and to increase the role and status of pre-school teachers in the society (Ministry of Education, Youth and Science 2010).

In Bulgarian public kindergartens, children are divided into separate groups, each taught by two teachers working in shifts, assisted by a full-time assistant educator. The group quota is 12 to 22 children; however, groups in large cities can have up to 30 children. There are four age groups (ages 3–4, ages 4–5, ages 5–6) and the preparatory group/class (ages 6–7). All preparatory groups and classes follow one of the aforementioned educational programme systems, chosen by the teachers. Parents are free to choose whether to enrol their children either in the preparatory group in kindergarten or a preparatory class in primary school.

In Bulgaria, the percentage of children regularly attending kindergartens is high. In the 2008/2009 school year, the average net rate of children enrolled in kindergartens was 73.8 per cent (National Statistical Institute n.d.) Table 3.1 summarises the overall distribution of children in different types of kindergarten during the 2008/2009 school year. It is evident that the majority of children attend *full-day kindergartens*, where parents can leave them from 7.00 am until 7.00 pm on weekdays. Besides pedagogical interactions, full-day kindergartens provide three meals (breakfast, lunch and an afternoon snack) and an afternoon siesta before the snack. For this, pre-schools are usually equipped with children's bunk beds.

Half-day kindergartens can keep children only until noon, while *weekly kindergartens* allow parents who work night shifts to leave children in their care on weeknights. Only a small number of children attend private kindergartens (Table 3.1). This can be attributed to the facts that public kindergartens have a very high level of education and that private kindergartens charge very high prices (approximately equal to the average monthly salary in Bulgaria).

A comparison of Table 3.1 with Table 3.2 shows that the places available in kindergartens surpass the corresponding demand. However, this data is averaged for the entire country and it applies primarily to smaller population centres. The situation is different in the capital and large cities, where there is a shortage of places in kindergartens and groups often have about 30 children.

Table 3.3 shows an approximately even distribution of children enrolled in kindergartens at ages 4 and 5; the numbers for children enrolled at age 3 are slightly lower. This is attributed primarily to the desire of some parents to look after their children at home in this lower age range. A significant increase can be seen in the number of children in kindergartens at the age of 6, which is related to the fact that preparatory groups are mandatory.

TABLE 3.1 Distribution of children in different types of kindergarten during the 2008/2009 school year

Type of kindergarten	No. of children
Full-day kindergartens	192,273
Half-day kindergartens	16,377
Weekly kindergartens	2,438
Other types of kindergarten (special, seasonal, etc.)	1,366
Total	212,454
Total for private kindergartens	1,620

Source: National Statistical Institute

TABLE 3.2 Distribution of places and groups available in kindergartens during the 2008/2009 school year

Type of kindergarten	Places	Groups
Full-day kindergartens	201,443	8,166
Half-day kindergartens	19,051	1,019
Other types of kindergarten (special, seasonal, etc.)	3,616	190
Total	224,110	9,375
Total for private kindergartens	1,854	141

Source: National Statistical Institute

TABLE 3.3 Distribution of children in kindergartens by age and gender during the 2008/2009 school year

Children's ages	Boys	Girls	Total
Age less than 3	4,654	4,477	9,131
Age 3	24,333	22,769	47,102
Age 4	25,804	24,246	50,050
Age 5	26,212	24,734	50,946
Age 6	28,292	26,104	54,396
Age 7	459	323	782
Age over 7	35	12	47
Total	109,789	102,665	212,454

Source: National Statistical Institute

Nurseries and nursery groups in Bulgaria

Parents of children before the age of 3 have the option of leaving them in the care of *nurseries* or *nursery groups*. This is another type of pre-school institution (not included in the data for Tables 3.1–3.3), which accepts children from 10 months to 3 years old. In practice, children usually go to nurseries after they have learned to walk. In 2008, there were 673 nursery groups in Bulgaria caring for 25,023 children (National Statistical Institute n.d.). The data in Table 3.4 shows that only a very small percentage of those children are younger than 1 year old.

In Bulgaria, there are independent public nurseries as well as nursery groups in some full-day kindergartens. Nurseries are further divided into two types: *daily* and *weekly* nurseries, the latter offering sleeping accommodation for children of night-shift workers. All nurseries are regulated by the Ministry of Health and staffed by qualified nurses, while a pedagogue with a degree in higher education is appointed per several nursery groups. Her/his responsibilities include arranging, planning and managing the educational activities for the children. The focus of education in nursery groups is on children's social development. The educational component is implemented by special educational programmes, approved by the Ministry of Education, Youth and Science in conjunction with the Ministry of Health.

TABLE 3.4 Distribution of children enrolled in nursery groups during the 2008/2009 school year

Children's ages	No. of children
Age less than 1	226
Age 1–2	12,146
Age 2–3	12,369
Age over 3	282
Total children in nursery groups	25,023

Source: National Statistical Institute

The education of Bulgarian kindergarten teachers

In Bulgaria, the professional qualification for a pre-school teacher is currently obtained in specialised faculties at universities after four years of vocational training (Bachelor degree) and a year of training in a Master's programme. From 2007 onwards, the so-called Professional Bachelor degree is also offered. This is a three-year training course for acquiring the pre-school teacher qualification. It is organised by pedagogical colleges and it has replaced the higher education Specialist degree. Successful completion of the Professional Bachelor degree allows students to continue their education for a Master's degree in the university. Students who have completed undergraduate programmes in other humanitarian disciplines are also given the opportunity to take an extended two-year Master's programme in order to acquire the qualification for working as a pre-school teacher. Furthermore, three-year training for a PhD degree in pre-school education is available.

The teaching positions in pre-schools are usually held by personnel who have completed a traditional degree or one of the relatively new degrees of Pre-school Pedagogy with [a] Foreign Language or Pre-school and Primary School Pedagogy. The first of the new degrees reflects the current need for qualified pre-school teachers who, in addition to the mainstream pedagogical work, are specially tutored for early foreign language teaching in one of several languages: English, German, French, Russian, Spanish or Italian. The second is a hybrid specialisation in pre-school and primary school pedagogy and it is premised on the idea of facilitating the transition of children from kindergarten to primary school by providing teaching professionals with a broad spectrum of competence; teachers who are well acquainted with the specifics of working with both pre-school and primary school children.

The university training ends with written state examinations. Students of the Pre-school Pedagogy with [a] Foreign Language are additionally tested on the respective foreign language, while students of the Pre-school and Primary School Pedagogy specialisation are tested in a state examination on a pooled questionnaire. For practical training of students in a real educational environment, universities have contractual agreements with specially selected nurseries, kindergartens and teachers/mentors. The practical training of teaching skills starts from as early as the first semester and ends with a practical state examination. Students gradually move from observation and analysis of teaching situations to independently performing in real pedagogical conditions.

According to the Bulgarian national system for postgraduate in-service training, all Bulgarian teachers (including pre-school teachers) can develop their qualifications in a five-level qualification scale. The first two levels involve education on contextual and technological innovation, as well as sharing of the teachers' individual experiences and pedagogical practices. The latter three levels focus on activities related to the practical application of innovations and the creation and practical testing of individual innovative practices, with the top-level qualification requiring dissemination of the results in suitable publications (Kusheva *et al.* 2006).

Profile of the Bulgarian kindergarten teacher

Traditionally, teachers in Bulgarian pre-school education have always been highly qualified. For the past ten years, the percentage of pre-school teachers with Bachelor's and Master's degrees in the total number of teaching staff in pre-school education has increased significantly. According to Kusheva *et al.* (2006), regarding the entire educational system for the 2003/2004 school year, teachers with higher education accounted for about 90 per cent of all teachers. The data regarding gender ratio in pre-school education professionals show that the overwhelming majority are women; in other words, there is a high feminisation of the pre-school teacher profession. According to Kusheva *et al.* (2006) and official data (shown in Table 3.5), the age distribution of pre-school teachers is mainly among older age groups. It is currently a worrying fact that a large percentage of pre-school graduates do not pursue a career working in kindergartens.

TABLE 3.5 Age distribution of teachers in kindergartens during the 2008/2009 school year

Teachers' ages	No. of teachers
Age less than 25	96
Age 25–29	750
Age 30–34	1,443
Age 35–39	1,854
Age 40–44	2,498
Age 45–49	3,454
Age 50–54	5,582
Age 55–59	3,423
Age 60 and older	248
Total teachers	*19,348*

Source: National Statistical Institute

Research on pre-school education in Bulgaria

The keen interest in reforming early childhood provision during the last two decades is also reflected in the large number of research projects and publications which focus on and contribute to the improvement of the quality of early childhood education and care. For the ten-year period from 1996 to 2006, 350 scientific dissertations have been defended before the Specialised Pedagogical Council, of which 30 have been in the area of pre-school education. The topics covered in most of these dissertations deal with issues that currently concern early childhood education in the light of the changing structure and demographics of Bulgarian society. These topics include (Boyadzhieva 2007):

- challenges with the upbringing and education of young children;
- personality formation;
- preparation and readiness for school;
- children's socialisation;
- family and the kindergarten as factors of children's development;
- intercultural pedagogy;
- integration of Roma children;
- mass media and pedagogy;
- educational activities in health and social care institutions (nurseries);
- inclusive education of disadvantaged children;
- surrogate families as an alternative to social care institutions.

Scientific conferences, dealing with the improvement of pre-school teachers' qualifications and the introduction of innovative approaches in education, are conducted annually. Bulgaria is an active member of the World Organisation for Early Childhood Education (OMEP) and the Bulgarian OMEP Committee has initiated programmes for improving the quality of early childhood education and professional development of pre-school education professionals; currently, more than 300 teachers throughout Bulgaria are participating in such programmes.

There is also an increased number of national and international projects which focus on the same issues. These are implemented by the regional inspectorates at the Ministry of Education, Youth and Science and various kindergartens across the country as well as with international partnerships.

Challenges for pre-school education in Bulgaria

In light of the national and global situation, when examining the need for the continuing education of pre-school teachers, the main priorities arising as challenges for pre-school education in Bulgaria are related to:

- practical application of digital literacy and informational culture as part of the professional pedagogical qualification of the pre-school teacher;

- extending the practical skills of qualified pre-school teachers specialising in early language tuition, so they can assist the development of the relevant competences among children, as well as stimulating bilingual skills where appropriate;
- updating the existing pedagogical policy and technology for equal tuition opportunities for children with special educational needs and children who are socially disadvantaged and/or at risk;
- raising the social status of pre-school teachers via state initiatives for improving their qualifications and creating models for career development, including a new remuneration system;
- applying good practices to the training of kindergarten directors in effective school management and promoting educational entrepreneurship in a competitive environment;
- encouragement of publications by Bulgarian teachers and pedagogical scientists in international peer-reviewed journals in the field of pre-school education; translation of selected monographs into English, in order to disseminate the results of their studies among foreign colleagues.

These challenges also define the scope and potential of improving and enhancing theory and practice for pre-school education.

Challenges for pre-school education of Bulgarian emigrant children

The political changes in the early 1990s have contributed to the increased emigration of Bulgarians to other European countries such as Greece, Spain, Italy, Germany, the United Kingdom, as well as the USA, Canada, etc. This number increased further after Bulgaria joined the European Union in January 2007. The emigration trends highlight the need for researching the process of the education of Bulgarian children living abroad.

There are two interdependent and mutually complementary aspects of the education of children who live in a foreign country. On the one hand, children need to preserve their mother tongue and national identity; and, on the other hand, they need to attain intercultural education for their natural integration into a foreign society. The necessity for development in these two directions is apparent in the concurrent publication of European directives (e.g. Lisbon European Council 2000; Barcelona European Council 2002) which examine and redefine the role of the teachers. These directives mandate the development of teachers' pedagogical methods and skills for increasing children's motivation for learning and for establishing their identity in the context of cultural pluralism and variety.

Much research has been conducted with regard to creating high-quality methodological handbooks, books for children and other publications aimed at Bulgarian children living abroad. These resources aim at facilitating children's learning of the mother tongue and national culture, while, at the same time, considering the specifics of the language and culture of their host country. The mother tongue and national cultural identity of Bulgarian children living abroad is now systematically supported by the Bulgarian government and national institutions. Starting from the 2009/2010 school year, the Bulgarian Ministry of Education, Youth and Science (2009) has initiated a project called Mother Tongue and National Culture beyond Borders. The project supports educational activities aimed at preserving ties with the Bulgarian nationality, culture and spirituality as well as strengthening the national affiliations. Under the terms of this project, 53 Bulgarian schools from all around the world have received financial support for the educational activities they are performing.

Conclusion

Building upon a solid historical and theoretical basis and encompassing the overall transformation of social life in the country, Bulgarian pre-school education is now being reformed to meet the standards of other European countries. The child and her/his needs are firmly established as the core focus of contemporary pre-school pedagogy. In this respect, the continuing education of pre-school teachers accentuates training that allows educators to adapt to the constantly changing educational needs of children and demands of the educational system. The modernisation of the Bulgarian educational system incorporates a desire for the harmonisation of its pedagogical practices with requirements adopted by various European and international organisations and fora. At the same time, it constantly looks for the means and forms which will allow the preservation and promotion of national traditions in education.

QUESTIONS FOR THINKING ABOUT POLICY AND PRACTICE

1. What can pre-school teachers do to keep the idea of the 'preciousness' of childhood at the core of their practice in their own context?
2. How can pre-school teachers counter the early onset of didactical methodologies, due to compulsory pre-school education at earlier ages (4–5 years old)?
3. What are the challenges of pre-school teachers in your context in supporting policy requirements with regard to the identity of children from different cultural and ethnic groups?

References

Barcelona European Council (2002) *Presidency Conclusions, 15 and 16 March*, available online at: http://www.bologna-berlin2003.de/pdf/Pres_Concl_Barcelona.pdf (accessed 21 February 2012).

Boyadzhieva, N. (2007) Analysis of the thematic field of the dissertations on theory of education and social pedagogy (1996–2006), in *Conference Proceedings on Social Pedagogy, History and Practice*, Sofia: Farago (pp. 65–85).

Bulgarian Government Gazette (2002), issue 90/2002.

Bulgarian Government Gazette (2010), issue 78/2010.

Kusheva, R., Zahariev, Z., Pillev, D. and Krumova, P. (2006) *National Report on International Research Project 'Raising the Professional Qualification of Teachers and Development of Pedagogical Practice in the Countries of South-Eastern Europe'*, available online at: www.see-educoop.net/education_in/pdf/workshop/tesee/dokumenti/tesee-report-bulgaria_bg.pdf (accessed 25 May 2011).

Lisbon European Council (2000) *Presidency Conclusions, 23 and 24 March*, available online at: http://consilium.europa.eu/ueDocs/cms_Data/docs/pressData/en/ec/00100-r1.en0.htm (accessed 21 February 2012).

Ministry of Education, Youth and Science (2000) Decree No. 4 for Early Childhood Education, available online (in Bulgarian) at: www.minedu.government.bg/opencms/export/sites/mon/left_menu/documents/process/nrdb_4-00_preduchilishtno_obr.pdf (accessed 1 June 2011).

Ministry of Education, Youth and Science (2009) *The National Programme: Mother Tongue and National Culture beyond Borders*, available online (in Bulgarian) at: www.minedu.government.bg/opencms/export/sites/mon/left_menu/projects/national_programs/2009-01_roden_ezik.pdf (accessed 3 June 2011).

Ministry of Education, Youth and Science (2010) *Report of the Minister of Education, Youth and Science on Pre-school Education*, available online (in Bulgarian) at: www. podkrepa-obrazovanie.com/Document/doklad.doc (accessed 1 June 2011).

Ministry of Education, Youth and Science (n.d.) *National Programme for Development of School and Pre-school Education (2006–2015)*, available online (in Bulgarian) at: www. minedu.government.bg/left_menu/documents/strategies/nac_programa.html (accessed 28 May 2011).

National Statistical Institute (n.d.) Children in kindergartens – statistical data, available online at: http://www.nsi.bg/otrasal.php?otr=23&a1=15&a2=16&a3 (accessed 1 June 2011).

Roussinova, E. (ed.) (1993) *Educational Program for Children Aged 2–7 Years*, Sofia: Daniela Ubenova.

Roussinova, E. and Angelov, B. (2008) *System of Early Education/Care and Professionalisation in Bulgaria*, Report commissioned by the State Institute of Early Childhood Research (IFP) Munich, Germany, available online at: www.ifp.bayern.de/imperia/md/content/stmas/ifp/commissioned_report_bulgaria.pdf (accessed 4 June 2011).

Vitanova, N. (ed.) (1993) *Children's Kindergarten Activities*, Sofia: Prosveta.

Educational programmes (cited in the text) approved by the Ministry of Education, Youth and Science

Programme System 'Friends' (2008), Sofia: Anubis.

Programme System 'Hand by Hand' (2003), Sofia: Prosveta.

Programme System 'I am in the Kindergarten' (2007), Sofia: Izkustva.

Programme System 'Molivko' (2003), Veliko Tarnovo: Slovo.

4

EARLY CHILDHOOD CARE AND EDUCATION IN UZBEKISTAN

Carol Aubrey

OVERVIEW

History, infrastructure and capacity for early childhood development (ECD) policies in Central and Eastern Europe (CEE) and the Commonwealth of Independent States (CIS) have traditionally been positive and strong. The period of transition from Soviet control in the early 1990s was marked by economic decline, decrease in availability of services and reduced ECD outcomes. This chapter describes the approach of one international organisation to tackling challenges for young children and families in Uzbekistan. Findings indicated that a range of strategies – from home visits and one-to-one contacts to targeted community and service-provider engagement and national partnerships – delivered key messages about safe motherhood, public health and practice of child nutrition, sanitation and hygiene, psychological, physical and social development of children. Kindergarten enrolment was most neglected at 16.5 per cent of eligible children. By focusing on the most vulnerable children, families and communities and their health, social care and welfare needs, it was possible to scale up coverage and incorporate ECD for basic schooling. Postcolonial theory served as a tool to uncover forms of power and control that are old and new.

Key words: Uzbekistan; early childhood; care and education.

Introduction

This chapter reports an evaluation of a Family Education Project (FEP) focusing on care and education of mother and child in the family and community. Uzbekistan can be regarded as a postcolonial state, having recently thrown off Russian occupation. Critical and postcolonial theory provided a tool for interrogation of findings, a means of unsettling Western ways of thinking about early child development (ECD) introduced recently through international donors, and a way of clearing space for multiple and possibly marginalised voices (Bhabha 1994). It was recognised that colonialism had remained, both through the old forms of Soviet power and control and production of new forms of dominant ECD knowledge by international donors.

Global context

Underpinning international donors' approach to ECD is the premise that in order to meet the rights of all children, particularly those in contexts of socio-economic disparity, poverty and vulnerability, the goal is to develop innovative models for promoting overall development and hence developmental readiness for formal primary schooling (UNICEF 2008). This suggests that the focus of effort should be knowledge, skills and access to resources offering a nurturing, safe, supportive and stimulating environment for children by families, community and service providers. It emphasises the inter-dependence of safe motherhood, public health services and child health, sanitation and hygiene, with the psychological, physical and social development of the child. It recognises that ECD aims to improve the lives of children and families and, hence, support poverty reduction, universal and successful completion of basic education and progress towards the anti-poverty Millennium Development Goals (MDGs) set by the United Nations (UN 2000). These range from halving extreme poverty to halting the spread of HIV/AIDS and providing universal primary education by 2015. These goals, in turn, are dependent upon enabling policies and investments for young children and families.

Successful transitions to school depend upon 'three pillars of readiness: child readiness for school; family readiness to support learning; and school readiness for children' (UNICEF 2008: 10). Global evidence has been marshalled to demonstrate the fundamental importance of early development and learning to later outcomes in school and beyond in adult life, (e.g. Engle *et al.* 2007; Grantham-McGregor *et al.* 2007; Sylva *et al.* 2004; Walker *et al.* 2007).

Context of Uzbekistan

In Uzbek culture, marriages are traditionally arranged. After marriage, the bride moves to the home of in-laws, thereafter spending more time with her mother-in-law and sisters-in-law than her husband (Alexander 2010). The mother-in-law may then retire from housework, leaving the girl to rise early to milk the cow, clean the house, prepare food and generally support the family economy. Beatings at the hands of the husband's family are common and lead to high rates of attempted suicides, estimated to be many thousands a year (Murray 2007). Gender is political, a taboo subject and domestic violence is described as 'family atmosphere' (Interview with UN agency representative 2009).

Views on the impact of Soviet rule vary. Women across Central Asia, previously veiled, largely house-bound and regarded as the property of husbands, had their rights transformed under Communism (Alexander 2010). Murray (2007: 147), on the other hand, suggested that 'hundreds of thousands of women led absolutely dreadful lives' following the Soviet destruction of traditional societal mechanisms and that their lives were worsened by the general brutalisation of society since independence. Job migration exacerbates split families, with an estimated 2 million working abroad, and HIV/AIDS is increasing with migration, with evidence now of mother–child infection (UN agency representative 2009).

The period of transition initiated in the 1990s created economic and social upheaval. President Islam Karimov reluctantly supported change from the Communist Party of Uzbekistan to the People's Democratic Party that espoused democracy, capitalism and liberal reform. In practice, independent political parties and Islamic groups have been crushed (MacLeod and Mayhew 2008). The Soviet KGB became the National Security Service (SNB). Reported numbers of political prisoners vary with an estimated 7,000 prisoners of conscience in Uzbek jails (Murray 2007) where torture, rape and murder are routine.

Despite a declared objective of transition to a market economy, the government retains rigid controls over the economy which relies mainly on commodity production of cotton, gold, uranium, potassium and natural gas. The economy has remained weak with social policy and investment at low levels. In response, the International Monetary Fund (IMF) closed its office and left, impacting on aid projects. The Uzbek cotton industry is the world's fifth largest producer and second largest exporter, but with only two state monopoly purchasers of cotton, there is wide scope for government corruption, leaving cotton workers a tied labour force, unable to pay the bribe to leave. This has led to increasing marginalisation of vulnerable populations, high rates of child poverty and growing inequalities among young children and families. Over this period several MDG indicators plateaued and in some cases declined (UNICEF 2007).

Abdurakhmanov and Marnie (2006) estimated that in 2001, 6.8 million people or 27.5 per cent were living below the poverty line (based on the cost of a minimum food basket that would produce 2,100 calories a day); 70 per cent were in rural areas and small towns with limited land access. In over 50 per cent of households, the head was in work, reflecting low wages in the public sector and agriculture. By 2003, there was a slight reduction in poverty from 27.5 per cent to 26.2 per cent.

Uzbekistan has a high literacy rate among adults (older than 15), attributable to the free and universal Soviet education system. A recent survey showed secondary schooling to be the highest level of education for nearly 78 per cent of the population and primary for 8.9 per cent with higher education enjoyed by only 8.9 per cent. Attendance at some form of early childhood education has been reported to be 20.2 per cent. More than 32,000 ECD programmes closed over the CEE/CIS region in the 1990s, with pre-primary enrolment falling in 12 countries (UNICEF 2008).

More than 75 per cent of children are not attending organised ECD programmes prior to school entry in most CEE/CIS countries. Poor children are at least twice as unlikely to attend as wealthier children (Stewart and Huerta 2006). It appears that not much has changed since Soviet times. Despite the long Soviet history of centralised child care in the region and allowing for inaccuracies in the collection of statistics at the time, Grant (1978) suggested that 33 per cent of children experienced some pre-school education, with enrolment clustering heavily at upper-age pre-school levels. In some areas of the Russian Republic at least, substantial majorities of five- and six-year-olds attended kindergarten from the mid-1960s, but a figure of 55 per cent concealed a much lower enrolment in the countryside. Bronfenbrenner (1969), at a similar time, reported that over 10 per cent of all Soviet children under two years old were enrolled in public nurseries; about 20 per cent of children between three and six years attended pre-school. Even in Moscow, with more facilities than any other Soviet city, only 50 per cent of all applicants could be accepted.

It is likely that some Uzbek families now, as in Soviet times, are ill-equipped in terms of knowledge of proper nutrition and health care, learning opportunities and protection from risk. They may depend on long-established cultural practices and out-dated cultural traditions such as extended use of the *beshiq*, a form of tight binding or swaddling of young infants into a small crib during the night and/or day that severely restricts freedom of movement.

Dependence on traditional cultural beliefs is further exacerbated by high rates of migration as men travel abroad to find work. Husbands are unavailable to share child-care arrangements and leave wives susceptible to the influence of grandparents who may lack reliable information and resources related to child health, early stimulation, nutrition and safety which are required to provide the 'family readiness'. None of this, however, warrants the claim of a 'lost culture of parenting . . . where systems for supporting parents are rare' (UNICEF 2008: 29).

One outcome of institutionalised child care is the social stigma attached to children with disabilities, where Soviet traditions of 'defectology' have seen children continuing to be assigned to special institutions with under-stimulating environments. Some special-school teachers have been reported to express an unwillingness to change (Alexander 2010) and the general public is suspicious of moves towards including children with disabilities.

Across the CEE/CIS, ECD and developmental readiness programmes have lacked investment. Soviet centralised education, health and social-protection systems, ideology and methods leave a valuable legacy in the form of a culture and infrastructure for universal education, large numbers of trained teachers and teacher-training institutions. Lack of public spending has, however, led to reduced teacher salaries, decaying school buildings and lack of or deterioration in resources. Pedagogy and curriculum have changed little in the absence of professional development and a downward pressure from the formal instructional methods of the primary school is experienced (UNICEF 2008).

There is a Soviet legacy of top-down planning and implementation of social and economic policies, encouraging a culture of inertia and low participation by families and communities. This does provide infrastructure for new projects and a framework for delivery that international development partners exploit.

The role of international development partners

Uzbekistan ratified the United Nations Convention on the Rights of the Child (UNCRC) in 1992 and the Convention on the Elimination of All Forms of Discrimination against Women (CEDAW) in 1995. In 2001, Uzbekistan submitted its first period report to the UNCRC Committee which raised a number of concerns. In June 2006, it submitted its second period report; the Committee had remaining concerns about this, despite noting that various previous recommendations had been addressed. Adoption of a comprehensive children's code, non-discrimination, ill-treatment and abuse of children, protection of refugees, displaced and street children, child labour and administration of juvenile justice, it was judged, had not been given sufficient follow-up. The three MDGs related to child mortality, maternal mortality rates and HIV/AIDS are still regarded as a challenge; ECD policies are lacking. There may be low family awareness of factors affecting well-being of women and children. Traditional cultural values and beliefs may militate against addressing family and social issues (Aubrey and Gittins 2009). Major international development partners such as the World Bank, Asian Development Bank and World Health Organization (WHO) have provided loans and support to the Uzbek government, priorities being reproductive health (infant and maternal health), community education, nutrition and food safety, and education of children of compulsory school age.

Convergence of action on delivery of basic services in health and nutrition, pre-school education, child protection and well-being contributed to attaining at least five of eight MDGs. This was the distinctive feature of the Family Education Project (FEP). Child protection is political, while mother and child health is not (Representative of a health organisation 2009).

The international FEP sponsor was strategically placed to promote new ECD policy and co-ordinate existing regional governance in systematic reform of local services for young children. This promoted knowledge skills in families and communities, particularly for vulnerable groups, laying foundations for developmental readiness for schooling, poverty reduction and progress towards MDGs.

The final year of the FEP programme cycle, initiated by the Government of Uzbekistan with technical assistance from the international FEP sponsor and with a vision of integrated ECD came in 2009. It was important to have reliable data on FEP impact, achievements and constraints, and to generate relevant recommendations for the next programme cycle. A national social-research centre carried out the last in a series of monitoring surveys in 19 districts of six regions to understand and explore quantitative evidence of reported behaviour change at the household level. The writer and a colleague carried out the qualitative aspect, with review and analysis of documents, observation, focus-group discussions and in-depth interviews. Key questions were:

• What is early care and education in Uzbekistan?
• What philosophies and values underpin practice?
• Are there conflicts between values underpinning policy and practice?

- What pedagogical models predominate?
- How (if at all) can these inform current practice internationally?

Methodology

A participative and reflective approach was adopted. The intention was to learn from reflections on experience by multiple stakeholders and families, to increase awareness and understanding of factors affecting their situation. Informants included government ministers and heads of department, other donors and UN partners, regional, district and local government officials, volunteers (doctors, nurses and teachers) and families. A maximum variation sample included ten families, five deputy governors and five community advisers, allowing for participants' meanings and perspectives to be captured.

Interview and focus-group schedules were developed for different stakeholders, addressing the relevance, efficiency, effectiveness, impact and sustainability of the FEP coverage, co-ordination and coherence. Two weeks were spent gathering data in different districts of two regions of Ferghana and Bukhara, as well as Tashkent. Two days were spent in national workshops enabling a larger sample of stakeholders the opportunity for sharing lessons learned, reviewing challenges and identifying future plans for the development of ECD standards. Findings were grouped according to the question they addressed and key themes were identified, drawing on postcolonial theory, and implications for ECD were considered.

Ethical safeguards were upheld and strict confidentiality maintained. Children were not formally interviewed, though parents might, for example, encourage reciting of poems or demonstrating *tae kwondo*. Government permissions were obtained in advance. Family visits were marked by displays of hospitality, sharing of food and exchange of gifts. Additional visits were made to two low-income families who had not received FEP training. Their poverty was significantly greater than the intervention families which included farmers, nurses and teachers whom one might not normally expect to receive social welfare.

Early childhood care and education

Document analysis revealed that programme goals were to promote ECD and school readiness by six years of age; service providers' incorporation of ECD principles in their practice; and families having knowledge, skills and access to resources providing a nurturing, safe and stimulating environment (UNICEF 2008).

Key FEP components were:

- capacity building, through training of personnel;
- advocacy and communication, through development of materials and popularisation of FEP messages;
- support for community initiatives and action;
- monitoring and evaluation.

Stakeholders acknowledged the distinctive cross–cutting nature of the FEP: 'We are most pleased with the FEP. Since the first days of independence, mother and child have been a priority for the Government' (Government official 2009).

Doctors, nurses and teachers worked as volunteers for the programme and utilised a traditional feature of Uzbek society, the 'street head', as 'a tool to reach every family' (Government official 2009). All members of the family were addressed through both traditional and professional leaders in the community. 'With increased knowledge, community advisers work at the level of every street. 10,000 community advisers go directly to reach families in communities. This will create a sustainability to work in the future' (National lead trainer 2009). The community advisers' role has never received systematic evaluation. Officially, they are required to work on moral upbringing and religious issues, following a decree to strengthen religious issues in the wake of a female suicide bombing. International donors work through them to reach communities (UN agency worker 2009).

Reproductive health was a cross–cutting area, creating synergy for co-operation between donors, though a UN agency worker noted that collaboration was not encouraged: 'They don't want us to work together . . . then we are easier to control.' It was agreed that a distinctive strength of FEP was its 'strategy to change behaviour creating a programme to reach families . . . achieved through levels of implementation with relevant ministries'. 'Government and programme work together . . . it gives motivation, a methodology, a form of communication, a structure and purposes' (Director of the social research centre 2009). Messages related to breast feeding were delivered by nurses at delivery. Community advisers worked with mothers, so from the beginning, FEP messages were received. Training took place at colleges, community centres and FEP learning resource centres, encouraging the participation of fathers and grandmothers, too.

Advocacy events were held at community health clinics, state kindergartens and schools. Posters and local and national newspapers served as popularising devices. Annual contests took place between community advisers to increase motivation and participation. Stakeholders agreed that FEP messages should be more widely covered by mass media – television documentary films, human interest stories and radio-spots to reach parents, caregivers and families:

> There is mass media, television shows for new families. Young people are interested. Television is a powerful tool – *Baby TV Show* for Tashkent is a dream . . . Good video clips for FEP convey messages. Every family has a television. For ECD, I think that it is good. My attitude is very positive.
>
> (Government representative 2009)

In practice, though, Murray (2007: 61) has suggested that 'the media is completely censored. There is absolutely no real news – it's the most arrant propaganda.'

In 2006, a strategic shift in coverage refocused FEP from pilot communities, 'scaling up' to entire district and regional levels in six priority regions. This necessitated change in training – to a cascade model, using community advisers who might lack the necessary skills and knowledge, affecting the training experience of volunteers. Volunteer dropout compromised 'the level of sustainability' (National lead trainer 2009). Monitoring of training activities of volunteers took place in some districts. Results of bi-annual monitoring ensured that changes in attitudes and practices were assessed at family level (Yakupov 2009).

A challenge was that 'they want to show reduction of 20–30 per cent in infant and child mortality' (UN agency worker 2009). In the Soviet era, the whole system was punished for failing to show expected improvements in the statistics, so 'just in case, figures show good performance'. Document analysis showed that a need to strengthen the ECD component of FEP was recognised. The mid-term review observed that there was some awareness of health and nutrition issues, but this was surface knowledge with even lower awareness of early education issues.

By 2008, the annual review noted that a study was being made of child skills, using observation record forms based on globally accepted indicators. By June 2009 these indicators were being cross-referenced with the newly developed Uzbekistan National Early Learning and Development Standards (ELDS). The final impact study (Yakupov 2009) of 270 households (with a further 90 control households) indicated that the FEP had been successful in raising awareness and knowledge about safe motherhood, public health services and child health, child nutrition, sanitation and hygiene, and the psychological, physical and social development of the child. It was concluded that ECD messages needed elaboration: 'Preschool development of a child has been the most neglected area, for example, reading stories or showing pictures, teaching to count, draw or name items is practised by only around a third of family members' (Yakupov 2009).

Policy in annual reports and work plans for 2008–2009 had evolved with more emphasis being placed on working with government departments on quality assurance of ECD standards and validation. 'Our biggest achievement has been maternal health and child health, growth and development, strength of the family . . . development of the whole child. Next most important is making families better organised to help the whole child' (FEP volunteer).

State ECD standards had been prepared in draft form and were subject to consultation at a Standards Validation Workshop held in June 2009. These described development from around three months to seven years (birth to three, three to five, and five to seven years). The *Early Learning and Development Standards (ELDS) 'Going Global'* from the USA (Kagan and Britto 2000) had been translated and guidance sought on development and implementation in Russia. A visit to the Republican Centre for Training of Pre-school Educators established that the standards would form the basis for professional training in all 14 regions and Tashkent. Another influence was a child-centred programme supported by the International Step-by-Step Association (ISSA), an NGO operating in 26 countries. As noted by the FEP officer: 'FEP health messages work. Education messages have not been developed. There is a need to develop standards for teachers and parents/caregivers to see what children know and can do. How do we integrate standards with school-age competencies?' This officer reported that implementation claimed a modest level of funding (6.5 per cent of the overall country budget) *if*, as claimed, it reached 10 per cent of all low-income families nationwide each year.

Values and philosophies

Historical trade routes through Uzbekistan produced a rich exchange of ideas (religious, intellectual and artistic) and goods (MacLeod and Mayhew 2008). Since independence, Uzbekistan attempted to re-establish its identity. Textbooks and street names were rewritten. At the same time, the Tajik cultural and literary traditions of Samarkand and Bukhara were being suppressed. Tajik schools had closed, newspapers halted and broadcasting stopped. Bringing Russian literature into Uzbekistan became illegal. There was less personal freedom, living standards were plummeting and there was a disastrous brain drain of Russians (Murray 2007).

Despite the impact of recent colonialism through Soviet centralised child care and Western ECD standards, Uzbekistan has its own ethnic, cultural and ideological traditions. Islamic beliefs have survived 70 years of Soviet rule. Whilst Western imperialist models of universal pre school for three- to five-year-olds may underpin the thinking of international donors, both previously under Soviet colonial influence and since independence, a minority of children have attended kindergarten. A hybridity in delivery models existed, from home-based care and home-visiting, through community pre-schools for three- to five-year-olds, to Saturday schools, providing preparation for school for low-income families. These have emerged reflecting local histories, needs and constraints.

Global knowledge, 'readiness' and 'standards' are being appropriated by government through the Ministry of Public Education, Department of Pre-school Education and Republican Centre for Training of Pre-school Educators. These standards are being developed in association with regional and district stakeholders who reflect their own sub-cultures and experiences. Through international donors, Western standards and curricular knowledge are being injected into Uzbekistan pre-school education, and its training and professional development. Traditional parental knowledge, through the FEP programme of health, welfare and sanitation knowledge, is being replaced by Western views of good parenting, developmental standards and education, as a regime of truth.

Pedagogic models

With the introduction of standards will come the notion of Developmentally Appropriate Practice (DAP), influenced by child-centred ISSA values, producing a common pre-school educational ideology for children's learning. One form of centralisation (Soviet) will be replaced by another (Western-styled). Colonial legacies *and* global discourses reveal how the Uzbekistan pre-school curriculum is being reconstructed and reinterpreted through an interplay of contradictory discourses, values and practices, as globally constructed notions of readiness are espoused. At the local level, teachers are oriented towards academic teacher-directed learning and respect for adults, influenced by limited space, lack of material resources and educational materials, training and teacher–pupil ratios. How the curriculum and pedagogy is adapted and implemented will depend upon the interplay of national and local knowledge and traditional value systems. Policy-makers' *and* parents' attitudes and expectations of school readiness will influence curriculum implementation.

Observation of adult–child interactions was curtailed. One pre-school visit revealed children taking a closely supervised nap. Another visit to an experimental community pre-school was intercepted by an official from the Margilan regional office who denied us access despite long delays and deliberation over our passports. Overall, in the company of adults, there was an impression of confident, exuberant and much petted infants, but quieter, more watchful, obedient and subdued older children. The National Training Centre was lavishly appointed and resourced but there were no children or professionals to disturb the order.

Conclusion

Postcolonial analysis of ECD in Uzbekistan reveals complexity and multiplicity of historical and cultural forces at play, with Islamic and Uzbek traditions overlaid with Soviet methods. Postcolonial global knowledge of Developmentally Appropriate Practice (DAP) and child development now dominate, sanctioning certain modes of teaching and learning practices. But ECD is culturally and historically constituted and will remain hybrid in its practices as multiple knowledges are interwoven. Rethinking Uzbek ECD is at an early stage. Global knowledge will continue to collide with local practices. How and what children will learn hinges on power relations and interacting historical and cultural forces.

QUESTIONS FOR THINKING ABOUT POLICY AND PRACTICE

Postcolonialism means a time after colonisation has ended, but concerns a way of thinking that seeks its continuing effects in terms of power/knowledge relationships in the present.

1. How is Western ECD knowledge embedded in power relations between the developed and developing world?
2. How do Western ECD ideas negate cultural difference and the value of what is non-Western?
3. How might our knowledge of young children be shaped differently?

References

Abdurakhmanov, U. and Marnie, S. (2006) *Poverty and Inequality in Uzbekistan*, London: United Nations Development Fund/London School of Economics.

Alexander, C. A. (2010) *A Carpet Ride to Khiva*, London: Icon Books.

Aubrey, C. and Gittins, C. (2009) *External Summative Evaluation of the Family Education Project for the Period January, 2005–July, 2009*, Coventry: University of Warwick.

Bhabha. H. (1994) *The Location of Culture*, London: Routledge.

Bronfenbrenner, U. (1969) Introduction, in H. Chauncey (ed.) *Soviet Preschool Education, Volume 11: Teacher's Commentary*, New York: Holt, Rinehart & Winston, Inc.

Engle, P., Black, M. M., Behrman, J. R., Cabral de Mello, M., Gertler, P. J., Kapiriri, L. and Martorell, R. (2007) Strategies to avoid the loss of developmental potential in more than 299 million children in the developing world, *The Lancet*, 36: 229–242.

Grant, N. (1978) USSR, in M. Chazan (ed.) *International Research in Early Childhood Education*, Windsor: National Foundation for Educational Research Publishing Company.

Grantham-McGregor, S., Cheung, Y. B., Cueto, S., Glewwe, P., Richter, L. and Strupp, B. (2007) Developmental potential in the first 5 years for children in developing countries, *The Lancet*, 369: 60–70.

Kagan, S. L. and Britto, P. B. (2000) *Early Learning and Development Standards (ELDS) 'Going Global'. Frequently Asked Questions*, Geneva: UNICEF Regional Office CEE/CIS.

MacLeod, C. and Mayhew, B. (2008) *Uzbekistan: The Golden Road to Samarkand*, Hong Kong: Odyssey Publications.

Murray, C. (2007) *Murder in Samarkand*, London: Mainstream.

Stewart, K. and Huerta, C. (2006) *Reinvesting in Children? Policies for the Very Young in South Eastern Europe and the CIS*, Innocenti Working Paper No. 2006–01, Florence: UNICEF Innocenti Research Centre.

Sylva, C., Melhuish, E. C., Sammons, E. C., Siraj-Blatchford, I. and Taggart, B. (2004) *The Effective Provision of Pre-school Education (EPPE) Project: Final Report: A Longitudinal Study Funded by the DfES 1997–2004*, London: DfES and Institute of Education, University of London.

UN (2000) *UN Millennium Development Goals*, New York: UN.

UNICEF (2007) *Uzbekistan Multiple Indicator Cluster Survey 2006*, Tashkent: UNICEF.

UNICEF (2008) *Early Childhood Development in the CEE/CIS Region: Situation and Guidance*, Geneva: UNICEF.

Walker, S. P., Wachs, T. D., Gardner, J. M., Lozoff, B., Wasserman, G. and Pollitt, E. (2007) Child development: risk factors for adverse outcomes in developing countries, *The Lancet*, 369: 145–157.

Yakupov, S. (ed.) (2009) *Impact Assessment: Family Education Project*, Tashkent: The Sharh va Tavsiya Sociology Center.

5

EMERGING MODELS FOR EARLY CHILDHOOD DEVELOPMENT FROM BIRTH TO FOUR IN SOUTH AFRICA

Hasina Banu Ebrahim

OVERVIEW

Centre-based provision is commonly accepted as the dominant model for locating good early care and education in the North. In South Africa, this model is inaccessible to the majority of young children (birth to 4 years old) and especially those living in poor and vulnerable circumstances. This chapter illuminates two emerging models as alternatives to centre-based provision. Both these models were developed through the innovative practices of two non-government organisations – one in KwaZulu-Natal and the other in the Free State province. The first model uses the community as an entry point for a family support programme in a rural context. The second model uses the early childhood centre for family and community outreach in an urban context. At grassroots both the models use practitioners to reach young children and their families. Policy challenges related to the scaling up of these models are presented.

Key words: Early childhood development; models; centre-based provision; family; community.

Introduction

At the outset it is necessary to sketch a picture of the lives of children from birth to 4 years in the South African context. The mid–2007 population of South Africa was 46.9 million, of whom 18.3 million were children under 18 years (Hall 2009a). Children between birth and 5 years make up 33 per cent of the child population.

Children from birth to 4 years live in environments that pose a risk to their survival, growth, development and learning. This age group has the highest rate of mortality in the South African population (at 57.6 per 1,000), and over a quarter of child deaths result from diseases related to poor living conditions (Biersteker & Streak 2008). For children between the ages of 1 and 3 years, poor nutritional status results in stunting and underweight rates.

Children also live in homes that experience high poverty levels. In 2007, two-thirds of children (68 per cent) lived in households with a per capita monthly income below R350. Although child support grants are providing relief, this is inadequate, especially for poor African children. Hall (2009b) notes that in 2007, three-quarters (75 per cent) of African children lived in poor households in contrast to 5 per cent of white children who lived below the poverty line.

The lives of young children have been tremendously effected by HIV/AIDS. Johnson (n.d.) argues that the majority of children are infected before and during the birth process and some later through breastfeeding. Sexual abuse also results in infecting young children, and HIV/AIDS has hampered the country's efforts to promote the survival of young children. Infected mothers and the limited availability of treatment have compounded the problem.

The caregiving environment is also an area of concern. Meintjies (2009) states that South Africa has a long history of children living apart from their biological parents; she contends that this practice emerged from labour migration, educational opportunities and cultural practices where the extended family shares the responsibility of child rearing. Children are brought up by grandparents and relatives, mostly in the absence of fathers.

In disadvantaged contexts, ECD programmes can play a critical role to improve survival, growth and development of young children, prevent the occurrence of risk and the negative effects of risk (Walker *et al.* 2007). This paper presents models that attempt to curb risk and increase the developmental potential of young children from birth to 4 years.

The inadequacy of centre-based provision

Centre-based programmes are accepted as having value for the improvement of young children's preparation for school. Engle *et al.* (2007) report that evaluations in eight countries in the developing world context show that centre-based programmes have a substantial effect on children's cognitive development. Most of these countries also reported gains in non-cognitive skills such as sociabillity, self-confidence, motivation and willingness to talk to non-familial adults. Longitudinal studies tracking children exposed to centre-based pre-school education recorded improvement in the number of children entering school, children remaining at school and performance at grade level.

Centre-based provision in South Africa is problematic. Ebrahim (2010), in tracing the trajectory of early care and education, argues that history shows a complex relationship between provision for the early years and the political, economic, social and cultural features of South African society. She notes that during the apartheid era, centre-based provision for children was limited. The discriminatory policies based on race created a polarisation between centre-based education and care. Nursery schools for whites were aimed at middle-class children whilst crèches and day care centres catered for working mothers of other race groups (Webber 1978). Centre-based provision became associated with stimulating education activities for middle-class whites and custodial care in questionable environments for other race groups, especially black Africans (Ebrahim 2010).

In the turn to democracy the concerns for equity led to a national audit of ECD provision (Department of Education 2001). It was noted that only 16 per cent of children were able to access centre-based provision funded directly or indirectly through the government. In a 10-year review on ECD, Porteus (2004) noted that centre-based provision was inadequate for meeting the needs of all pre-school children; in some areas, centre-based provision could be likened to warehousing – too many children confined to a restricted space. The lack of practitioner training further compounded the delivery of quality centre-based provision.

There is still a severe lack of demand for formal centre-based programmes. Dawes *et al.* (2008), writing after the 10-year review, noted that less than 20 per cent of South African children are likely to attend formal centre-based programmes. While it is laudable that the State of the Nation Address by President Thabo Mbeki (2008) referred to speeding up of ECD programmes by doubling the number of delivery sites and child beneficiaries in 2009 and 2010, this process is challenging. Most children reside with families in home-based care – the result of families being poor and unable to afford fees. In rural and deep rural areas, centre-based provision is difficult to access. The high rate of unemployed mothers lowers the demand for centre-based provision.

For those children whose development and learning is compromised by not attending centre-based provision, alternative models of provision are necessary. Engle *et al.* (2007) state that for children younger than 3 years old, combining family and centre-based components is more effective than centre-based alone. Lee and Hayden (2009) argue that the needs of very young children require family and community-based programmes rather than centre-based pre-school programmes. These alternate models require a rethink on the content, intensity and combination of services required for children from birth to 4 years.

The National Integrated Plan (NIP)

The National Integrated Plan (NIP) (Department of Education *et al.* 2005) recognises the need to provide ECD programmes to meet the needs of poor and vulnerable children from birth to 4 years. It goes beyond centre-based provision and focuses on delivering comprehensive programmes aimed at young children, families and communities. Given the complexity of needs of these groups in disadvantaged contexts, it takes an integrated and multi-service delivery approach. Homes, formal ECD centres, community childcare settings and places of safety are accepted as sites for integrated service delivery.

In order to achieve the aims of integrated service delivery, the government values working in partnership with NGOs and communities. The Departments of Social Development, Education and Health form a social cluster to promote early learning, health, nutrition and social well-being. Each department has to foreground its particular focus on birth to 4 programmes and make budget commitments.

The *Tshwaragano Ka Bana* is a sub-programme within the NIP. It specifically aims at targeting poverty through delivering integrated services to the most vulnerable children. Efforts are directed towards upgrading of formal ECD programmes through training and infrastructure programmes. It also recognises the need for a new type of ECD worker who works directly with family and communities.

Investigating alternate models of early care and education

A rapid assessment and analysis of innovative community- and home-based early childhood programmes was conducted in 2007 by UNICEF, government departments and a local NGO (Early Learning Resource Unit *et al.* 2007). Findings on ECD programmes indicated that most programmes were located with the NGOs. Interventions aimed at families and communities were fairly recent. They included multiple elements such as using the ECD centres for community outreach, home visiting, parent education, playgroups, toy libraries, support for children affected by and infected with HIV/AIDS, support for child minders and community child-protection strategies. Contextual responsiveness, working within a rights-based framework, partnerships, monitoring and evaluations were noted as positive aspects in programmes. Further research was required in order to gain in-depth information on the alternate models to centre-based provision.

UNICEF was instrumental in selecting promising models for further investigation. The author and two other members of staff from the University of KwaZulu-Natal conducted research using a qualitative approach with multiple methods. The Little Elephant Training Centre for Early Education (LETCEE) was selected for the innovative ways in which it was dealing with young children and their families through using the community resources for ECD in rural KwaZulu-Natal. It offers a model of a Family Support Programme (FSP) with the community as the entry point (see Rule *et al.* 2008). Lesedi Educare Association in the Free State province was selected for the innovative ways in which it was using the ECD centres for outreach work playing a key role in initiating ECD in families and communities (see Ebrahim *et al.* 2008 for more).

Family Support Programme (FSP): community as an entry point

Central to this model is the well-being of poor and vulnerable young children in significant sites that affect their growth, development and learning. The model recognises that healthy ECD is dependent upon the nurturant qualities of the environments in which young children grow up. The structural space of the home is viewed as a hub for survival, growth and learning. The family is respected as the primary source of experience for young children's well-being. This is where children will receive the greatest amount of human contact. There is recognition that disadvantaged families will have multiple problems which affect how they connect and bond with their children. It is acknowledged that the social and economic resources together with the health status of family members determine the type of opportunities that become available to young children.

In the FSP model, the community is mobilised to actively promote ECD. In rural communities, project initiatives must gain the approval of the traditional leadership responsible for community governance. As a socially responsive organisation for ECD, LETCEE developed a good relationship with rural communities around the Greytown area. They approached the leadership and explained the project in terms of how the community would be involved, the activities and possible outcomes and benefits. Since the community trusted LETCEE and valued the idea of community intervention for ECD, permission was granted to begin the FSP, namely *Siyabathanda Abantwana* (We Cherish the Children) in March 2008. Another initiative of a similar nature began after the local chief and a retired health worker approached LETCEE as 'children's champions' for ECD.

The development of the FSP was facilitated through the formation of a community committee. The traditional and political leadership with respected members from the community formed this structure. Coordinators of the projects also joined this structure. They oversaw the intervention; addressed problems brought to the fore by coordinators, monitored the performance of the family facilitators (FFs) and discussed the budget.

The community committee was responsible for conducting a needs survey. This provided information on the type and levels of vulnerability families experienced – a process regarded as important for relevant interventions. The family facilitators (FFs) were identified by criteria developed by the community committee.

The FFs were responsible for home visiting, parent education, nutrition and health advice, early stimulation, giving logistical support to the elderly and moral support for those with HIV/AIDS. They assisted families with birth registration and immunisation and supported orphans and the elderly with documentation to access social grants. For early education, FFs conducted neighbourhood playgroups, where children were given the opportunity to learn through play in culturally appropriate ways through song, dance, rhyme and story reading in the mother tongue. The FFs also coordinated 'buddies', children from 8 to 13 years, who were responsible for organising playgroup activities after school and during weekends with children from targeted families. The FFs were monitored by project coordinators who mediated between them and the families. Through direct communication with the FFs and their reports, the project coordinators developed action plans to assist families.

In order to drive an integrated holistic model of ECD, the community leadership, the community development workers and LETCEE worked closely with the local clinic, the police, local schools and other non-profit organisations. The Departments of Health, Social Development, and Education and the local municipality needed greater collaboration to support the whole child in the context of the family.

ECD centre: entry point for community development and family support

This model subscribes to the same foundational ideas as the previous one. It respects the family as an important system in providing healthy ECD for young children. There are, however, two aspects that make this model different from the previous one. The ECD centre and not the community is the entry point for reaching young children in their families and in the community. This model provides a more established response to community development for ECD.

The Community Development and Family Support Programme (CDFSP) began with the need to address the vulnerabilities of urban families who were unable to send their children to ECD centres. The main focus of the programme was to provide quality outcomes for the well-being of young children in the context of family, home and broader community. The ECD centres were viewed as the nucleus of care and support for families and communities. The staff at the centres normally consisted of ECD practitioners, managers, the cook, a management committee and parent volunteers.

In the CDFSP, the managers were responsible for identifying the frontline workers known as Community Development Practitioners (CDPs). Since managers resided in the community, they had intimate knowledge of women best suited for intervention work in early childhood. Volunteers from the immediate vicinity of the centres were chosen. Criteria such as love for children, commitment, patience, passion and willingness to understand the problems of families and communities were used to select the CDPs.

In the immediate family environment, CDPs used the home visiting approach which began with CDPs joining the manager and the centre-based practitioners to conduct a needs survey. Entry to homes was gained through conversations and sometimes through picture books. Early stimulation activities and parent education were undertaken with sensitivity to cultural child-rearing practices. Families were given advice on health, nutrition and how to access services. Parents were assisted in the interpretations of a Road to Health Chart. The CDPs dealt with family crises stemming from child abuse, neglect, domestic violence and caregivers' ill health. In these instances, CDPs acted as case managers and made referrals to the centre managers.

The CDPs also served as facilitators of projects in community development. Each CDP had the choice of being involved in one or two projects. Once the children outside the ECD centres were identified, CDPs clustered them into informal neighbourhood playgroups; some were formed at clinics with children awaiting anti-retroviral treatment for HIV/AIDS. The CDPs facilitated play sessions with toys aimed at early stimulation. Parents/caregivers were encouraged to join the playgroups to help strengthen adult–child interactions in play-based ways. In order to introduce a variety of early stimulation activities, the CDPs facilitated sessions with children and parents/caregivers in a toy library bus which visited the centres intermittently. Given the number of orphans and vulnerable children in the project areas, CDPs used the ECD centres as a support base for homework clubs, computer literacy and opportunities for participation in music, art and cultural activities. In order to encourage income generation to alleviate poverty, CDPs supported self-help groups. Community members were encouraged to use their skills to start a small business. The CDPs were also involved in setting up support groups for women who experienced high levels of stress. In order to raise awareness of the importance of a healthy environment for young children, CDPs were active in organising advocacy campaigns.

The centre-based managers and the project staff of Lesedi Educare Association served as coordinators who helped the CDPs by making available necessary resources to help children and their families. Coordinators mediated between the CDPs and the families/communities.

The community structure consisted of the managers' forum and the community support committee. The former was made up of managers from a particular area. They were responsible for responding to the needs of managers. The community support committee served as a platform for managers, CDPs, community members and ward councillors to discuss issues in the community. It monitored the activities of the projects in the community and facilitated feedback on the elements of the programme. It prepared for community ownership once the NGO withdrew.

Members from the community support committee had representation in the provincial stakeholders' forum. The committee had representation from the Departments of Health, Social Development, Education and civil society. Stakeholders met to deliberate on issues related to ECD in the province.

Policy challenges

Biersteker and Streak (2008), writing in the context of scaling up ECD programmes for birth to 4 years, note that whilst there are legislative and policy commitments for providing services beyond centre-based provision, the enabling mechanisms for integrated service delivery is weak. The regulatory framework for ECD services up until recently did not incorporate integrated family- and community-based ECD programmes. Both the Children's Act 38 of 2005 and the Children's Amendment Act 41 of 2007 (*Government Gazette* 2005, 2008) were revised. The Children's Act 38 of 2005 (as amended by Act 41 of 2007) took these alternative models to centre-based provision into consideration.

The functioning of key departments in separate compartments runs counter to the vision of an integrated approach. The Departments of Social Development, Health and Education need to work as a strong team together with civil society. At present, systems promote working in isolation with sector programmes. At the provincial level, the inter-departmental committees and inter-sectoral committees still need to become a driving force for integrated ECD programmes in families and communities. The municipality is key in implementing family- and community-based programmes. At present this is a weak structure. The lack of capacity and the marginalised status of ECD are two of the factors inhibiting the delivery of integrated family- and community-based models of ECD.

Funding is problematic. Each province receives an equitable share allocation from the national treasury. The budget for ECD is not ring-fenced. ECD programmes outside centre-based provision have to compete for funding amongst other priorities. These programmes run the risk of receiving inadequate funding which ultimately affects the nature of outcomes for young children and their families. Additionally, the funding formulae tend to be more geared towards centre-based provision. Funding for family and community ECD programmes is complex. A variety of elements needs to be considered to fully fund comprehensive programmes. This is being explored by the Human Sciences Research Council in partnership with the Department of Social Development.

Another area that poses a challenge is the recognition of frontline workers (FFs, CDPs) as a legitimate workforce for ECD. These workers volunteer their labour for little or no income. Donor funding and the Expanded Public Works Programme are used to provide stipends which are inadequate for the needs of these workers. In order to retain a stable workforce for children from birth to 4 years in family- and community-based programmes, the minimum wage and the conditions of service have to be attractive.

Conclusion

The two models described in this chapter show a way of reaching poor and vulnerable children in the contexts which matter most in their lives. Given the financial limitations in the context of the developing world to provide centre-based provision for all children, these alternative models are worth full exploration. In order to ascertain the medium- and long-term gains for children, more longitudinal studies would be required. To ensure that alternative models to centre-based provision remain high on the political agenda in South Africa, strong advocacy and ongoing research are needed to show their possibilities for breaking cycles of poverty and developing new horizons for poor families and their children.

QUESTIONS FOR THINKING ABOUT POLICY AND PRACTICE

1. What kinds of provision are most suitable to support young children from birth to 4 years in poor and vulnerable contexts?
2. How can the regulatory environment support alternative models to centre-based provision for children from birth to 4 years?
3. What structures are necessary for the implementation of an integrated approach to non-centre-based provision at national, provincial and local levels?

References

Biersteker, L. and Streak, J. (2008) *Scaling up ECD (0–4) in South Africa: Policy, demographics, child outcomes, service provision and targeting*, Centre for Poverty and Growth, Child, Youth, Family and Social Development Research Programme, Pretoria: Human Science Research Council.

Dawes, A., Biersteker, L. & Irvine, M. (2008) *Scaling up ECD (0–4) in South Africa. What makes a difference to child outcomes in the period 0–4? Input for quality ECD interventions*, Centre for Poverty and Growth, Child, Youth, Family and Social Development Research Programme, Pretoria: Human Science Research Council.

Department of Education (2001) *The nationwide audit of ECD provisioning in South Africa*, Pretoria: Government Printers.

Department of Education, Department of Social Development and Department of Health (2005) *National integrated plan for early childhood development in South Africa 2005–2010*, Pretoria: UNICEF.

Early Learning Resource Unit (ELRU), Department of Education and Department of Social Development (2007) *Early childhood development: Rapid assessment and analysis of innovative community and home-based childminding and early childhood development programmes in support of poor and vulnerable babies and young children in South Africa*, Pretoria: UNICEF.

Ebrahim, H.B. (2010) Tracing historical shifts in early care and education in South Africa, *Journal of Education*, 48: 119–135.

Ebrahim, H.B, Killian, B. and Rule, P. (2008) *Report on the practice, principles, methodologies, core interventions, networking, stakeholder analysis, cost drivers, outcomes and benefits of an intervention based concept of ECD programmes as resources for care and support of poor and vulnerable young children: Lesedi Educare Community Development and Family Support Programme*, Pretoria: UNICEF.

Engle, P., Black, M.M, Behrman, J.R., de Mello, M.C., Gertler, P.J., Martorell, R. and Young, M.E. (2007) Child development in developing countries 3: Strategies to avoid the loss of developmental potential in more than 200 million children in the developing world, *The Lancet*, 369: 229–242.

Government Gazette (2005) Children's Act, Vol. 492, No. 28944 (19 June), Cape Town: Republic of South Africa.

Government Gazette (2008) Children's Amendment Act 2007, Vol. 513, No. 30884 (18 March), Cape Town: Republic of South Africa.

Hall, K. (2009a) *Children count: Statistics on children in South Africa – the number of children in South Africa*, Cape Town: University of Cape Town, available online at: www.childrencount.ci.org.za (accessed 9 January 2010).

Hall, K. (2009b) *Children count: Income and social grants – children living in poverty*, Cape Town: University of Cape Town, available online at: www.childrencount.ci.org.za (accessed 20 January 2010).

Johnson, L. (n.d.) *HIV and health: HIV prevalence amongst children*, Cape Town: University of Cape Town, available online at: www.childrencount.ci.org.za (accessed 12 February 2010).

Lee, Y. and Hayden, M. (2009) Editorial introduction: Early childhood care and education: World challenges and progresses, *Current Issues in Comparative Education*, 11: 3–5.

Mbeki, T. (2008) *State of the Nation Address*, available online at: www.allafrica.com (accessed 23 February 2012).

Meintjies, H. (2009) *Demography: Children living with biological parents*, Cape Town: University of Cape Town, available online at: www.childrencount.ci.org.za (accessed 12 February 2010).

Porteus, K. (2004) The state of play in early childhood development, in L. Chisholm (ed.) *Changing class: Education and social change in post apartheid South Africa*, Cape Town: Human Science Research Council.

Rule, P., Ebrahim, H.B. and Killian, B. (2008) *Report on the practice, principles, cost drivers, interventions, methodologies and stakeholder analysis of the project based on the concept of ECD programmes as resources for the care and support of poor and vulnerable young children: LETCEE – Siyabathanda Abantwana and Sikhulakahle interventions*, Pretoria: UNICEF.

Walker, S.P., Wachs, T.D., Gardener, J.M., Lozoff, B. Wasserman, G.A., Pollitt, E., Carter, J.A. and the International Child Development Steering Group (2007) Child development in developing countries 2, *The Lancet*, 369: 145–157.

Webber, V.K. (1978) *An outline of the development of preschool children in South Africa: 1930– 1977*, Pretoria: South African Association for Early Childhood Education.

6

EARLY CHILDHOOD EDUCATION IN THE PHILIPPINES

Administration and teaching practices

Percyveranda A. Lubrica, Chul Woo Lee and Evelyn Angiwan

OVERVIEW

In recent years, increasing attention has been paid to early childhood provision in the Philippines and it is now a policy goal to expand and improve comprehensive services. Currently, however, there are limited rigorous studies on the effectiveness of the provision. The study, discussed in this chapter, was conducted with the aim to address this issue. A questionnaire was administered and interviews were conducted among personnel in pre-schools in Baguio City and Benguet. The results showed that pre-schools carry out comprehensive administrative programmes, implement the curriculum, and adhere to teaching and learning instruction requirements. In general, teaching practices were perceived to be very effective, but the family involvement, culture and community relations significantly affected the learning environment. It is recommended that the Department of Education in the Philippines should develop benchmarking requirements for best and effective practices among pre-schools and establish models of successful administration to improve ECCE in the country.

Key words: Philippines; administration; determinant factors; benchmarking.

Introduction

The benefits of ECCD provision for children, families and communities are now well established in international research undertaken mainly in developed countries (see Introduction to this book). Research studies which focused on low and middle economy countries also present similar patterns. For example, research conducted in the Philippines by Armecin *et al.* (2006) showed that children, especially those from disadvantaged backgrounds, make great gains in cognitive, social and motor skills and language development. Children under 3 years old, in particular, exhibit faster rates of change in psycho-social development than do older children.

The critical importance of the educational experiences and the development that occurs during the early years has increasingly attracted the attention and interest of government and policy makers. The Early Childhood Care and Development (ECCD) Law, enacted in 2000, recognises the importance of early childhood and requires the establishment of a Council for the Welfare of Children (CWC) with responsibility to: establish guidelines and standards for early childhood programmes; develop a national system for staff recruitment and training; monitor the delivery of services; provide additional resources to increase the supply of programmes; and encourage the development of private sector initiatives (cited in UNESCO International Bureau of Education [IBE] 2006).

Pre-schools in the country are governed by two laws: the Republic Act 6972 (Daycare Law 1990) which seeks to establish at least one daycare centre in every *Barangay* (village) in local communities in the country; and the Republic Act 8980 (ECCD Law 2000) which seeks to provide a comprehensive and integrated approach in the delivery, monitoring and planning of early childhood care and education in the country (cited in UNESCO International Bureau of Education [IBE] 2006).

There are two types of early childhood provision in the Philippines: graded and non-graded. The graded provision uses age as the criterion for pupils' admission to each grade of provision and for informing practices for assessing pupils' progress. It implements a curriculum that is designed for all children attending the same grade of provision. The graded provision is mostly used in private pre-elementary education. The non-graded provision admits children of different ages in the same class. The assessment is based on the child's ability to do developmental tasks required by the school programme.

Early childhood provision can be private, centre-based or attached to schools. Private and centre-based types of provision operate independently using their own funds, while types of provision attached to schools operate under the basic education schools. All operate with permission granted by the Department of Education. The pre-school curriculum explicitly focuses on supporting school readiness. Teachers are provided with a *Pre-school Handbook* which describes the instructional objectives and concepts or content to be covered, recommended classroom activities and learning materials (UNESCO International Bureau of Education [IBE] 2006).

In pursuit of its mission to contribute to the attainment of quality early childhood education, the Department of Education has strategically put in place a system that externally assesses the quality of pre-school education in the country. It is assumed that the external assessment will drive all pre-schools to continuously improve and further enhance the quality of early education provision and the overall quality of the programmes offered by schools (DECS Order No. 107, S.1989)

Despite the efforts to increase provision and quality of early childhood services, a UNESCO (2004) report has identified the following issues to be pertinent in the sector:

- The poor quality of the physical environment and lack of appropriate resources and materials that compromise the safety, hygiene and well-being of children.
- Teachers' overall profile is low, with most of them not having the qualifications or standards required to teach young children.
- There are increasing disparities in school readiness of children attending public schools and community childcare centres.

The differential effect of different models of early childhood provision and teaching practices on pre-schoolers' competencies is now documented. Myers (2006) observed that if the characteristics and processes of an educational environment are not consistent with the kind of world, country and citizenry desired and/or consistent with widely agreed rights for children, it is difficult to ascertain the quality of the programme. It is therefore important that a conscious effort is made to harmonise policies, systems and interventions in order to enable delivery of services that are of high quality and achieve the intended policy goals (Asian Development Bank 2007). Accordingly, early childhood providers need information about the standards required to provide quality services.

Methodology

Within this context, it was imperative to evaluate the present status of early childhood provision in the Philippines in order to investigate the factors that determine its quality.

More specifically, the study sought to answer the following questions:

1. How is the early years curriculum implemented by graded and non-graded schools?
2. To what extent are programme administration and teaching practices implemented in early childhood programmes?
3. What are the strengths and weaknesses of the programme administration in early childhood education?
4. What areas of programme administration correlate with teaching practices of pre-school teachers?

The study was based on the premise that pre-schools significantly vary in their perceptions with regard to:

- the comprehensiveness of the curriculum, its degree of relevance and level of effectiveness, and the extent of attainment of its objectives;
- the extent of implementation of quality indicators related to programme administration and the level of effectiveness of teaching practices;

- how the school administrators administer the programmes in their respective schools;
- the relationship between the programme administration and degree of effectiveness of teaching practices.

The study adopted the Stufflebeam's Context–Input–Process–Product (CIPP) model (Bilbao *et al.* 2008) which ascertains that the quality of the programme (product) is affected by the kind of inputs and type of processes involved (see Figure 6.1).

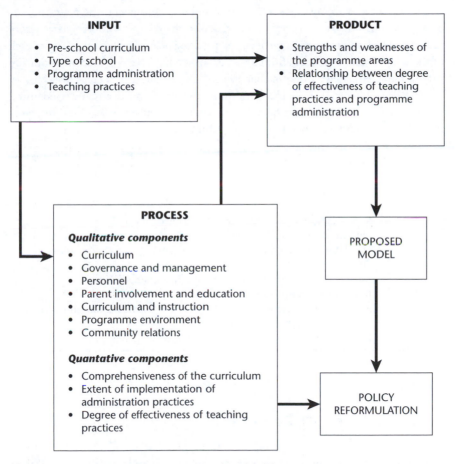

FIGURE 6.1 Context–Inputs–Process–Product model

Inputs included: type of pre-school; pre-school curriculum; teaching practices and programme administration. Processes included qualitative and quantitative components. Qualitative components were: curriculum; government and management; personnel; parent involvement; curriculum and instruction; programme environment and community relations. Quantitative components comprised:

- the perceived level of comprehensiveness and degree of relevance of the curriculum;
- the extent of the perceived effectiveness of teaching practices;
- the extent of the implementation of variables of administration of pre-schools;
- the relationship between administration variables and teaching practices.

The study was conducted among 85 pre-schools, which have operated for 5 years in the region of Benguet. Of these, 68 were graded pre-schools and 17 non-graded; one was a public pre-school and 84 were private. The respondents comprised 85 administrators and 255 teachers who completed a questionnaire, the main tool for data gathering. The data collected were related to three areas: comprehensiveness of the curriculum, administrative practices, and teaching practices. Statements under each of these three areas were rated from 5 to 1 as shown in Table 6.1. The questionnaire was also supplemented by informal interviews for qualitative data collection.

The data, collected from the questionnaire, were statistically analysed using descriptive and inferential statistics. A 0.05 level of significance was used to determine significant differences among the variables studied.

TABLE 6.1 Definition of the rating scale

Rating	Adjectival Rating
5	Very significantly relevant, effective, attained/Exemplary implementation/Very strong/Excellent
4	Significantly relevant, effective, attained/Complete implementation/Strong/Very satisfactory
3	Moderately relevant, effective, attained/Moderate implementation/Moderately strong/Satisfactory
2	Fairly relevant, effective, attained/Minimal implementation/Fairly strong/Fair
1	Not relevant, effective, attained/No implementation/Poor

Findings

Comprehensiveness of the curriculum

Table 6.2 (below) shows the perceived comprehensiveness of the curriculum by respondents in the graded and non-graded schools. The weighted mean values (second and fourth columns), related to the three dimensions of the comprehensiveness of the curriculum, ranging from 4.18 to 4.32 of the rating scale. These findings indicate that the curriculum was perceived as being relevant, effective and attaining its objectives. Statistically, the two types of schools are not significantly different (see sixth column for the computed F-values using ANOVA [Analysis of Variance]), implying that graded and non-graded pre-schools do not vary in the implementation of the curriculum.

TABLE 6.2 Level of perceived comprehensiveness of the pre-school curriculum

Indicators	Graded school		Non-graded school		Computed F-value (Fc)	Tabled F-value (F0.05)
	Weighted mean	Description	Weighted mean	Description		
Relevance	4.28	Significantly relevant	4.32	Significantly relevant	1.17^{ns}	3.226
Effectiveness	4.20	Significantly effective	4.18	Significantly effective	0.17^{ns}	4.079
Extent of attainment of curriculum objectives	4.31	Significantly attained	4.25	Significantly attained	1.63^{ns}	4.238

Teaching practices

Table 6.3 shows the perceived level of satisfaction with regard to effectiveness of teaching practices related to: instructional delivery; classroom management; dealing with family culture and community. All three dimensions are perceived as being very effective with the weighted mean for each of them above 4 of the rating scale.

The *instructional delivery* indicator of teaching practices was related to such aspects as: choosing alternative teaching strategies and materials to achieve differential instructional purposes; assessing children's learning to achieve learning goals; and assessing children through the use of performance-based assessments. The *classroom management* indicator was related to the following components: classroom management including administering first aid to children; encouraging independent learning; creating and maintaining a healthy, safe, clean environment; and using strategies to prevent accidents in the classroom. The *dealing with the family culture and community* indicator included: practices of modelling respect for all individuals; and the development and implementation of an integrated curriculum which focused on children's needs and interests, and took into account culturally valued content and the children's home experiences.

The teaching practices which were perceived as satisfactory included: stimulation of young children's reflection; promotion of critical and thinking skills; the linking of new ideas to familiar ones by using inquiry methods; and providing opportunities

TABLE 6.3 Level of perceived satisfaction with the effectiveness of pre-school practice

Teaching practices	Weighted mean	Adjectival rating
Instructional delivery	4.24	Very satisfactory
Classroom management	4.14	Very satisfactory
Dealing with family culture and community	4.10	Very satisfactory

for active management. The usage of media communication tools and other appropriate learning technologies to facilitate learning was given the least attention.

Programme administration

Table 6.4 indicates that there is strong implementation of administration with regard to: curriculum and instruction (weighted mean 4.05), followed by staff professional development and record keeping (weighted means of 4.02 and 4.00, respectively). Parental involvement and parent education received lower weighted means (3.56 and 3.55, respectively), implying that these are the areas that get the least attention.

Results of the study suggested that the high rating of curriculum and instruction was due to perceived alignment of learning standards with those prescribed by the Department of Education. Despite the variation in curriculum implementation, the infusion of standards for learning competencies was an important element in instructional designing. This implies that there is convergence of teaching practices with the prescribed standards of learning, supporting arguments that teaching practices should respond sensitively and appropriately to the range of children's diverse needs and encompass both knowledge of child development and curriculum content.

The staff professional development draws its strength from staff participation in professional development activities that were explicitly related to the philosophy of the school and guided by the comprehensive development plan (in the ECCD Law 2000), and the assessment of staff needs. Record keeping draws its strength from the presence of safeguards to ensure confidentiality of personal data and information and/or other relevant information such as: provisions for individualised programmes for children and families; monitoring programme services; assisting programme planning and management to ensure quality services. This information is used for the generation of annual reports.

TABLE 6.4 Extent of programme administration among pre-schools

Area of administration	Weighted mean	Adjectival rating	t-value
Governance and management	3.93	CI	8.71**
Communication systems	3.98	CI	10.27**
Record keeping/reporting	4.00	CI	8.32**
Fiscal resources	3.75	CI	6.04**
Staff qualification	3.91	CI	9.17**
Staff professional development	4.02	CI	8.64**
Parent involvement	3.56	CI	4.54**
Parent education	3.55	CI	3.53**
Curriculum and instruction	4.05	CI	10.38**
Programme environment	3.98	CI	9.00**
School community relations	3.87	CI	6.80**

Note: ** significant 0.01 level of significance.

Comparatively, pre-schools in the study differ significantly in their extent of implementation of the quality indicators. The computed t-values (which express the significant differences between the variables) far exceeded the probability values at 1 per cent level of significance for all quality indicators, especially for curriculum and instruction (t-value at 10.38★★) and communication systems (t-value at 10.27★★). Although statistically significant, the low computed t-values for parent involvement (t-value at 4.54★★) and parent education (t-value at 3.53★★) indicate that these two quality indicators receive less attention in both types of pre-school.

Statistically, the significant difference in the extent of implementation of the various areas of administration implies that graded and non-graded pre-schools vary in the foci of their administration along the identified areas.

Relationship between the programme administration and teaching practices

The relationships between teaching practice indicators and variables of administration are shown in Table 6.5. Correlations show a positive but low relationship between instructional delivery and administration variables such as: governance and management; fiscal resources; staff qualifications; family involvement and education; curriculum and instruction; and community relations. There is a negative correlation however between instructional delivery and the administration of record systems and programme environment. This is a finding that is worth exploring further, as it may imply the burden of paper work and the inadequacy of the existing environment of the programmes. Thus, instructional delivery is not significantly affected by programme administration.

Teaching practices with regard to classroom management were positively correlated with: governance and management; fiscal resources; staff qualifications; family

TABLE 6.5 Relationship between the programme administration and teaching practices

Program administration	Teaching practices		
	Instructional delivery	Classroom management	Family culture and community
Governance and management	0.095	0.173	0.143
Record keeping/reporting	−0.015	0.013	−0.059
Fiscal resources	0.161	0.102	0.159
Staff qualifications	0.122	0.313	0.336
Family involvement	0.310	0.349	0.431★
Family education	0.319	0.348	0.351
Curriculum and instruction	0.153	−0.219	−0.049
Program environment	−0.078	−0.191	−0.145
Community relations	0.275	0.433★	0.523★★

Note: ★ significant at 5% , ★★ significant at 1%.

involvement and education; and community relations. The correlation with record keeping/reporting wa also positive but very low. There were negative correlations with: the administration of curriculum and instruction and programme environment. The latter finding is consistent with other research which shows that classroom management is affected by the learning environment as well as the pre-school curriculum and teaching strategies (Papatheodorou 2005). Again, this is a finding that may need to be further investigated in the Philippine context.

Teaching practices with regard to family culture and community relations were positively correlated with: governance and management; fiscal resources; staff qualifications and family education. There was a negative correlation with record keeping/reporting,curriculum and instruction, and program environment. A significant difference was found in the administration of family involvement and community relations themselves. The latter finding implies that the administration of family involvement and community relations are recognised as significant variables in supporting teaching practices that relate to this area. This is a particularly interesting finding, as parental involvement is recognised as being an important factor in children's cognitive and non-cognitive development (Cotton and Green 1988).

Conclusion

Under the present conditions of pre-schools in Baguio and Benguet, in the Philippines, the following conclusion may be drawn:

- The curriculum implemented in pre-schools is perceived as being relevant and effective, and aligned with its objectives.
- The perceived level of effectiveness of teaching practices (instructional delivery, classroom management, and family culture and community relations) was rated as very satisfactory. However, the evidence showed that teaching practices were limited in terms of encouraging children's reflection, critical thinking and inquiry-based learning.
- The administration of pre-schools was particularly strong in record keeping/ reporting and curriculum and instruction. Administration of parental involvement/education and community relations were the weakest areas.
- Correlations between variables of administration and teaching practices showed a positive, although low, relationship among most of them. Three findings are of particular interest. First, the negative correlation of the administration variables of: record keeping/reporting and programme environment with instruction and delivery. Second, the negative correlation of the administration variables of: curriculum/instruction and programme environment with classroom management. Third, the significant differences of the administration of family involvement and community relations compared with the practices that relate to these aspects of teaching. These findings call for further research to explore their impact on children's experience and the quality of pre-school provision.

The findings and conclusions of the study point to the following recommendations:

- Benchmarking is required by pre-schools in order to monitor the implementation of administration variables/components and teaching practices; to find out from other pre-schools most effective and best practices; and to share information and practices for the improvement of their respective pre-schools.
- Action plans are needed in order to address areas of pre-school provision that require improvement; to identify support for staff as they undergo the processes of change; and to emphasise teaching enhancement and educational qualifications.
- The pre-school curriculum should focus more on children's reflection, critical thinking and inquiry/exploration-based learning to acquire life skills.
- The pre-school administrators should establish a programme that would promote parental involvement and community engagement by, for example, organising school-visiting days for parents; seeking public participation in school-community problems; making the school the centre of community improvement and welfare promotion; encouraging the community to serve the school; conducting home visits; and forming parent-teacher organisations as an avenue for parental education.
- Further study should be conducted in identifying models of successful administration and teaching practices in early childhood provision.

QUESTIONS FOR THINKING ABOUT POLICY AND PRACTICE

1. Is standardised administration a determinant factor for the quality of early childhood provision?
2. What support services could increase the quality of experience of learners and their teachers?
3. How could administration improve teaching practices?

References

Armecin, G., Behrman, J.R., Duazo, P., Ghuman, S., Gultiano, S., King, E.M. and Lee, N. (2006) Early childhood development through an integrated program: Evidence from the Philippines, Impact Evaluation Series No. 2, World Bank Policy Research Working Paper 3922, May 2006, available online at: www-wds.worldbank.org/servlet/WDSContentServer/WDSP/IB/2006/05/11/000016406_20060511122104/Rendered/PDF/wps3922.pdf (accessed 10 August 2011).

Asian Development Bank (2007) *Project Completion Report Philippines: Early Childhood Development Project*, Project Number: 27086, Loan Number: 1606/1607, available online at: www.adb.org/documents/pcrs/phi/27086-phi-pcr.pdf (accessed 10 August 2011).

Bilbao, P.P., Lucido, P.I., Iringan, T.C. and Javier, R.B. (2008) *Curriculum Development*, Quezon City, the Philippines: Adriana Printing Co., Inc.

Cotton, K. and Green, K.R. (1988) *Parent Involvement in Education*, Portland, OR: Northwest Regional Education Laboratory.

DECS Order N0 107 s. (1989) *Standards for the Organisation and Operation of Preschools (Kindergarten Level)*, Issued on 10 November 1989, available online at: www.scribd.com/doc/48255095/DECS-ORDER-107-s1989-Standards-in-Preschool (accessed 26 August 2011).

Myers, R.G. (2006) *Quality in program[s] of early childhood care and education (ECCE)*, Background Paper prepared for the *EFA Global Monitoring Report 2007 Strong Foundations: Early Childhood Care and Education*, Paris: UNESCO, available online at: http://unesdoc.unesco.org/images/ 0014/001474/147473e.pdf (accessed 11 August 2011).

Papatheodorou, T. (2005) *Behaviour Problems in the Early Years: A Guide for Understanding and Support*, London: Routledge.

Republic Act 6972 (Daycare Law) (1990) Barangay-Level Total Development and Protection of Children Programme, approved 23 November, available online at: http://www.chanrobles.com/republicactno6972.htm (accessed 9 August 2011).

Republic Act 8980 (ECCD Law) (2000) An Act Promulgating a Comprehensive Policy and a National System for Early Childhood Care and Development (ECCD), Providing Funds therefore and for Other Purposes, Early Childhood Care and Development Act, approved December 05, 2000, available online at: www.lawphil.net/statutes/repacts/ra2000/ra_8980_2000.html (accessed 26 August 2011).

UNESCO (2004) *Education for All: The Quality Imperative*, Global Monitoring Report 2005, Paris: UNESCO, available online at: http://unesdoc.unesco.org/images/0013/001373/137333e.pdf (accessed 9 August 2011).

UNESCO International Bureau of Education (IBE) (2006) Philippines: Early childhood care and education (ECCE) programmes, Country Profile prepared for the *EFA Global Monitoring Report 2007 Strong Foundations: Early Childhood Care and Education*, Geneva, Switzerland: UNESCO, available online at: http://unesdoc.unesco.org/images/0014/001472/147225e.pdf (accessed 10 August 2011).

7

EARLY CHILDHOOD POLICIES AND PRACTICES IN NIGERIA

Monica Odinko

OVERVIEW

In Nigeria, pre-school education is seen by the Government as one of the compulsory levels of education that young children must be exposed to. To ensure uniformity and good quality provision, the Government has set out guidelines for provision and curriculum development. This chapter discusses the findings of research which was conducted with the aim to investigate providers' compliance with policy requirements. The study sample consisted of 216 pre-school teachers, teaching 3,150 pupils, aged 3–5 years. Two observational instruments, the Classroom Interaction Sheet (CIS) and the Ten-Minute Interaction (TMI), were used to record teaching–learning processes. Policy and curriculum documents were also analysed.

The results revealed that there was a discrepancy between policy guidelines and pre-school practices, especially with regard to class size, teaching method, language of instruction and site facilities and resources. Teacher-initiated interactions and whole-class activities prevailed, while learner-initiated interactions and individual/small-group activities were less frequently observed. The language of instruction was English instead of the language of the home or immediate environment. Suggestions and recommendations for improving pre-school provision in Nigeria are discussed in the light of these findings.

Key words: Nigeria; pre-school education; curriculum; policy; pedagogy.

Introduction

The importance of giving young children quality care and education has received recognition both internationally and within Nigeria. Issues pertinent to early childhood care and education (ECCE) were prominent in the UN Convention on the Rights of the Child (United Nations General Assembly 1989), the World Conference on Education for All (EFA) (UNESCO 1990) and the Dakar Framework for Action (UNESCO 2000). The latter included ECCE as number one of the six EFA goals, by placing emphasis on 'expanding and improving comprehensive early childhood care and education, especially for the most vulnerable and disadvantaged children' (UNESCO 2000: 17).

The Nigerian Government is a signatory to each of these decisions and it has included ECCE as one of the compulsory levels of Universal Basic Education (UBE) through which every Nigerian child must pass. As articulated by the Nigerian Government, UBE focuses on provision of nine years of schooling which includes ECCE provision, primary education and the first three years of secondary education. The government has prescribed that this level of education must be free, universal, compulsory, functional and of high quality. Pre-school services are offered by central and local government departments, non-governmental organisations (NGOs), community-based organisations (CBOs) and private entrepreneurs.

Pre-school education in Nigeria: policy issues

The formal education of pre-school children, 3 to 5 years old, was first mentioned in the Nigerian National Curriculum Conference in 1969, but it only appeared in the nation's educational document in 1977 (Osokoya 1989). Prior to its formal inclusion in the Nigerian policy, there were pre-school institutions in some cities and towns, run by individuals or or organisations (Osokoya 2000; Ukeje and Aisiku 1982). In the past two decades, the opinion of the Nigerian Government on pre-school education has changed, as a result of the nation's educational goals which are geared towards 'creating an enabling environment for the Nigerian child to thrive and develop to the fullest potential as well as the aspiration of building a land full of bright opportunities for all citizens' (FRN 1977–2011, section 1: 3e: 5–6). Research results on the importance of giving children appropriate stimulation during the early years of life to ensure a reasonable and healthy development have also contributed to the emphasis given to pre-school education.

In the nation's policy document of 1977 (revised in 1981, 1985, 1998, 2004), pre-school education was referred to as early childhood education. It was defined as 'the care, protection, stimulation and learning promoted in children from age 0–5 years in a crèche, nursery or kindergarten' (FRN 1997–2011, section 2: 10). This definition of pre-school education shows the Nigerian Government's commitment to the realisation of the first goal of EFA. Pre-primary education is viewed as a 'foundation stone and is considered indispensable to future or life-long education by the government' (Olorunfunmi 2000: 7). Educational settings where pre-school education is offered include the crèche, the nursery and the kindergarten. These settings cater for children from birth until the age they are ready to be admitted into the primary school (FRN 1977–2011, section 2: 11).

The Nigerian Government is now directly involved in the establishment of pre-school institutions and it is saddled with the responsibilities of:

> provision and distribution of policy guidelines for the establishment and management of pre-primary institutions; production and development of appropriate National Curriculum and textbooks in Nigerian Languages; approval of relevant supplementary reading materials and teachers/instructors' manual; supervision and control of quality of such institutions.
>
> (FRN 1977–2011, section 2: article 12: 11)

Objectives of pre-school education in Nigeria

The Federal Republic of Nigeria (FRN), after due consultations with stakeholders, concluded that the general goals for ECCE are to

> effect a smooth transition from the home to the school; prepare the Nigerian child for the primary level of education; inculcate social norms in the child; inculcate in the child, the spirit of enquiry and creativity through the exploration of nature, the environment, art, music and playing with toys, etc; develop a sense of co-operation and team spirit; learn good habits, especially good health habits; and teaching the rudiments of numbers, letters, colours, shapes, forms, etc, through play.
>
> (FRN 1977–2011, section 2: 11a–h: 4)

To achieve these goals, the Nigerian Government decided to do the following (FRN 1977–2011: 11–12):

- establish pre-primary sections in existing public schools and encourage both community/private efforts in the provision of pre-primary education;
- make provisions in teacher education programmes for specialisation in early childhood education;
- ensure that the medium of instruction is principally the mother-tongue or the language of the immediate community;
- ensure that the main method of teaching at this level shall be through play and that the curriculum of teacher education is oriented to achieve this;
- regulate and control the operation of pre-primary education – to this end, the Government recommended that the teacher–pupil ratio shall be 1:25;
- set up avenues for monitoring minimum standards for early childcare centres in the country;
- ensure that the staff of pre-primary institutions are adequately trained and that essential equipment [is] provided.

The objective of ECCE programmes in Nigeria, as stated in the policy document, is geared towards ensuring the *all-round* development of Nigerian children. This covers the cognitive, affective and psychomotor domains.

To monitor compliance, the government inaugurated the Integrated Early Childhood Care and Development project (IECCD) under the Nigerian Educational Research and Development Council (NERDC 2002). Minimum standards were prescribed by the NERDC in areas such as:

- types of ECCE centres to be opened;
- location of the ECCE centre close to children's homes;
- requirements for starting a centre and actions that could lead to closure of a centre;
- nature of the building and class size with enough space (at least 16 square metres for 20–25 children) to give room for free movement;
- classroom environment and seating arrangements that are flexible, not rigid as in a formal school setting;
- infrastructure and type of furniture (child-size);
- instructional materials (child-friendly reading materials, corners for science, health and nutrition, drama, shopping, resting and reading should be put in place);
- daily programmes;
- human resources/personnel;
- basic qualification for teachers.

The document also indicated that the government should be in charge of the licensing, supervision, monitoring and assessment of pre-schools to ensure quality control, training of suitably qualified personnel, provision of infrastructure, personnel and gender-fair instructional materials for both government and community-owned centres. All these were put together by the stakeholders to ensure uniformity as well as provision of services that are of high quality.

Nigerian pre-primary curriculum

As the name pre-primary education suggests, preparatory classes are available prior to primary school entry. Relevant qualitative and quantitative information and recommendations, received by stakeholders (policy makers, parents, teachers and school administrators) were considered for inclusion in the curriculum content of pre-primary education. The recommended learning experiences include: children's exposure to creative arts, social norms, physical and health education, language and communication skills, mathematical skills, as well as scientific and reflective thinking. The content shows that care was taken to ensure that the curriculum caters for the *all-round* development of Nigerian children. Teaching methods and instructional material were also recommended.

The curriculum content signifies that the Nigerian child who passes through a pre-school programme would be able to exhibit behaviours appropriate for transition to primary school. The child would be emotionally prepared to adjust to another environment outside of her/his home and/or the pre-school setting. Furthermore, the child should be able to express her/himself clearly, recite rhymes, use writing tools and materials correctly, identify letters of the alphabet in both small and capital forms, identify objects, shapes, colours, count freely up to each child's level of ability and recognise number symbols.

The extent to which these laudable policies and curriculum requirements are adhered to by providers and practitioners has not yet been investigated by Nigerian researchers. Therefore a study to evaluate the level of compliance with these policies was necessary. The study, discussed in this chapter, was conducted with the aim of gathering information and answering the following research questions:

1. What is the level of compliance by pre-school institutions in Nigeria with respect to (i) using the recommended curriculum; and (ii) meeting the objectives of setting up this level of education, as indicated by the policy?
2. What is the direction of communication during instructional practices?
3. What is the nature of class context in the schools observed?

Methodology

The target population for this study comprised Nigerian pre-school teachers working with 3–5+ year olds, enrolled in pre-schools located in three selected states of the country. The study sample was selected using stratified sampling (Kerlinger and Lee 2000). The country was stratified along the three major regions: Eastern, Western and Northern. Each of the regions has special characteristics as depicted by the socio-political history, geographical location, cultural orientation, educational development, linguistic propensity and religious background. A state that reflected the special characteristics of each region was selected for the study (see Figure 7.1).

In all, 24 pre-school institutions were randomly selected from each state. In each selected pre-school, three pre-school classrooms were randomly chosen to represent children aged 3+, 4+ and 5+. In total, 72 pre-primary schools were selected – 216 classrooms led by 216 teachers.

The researcher collected data using observational techniques and documentary analysis. More specifically, the CIS and TMI observational schedules were used (i) to monitor and record the teachers' and the learners' behaviour patterns in the classroom; (ii) to find out if the pupils learn through the methods recommended in the curriculum; and (iii) to determine the classroom climate – direction of interaction. These observational schedules provide information on the frequency and sequence of categories of behaviour observed in the classroom.

The data collection involved the training of five research assistants on the technicalities of using the observational schedules to ensure their consistent use. In all, six people were involved in the data collection exercise, including the researcher. Two researchers were sent to each state. Each teacher and the pupils were observed once. Each lesson was observed for 30 minutes using the instruments. Subjects

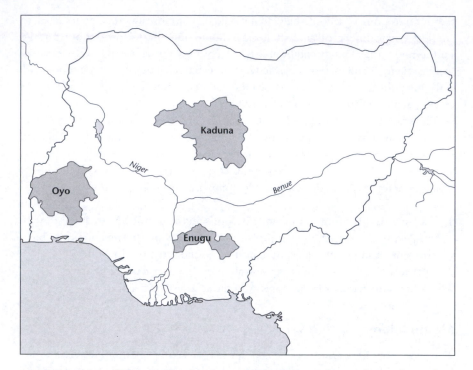

FIGURE 7.1 Map of Nigeria, showing the states where the study sample was drawn from

observed included: introduction to literacy; numeracy; science; and social skills. These subjects were chosen because they are the core subjects taught at pre-schools, considered to aid the learning in other subject areas. Data analysis involved the use of frequency, percentage and graphical illustrations.

Existing government policy documents on ECCE curriculum (e.g. NERDC 2002; FRN 1977–2011) and additional documents from individual private schools were also reviewed and content-analysed.

Results

Curriculum

Table 7.1 shows that the curriculum was adhered to by public schools (100 per cent), but this was not the case with the private sector (50 per cent). A large percentage of pre-schools did not have teaching and learning materials available (30 per cent and 70 per cent for public and private institutions, respectively). However, the materials provided were used during instructional delivery activities (100 per cent). The findings also showed that private pre-school providers have additional subjects included in the curriculum and their scheme of work. These included: computer studies; music; French language; dance (ballet) and swimming classes.

TABLE 7.1 Level of compliance with the curriculum

Curriculum items	Percentage of compliance	
	Public	Private
Recommended curriculum available in school	100	100
Structured scheme of work based on the curriculum	100	50
Prepares lesson activities based on what was recommended	100	50
Carries out teaching–learning activities based on what was recommended	100	100
Provided [with] teaching materials	30	70
Used the teaching materials provided	100	100

Policy

Table 7.2 shows that elements of the policy objectives were observed by all schools (100 per cent) with exception of language of instruction and pre-school teacher qualification, where no school adhered to policy recommendations. Nevertheless, the teachers were qualified to teach at other levels education, mostly primary and secondary. There was no compliance with the recommended teacher–pupil ratio; only 30 per cent of pre-schools had 25 pupils in the class. With regard to classroom environment, 60 per cent of public and 70 per cent of private institutions, respectively, complied. Finally, although there is a policy requirement that government officials in the Ministry of Education should supervise and accredit pre-schools, there is an absence of such functions and lack of government commitment to monitor

TABLE 7.2 Extent of compliance with the policy by schools

Policy items	Percentage of compliance	
	Public	Private
Effects smooth transition	100	100
Preparation for primary school	100	100
Inculcate social values	100	100
Inculcate the spirit of enquiry and creativity	100	100
Develop co-operation and team spirit/Learn good habits	100	100
Teach rudiment[s] of numbers, letters, etc.	100	90
Classroom environment	60	70
Teacher–pupil ratio	30	100
Location	100	100
Schools visited by government officials (before/after opening)	30	60
Teacher qualification	0	0
Language of instruction	0	0

and evaluate the compliance of providers with policy requirements. The language of children's immediate environment was minimally used.

Instructional approaches

Table 7.3 shows that none of the schools visited either used play or allowed the pupils to initiate the activity they were interested in. The table also shows that all teachers (in both public and private pre-schools) were at the centre of the instructional delivery and used direct teaching. The communication flow was usually from the teachers to the pre-schoolers with the pre-schoolers mostly at the receiving end. It is also worth noting that the responses from the pupils, either as a whole class or at individual level, were mere responses to either the teachers' questions or directive remarks.

Direction of communication

Table 7.4 shows that the direction of communication observed was from teacher to group and group to teacher. There were limited interactions at individual level; that is, teacher to pupil or pupil to teacher or towards others.

Classroom context

With respect to classroom context, Table 7.5 reveals that all pre-schools used whole-class teaching, monitoring and transition techniques with minimal small-group

TABLE 7.3 Instructional approaches observed

Instructional approaches	Percentage of compliance	
	Public	Private
Teaches through play	0	0
Teacher-initiated activities	100	100
Pupil-initiated activities	0	0
Direct teaching	100	100

TABLE 7.4 Direction of communication observed

Direction of communication items	Percentage of compliance	
	Public	Private
Teacher to group	100	100
Group to teacher	100	100
Teacher to pupil/Pupil to teacher/group	20	50
Teacher to other teacher/visitor	30	10

TABLE 7.5 Classroom context observed

Classroom context items	Percentage of compliance	
	Public	Private
Whole class	100	100
Small group	30	70
Monitoring	100	100
Transition	100	100
One-to-one	40	80
Non-involved	30	5

activities and one to one interaction, especially in public pre-schools. A large percentage of children were not involved, again, mainly in public pre-schools.

Discussion: what does the evidence tell us?

The impression created from these findings is that there is a wide gap between policy and practice in Nigerian pre-school settings. The findings run contrary to policy requirements which were put in place to achieve the first goal of EFA (Olorunfunmi 2000). These inadequacies may be seen as unexpected, considering that the Nigerian Government has attended most of the global educational conferences, where issues of quality of education have been discussed (NERDC 2002). However, the situation on the ground is explicable when one considers the amount of funds earmarked for the education sector by the Nigerian Government. Issues concerning funding of education in Nigeria have generated many controversies in the country. For instance, in the past decade, the entire budgetary allocation for education has been less than 4 per cent of the total budget, far below what is recommended by UNESCO (2000). This perhaps has contributed to the characteristics of the pre-schools observed.

Most importantly, these types of provision may not augur well for the development of Nigerian children, considering the advantages associated with pre-schoolers' experience of early education and care, prior to their entry into formal schooling. Such advantages include children's effective learning through active interactions with their environment (Vandeyar and Killen 2006); positive relationships between children; children's significant language ability and better mathematical skills (NICHD 2002); children's significant cognitive and social development (Sylva *et al.* 2006).

The results revealed that the observed practice of the pre-school teachers, school administrators, parents and owners emphasised formal learning, especially numeracy, reading and writing, and English language. This could be because pre-school in Nigeria is an important prerequisite for primary school entry, even though entry into primary school should be automatic and compulsory for all Nigerian children of school age, and experience of rigorous formal instruction in pre-school settings is unnecessary.

The interesting thing about the findings is that the differences observed occurred in both government-funded and privately owned pre-schools. For instance, the teachers did not adhere to the prescribed medium of instruction and the class size was larger than was recommended. These practices may not serve well either the learners or the education system. During instruction, it is important to consider the intricate values of using the languages in which both parties (the teacher and pupils) are conversant (Prah 2003), while small classes enable the teacher to have more contact periods with children on a one-to-one basis (Blatchford *et al.* 2002).

Implications of the findings

These findings have implications about the impact of the pre-school experience on the children's learning and development. Observed implementation of policy and pedagogical practices provides Nigerian pre-schoolers with limited experience of creativity and independence though learner-centred and learner-initiated activities. Teaching the rudiments of numbers, shapes and form, literacy and science skills through play and other types of learner-centred activities are important in inculcating in children the spirit of enquiry, exploration and autonomy. Research has now established that pre-schoolers learn best when they are enabled to construct knowledge through activities, and participation with others in activities, which foster experimentation, problem solving and social interaction.

The findings indicate that there is a need to review and potentially update the curriculum content of teacher preparation and continuing education programmes (in-service and professional support) to include both theory and practice that is appropriate for pre-schools. The aim is to produce teachers who can channel most aspects of their practice towards planning and facilitating learning tasks at both individual and small-group levels, with the children being at the centre stage of the interaction, without delivering monologues; to equip the teachers with skills and competencies in encouraging pupils to initiate activities and participate actively in classroom interactions; and to acquire adequate knowledge in child development and training in associated pedagogical methods that have been identified as important measures of pre-school quality.

Conclusion

Based on the findings of this study, the picture painted shows that the Nigerian Government appears not to be ready yet to implement the well-articulated policy and the curriculum content for pre-school education. Quality pre-school provision is well articulated in policy documents, but actual provision is far behind the standards set out. The introduction of pre-school education seems to have caught the Nigerian Government unaware and unprepared, although issues pertaining to this level of education have been on the education agenda since 1969.

It appears that the government and policy makers have found it politically desirable and convenient to start pre-school provision in existing public primary schools; something that has led to early formal instruction and children's 'schoolifi-cation' (discussed also in Chapter 1). However, further research and feasibility studies are required to ensure the development of infrastructures and instructional materials which are informed by the needs and context of the children, families and communities in Nigeria and the training of pre-school teachers who are familiar with appropriate theories and have the relevant pedagogical skills.

QUESTIONS FOR THINKING ABOUT POLICY AND PRACTICE

1. Should generating a policy document be an end in itself or a guide to quality compliance?
2. Should policy statements be politically motivated or a means to national development?
3. After generating a policy document, does implementation matter?

References

Blatchford, P., Moriarty, V., Edmonds, S. and Martin, C. (2002) Relationship between class size and teaching: A multi-method analysis of English infant schools, *American Educational Research Journal*, 39(1): 101–132.

FRN (Federal Republic of Nigeria) (1977–2011) *National Policy on Education*, Abuja: Nigerian Educational Research and Development Council.

Kerlinger, F.N. and Lee, H.B. (2000): *Foundations of Behavioural Research*, 4th edn, Orlando, FL: Harcourt.

NERDC (Nigerian Educational Research and Development Council) (2002) *National Minimum Standards for Early Child Care Centres in Nigeria*, Abuja: NERDC.

NICHD (Early Child Care Research Network) (2002) Early child care and children's development prior to school entry: Results from the NICHD study of early child care. *American Education Research Journal*, 39(1): 133–164.

Olorunfunmi, M.O.A. (2000) *Education For All: The Year 2000 Assessment: Nigeria*, Abuja: Federal Ministry of Education.

Osokoya, I.O. (1989) *History and Policy of Nigerian Education in World Perspective*, Ibadan: AMD Publishers.

Osokoya, I.O (2000) *Early Childhood Education Teaching Methods*, Ibadan: Centre for External Studies, University of Ibadan.

Prah, K.K. (2003) Going native: Language of instruction for education, development and African emancipation, in B. Brock-Utne, Z. Desai and M. Qorro (eds) *Language of Instruction in Tanzania and South Africa*, Dar-es-Salaam: LOITASA E & D Limited.

Sylva, K., Siraj-Blatchford, I., Taggart, B., Sammons, P., Melhuish, E., Elliot, K. and Totsika, V. (2006) Capturing quality in early childhood through environmental rating scales, *Early Childhood Research Quarterly*, 21(1): 76–92, available online at: www.sciencedirect.com/science/article/pii/S0885200606000044 (accessed 5 May 2011).

Ukeje, O. and Aisiku, J.U. (1982) Education in Nigeria, in A.B. Fafunwa and J.U Aisiku (eds) *Education in Africa: A Comparative Survey*, London: George Allen & Unwin.

UNESCO (1990) *Education For All: Framework for Action: Meeting Basic Learning Needs*, World Conference on Education, Jomtien, Thailand, available online at: www.unesco.org/education/efa/ed_for_all/background/world_conference_jomtien.shtml (accessed 5 May 2011).

UNESCO (2000) *World Education Forum: The Dakar Framework for Action. Education For All: Meeting Our Collective Commitments*, adopted by the World Education Forum, Dakar, Senegal, 26–28 April 2000, available online at: http://unesdoc.unesco.org/images/0012/001211/121147e.pdf (accessed 15 August 2011).

United Nations General Assembly (1989) *The Convention on the Rights of the Child*, adopted by the General Assembly of the United Nations on 20 November 1989 (UN Convention), available online at: www.unicef.org/crc/text.htm (accessed 21 May 2011).

Vandeyar, S. and Killen, R. (2006) Teacher–student interactions in desegregated classrooms in South Africa, *International Journal of Educational Development*, 26(4): 382–393, available online at: www.sciencedirect.com/science/article/pii/S0738059305001112 (accessed 15 August 2006).

8

A PEDAGOGY FOR EDUCATING 'NEW PROFESSIONALS'

An English perspective

Sue Callan, Michael Reed and Sharon Smith

OVERVIEW

This chapter critically explores the term 'new professional', by considering the roles, responsibilities and relationships expected of an early years practitioner. It will argue that these 'roles' are increasingly defined by government initiatives, directives and regulation. These place higher education (HE) establishments under pressure to design 'training' that is responsive to such initiatives. We suggest that there is a need to develop a pedagogic base to develop reflective practitioners who will question policy and challenge assumptions about the way their own learning is designed.

Key words: reflective practice; heutagogy; andragogy; professional development; new professionals.

Introduction: the context of professional change

In England the Childcare Act 2006 reinforced parents' expectations for the provision of high-quality childcare services and confirmed the role of Local Education Authorities (LEA) as leaders in forging partnerships across all sectors. This is also recognised within the Children's Plan (DCSF 2007) and changes to the 'early years curriculum' in England with the introduction of a statutory framework – the Early Years Foundation Stage (EYFS) (DCSF 2008). Indeed, this curriculum requires adherence to a variety of initiatives to support children and their families. Practitioners are asked to consider the 'whole child', ensuring that they work with professionals from other agencies and share information between the different settings a child may attend. There have also been changes in Scotland, Wales, and Northern Ireland which underline the importance of integrated working, safeguarding children's welfare, longitudinal assessment, specialised early years teaching, and the introduction of a defined curriculum framework.

Such change has not been enacted without debate. This focussed on new professional roles, as well as the appropriateness of introducing and reviewing curriculum frameworks, let alone their content. There have also been debates about the value of engaging in reflective practice, the importance of professional development and the nature of professionalism – with a particular focus on management and leadership approaches (Miller and Cable 2011; Murray 2009; Reed 2008 and 2009; Moss 2008; Pound 2008; Aubrey 2007; Nurse 2007). In terms of common working practice, the Common Core of Skills and Knowledge (CWDC 2010) identifies the practice components required by those (including volunteers) whose work brings them into regular contact with children, young people, and families. The 'core' underlines the need for professionals to work together and therefore be more effective in supporting the interests of the child. However, these components can also reflect a somewhat 'technocratic' view of early years practice and assume that competencies can be equated with qualities and what are increasingly known as 'professional dispositions' – values and ethics in practice (Rike and Sharp 2008).

In essence, practitioners today are required to support families and children based upon an interrelationship between the abilities to:

- provide a warm, caring and purposeful way of effectively communicating with children, young people and families, and being adept at sharing information with other professionals;
- see the value of multi-agency working;
- be curious about a child's development;
- be prepared to advocate and safeguard the welfare of the child;
- lead practice and have a positive response to change;
- understand and apply aspects of diversity and inclusion to promote the welfare of children;
- understand the importance of developing a positive learning environment;
- view continuing professional development as an important aspect of professional practice;
- engage in work-based research and enquiry, reflect on practice, lead, challenge, adapt and refine practice.

All of these are laudable aspects of early years professionalism. As to whether they can be taught as a set of all-encompassing 'requirements' is the key question. Perhaps they should be seen more as professional dispositions which may be explored, refined and developed in terms of values, beliefs, attributes, professional and personal heritage as well as professional competency.

The new professionals

The development of work-based learning and the emergence of the Foundation Degree (Fd) has provided a platform for practitioners to explore and develop their role. This includes the ability to share information with parents, share information with other agencies and engage in partnership working. Therefore, a new professional is expected to work within three different levels (Thompson 1997):

1. a structural level – understanding the aims and objectives of their nation's policy documentation and the implications this has for early years provision and practice;
2. a community level – considering how policy documentation can be applied in relation to the culture, values and attitudes which exist within the community in which the early years setting exists;
3. a personal level – interpreting the rhetoric of the policy documentation and the reality of working in the early years setting to enable staff, parents and the wider community to work together for the best interests of the child.

These levels are not static and there needs to be a fluid movement between them. For example, the ability to think critically and creatively in applying policy documentation requires an engagement in reflective practice and a holistic overview of ways to support children and parents. This not only develops a sense of shared values within the setting, but places emphasis on the child at the centre of the process. We therefore argue that making a difference in leading early years practice requires not only knowledge and understanding of structural aspects as well as a purposeful response to community, but also recognising values and beliefs at a personal level.

This is a view that Appleby (2010) sees as developing personal confidence and motivation to construct an interpretation of what it means for individuals to work in a particular context. This is important to enable practitioners to determine where they 'fit' in terms of contributing to early years change and development, a stance that Claxton (2003) views as a never-ending 'learning journey' involving personal and professional qualities that merge as we develop a personal sense of responsibility. This is becoming more widely known as forging a 'community or landscape of practice' (Wenger 1998, 2010; Wenger et al. 2002). It all requires early years practitioners to be responsive to change, develop their own views and reflections and, importantly, challenge practice in teaching and learning (Callan 2007; Smith 2008).

Emerging pedagogy in continuing professional development

The development of vocationally-based Foundation degrees has raised a new platform for practitioners to explore and develop their role. Practice and theory are merged within a framework that supports work-based learning and work-based enquiry. The benchmarks for Fds identified by the Quality Assurance Agency (QAA 2004) highlight that Fds have particular characteristics that cannot be found in other qualifications; in particular, the emphasis on a practice-based approach and practice-based reflection. These degrees are usually taught within universities, but also within further education institutions (FEIs), and attract students who traditionally would not have studied at HE level. However, there is evidence which shows that students make an effective transition into undergraduate education and many progress to further studies (Smith 2008). Access has been aided by government funding and a degree structure based upon practice-based learning alongside directed teaching. Many students enter this structure with expectations based on their formative education experiences of a teacher-led approach which is characterised by a formal pedagogy. Whether this is the most appropriate approach to meeting the complexity of engaging in a vocational programme is a key question.

We contend that the new professional requires training that moves away from a teacher-led approach and should be underpinned by what John Dewey, cited in Knowles (1990), sees as teaching and learning which require an interaction with experience and a process of student-led education – a process that Knowles (1990) recognised as an interaction between teacher and student with the teacher supporting the student's learning and encouraging a desire to learn. He defined this process as 'andragogy' and his main assumption was the learners' involvement in the process, through interacting in the decisions about what they wanted to learn and their self-motivation in the process. The learning process is therefore more self-directed and autonomous. Students become part of the 'journey' and are encouraged to co-construct learning alongside their peers. In this way, they are learning from experience and, importantly, sharing those experiences. For the new professionals this also means engaging with technology as this is now having a profound effect on adult learning as well as on children's learning (Tyler 2012).

The use of web-based tools and online learning environments has meant a rethinking about teaching strategies by lecturers. However, they have also enabled a more independent and flexible approach to learning, including the use of virtual learning environments and an almost instant communication between learners that can lead to increased dialogue and shared learning opportunities. Such environments promote self-directed learning which is essential in order to adapt to the demands of higher education. They also empower learners to seek information and find solutions which are pivotal to the learning process (Hyland and Merill 2003). Technology allows visual, auditory and interactive means of exploring work-based practice and engaging in professional reflection and 'collaborative enquiry'. It is a means of eliciting views on what is happening and what works (Reed 2011).

However, this is not to suggest that technology in itself can or should supersede effective teaching. It is a complement to ways of encouraging enquiry and research leading to a review and reflection on practice. This is usefully explained by Finlay and Gough (2003: 9) who suggest: 'Reflexive means to "bend back on oneself" . . . Reflexivity requires critical self-reflection of the ways in which researchers' social background, assumptions, positioning behaviour impact upon the research process.' This is a stance that is rooted in the concept of problem-based learning (PBL), which encourages student-focussed activities and teaching strategies that attempt to solve particular problems (McLinden *et al.* 2006). Cowan, cited in Littlejohn and Pegler (2007: 134), highlights that this requires an approach which involves a series of activities that are 'reflective and constructive, raising students' awareness and skills in solving complex problems' and it is a process that engages the learner in different levels of reflection 'before action, during action and after action'. More than this, it requires students to go beyond accepting regulatory levels of quality and to challenge, adapt and shape practice that is meaningful to the world they inhabit. In this model, the lecturer engages in the process as a conductor, who provides the tools for engaging the professionals in reflective practice (McLinden *et al.* 2006).

Of course, this requires high-quality teaching, structuring and promoting collective learning (Hase and Kenyon 2000). The function of lecturers is then to move beyond being pedagogues or andragogues and become knowledge brokers (Ashton and Newman 2006). All of which moves us some way from simply identifying the difference between pedagogy and andragogy; it takes us towards a model that celebrates an active and interactive engagement with the learner. This is the bedrock of 'heutagogy' (Hase and Kenyon 2000), which looks to the future, in which knowing how to learn will be a fundamental skill, given the pace of innovation and the changing structure of communities and workplaces.

So, when we engage actively in our own study it actually does make us better learners and educators. Hase and Kenyon (2000) acknowledge that this requires high-quality teaching. We argue that such an approach to learning and teaching recognises the strengths of the new twenty-first-century professionals. It builds upon inherent personal skills, improves personal confidence and celebrates a desire to share expertise with others. It provides the basis for practice-based enquiry and quality improvement and involves the practitioner in the active process of reflection on day-to-day practice.

A culture for communities of learning and practice

Where are we now? It is impossible to separate the discussion of experience in any form of education without reference to the wider context for policy and practice. At the time of writing, there are significant numbers of early years professionals (EYPs), working in early years settings and/or school classrooms, and the introduction of the EYFS (DCSF 2008) is embedded in their study. The design of professional development programmes is inevitably driven by these curriculum initiatives as well as government policies, reviews and regulatory requirements. These requirements set students on a particular learning journey as they continue to access professional development programmes.

Whilst HE has long-established quality and academic checks, it is unused to local levels of external scrutiny, but these examples are indicative of the social, cultural and political tension regarding shared meanings and expectation for HE programmes in particular. Staff in HE articulate the concern that the expanding role of HE early childhood centres in particular, in contributing to the quality of provision/

practitioners in children's services, has had significant impact on course focus in respect of the traditional 'ologies' of HE – the broad sweep of theory/practice discourse. Traditionally, there has been little crossover between the academic body of knowledge and 'training' (in the technical sense) which has been the remit of the FE sector. There appears to be a merging of the two in the process of implementing policy for change in practice, which has impacted on pedagogies, ethos and delivery. The experience of students in this process is that they have perceived 'goal posts' moving on more than one occasion and this leaves some practitioners facing professional dilemmas and becoming personally unsettled (Callan 2009). We see reflexivity as engaging practitioners in the process for quality improvement in child and family provision as well as personal development.

However, simply focussing on reflective practice does not offer a real possibility of change. Change requires FE institutions and HE centres to develop virtual learning environment (VLE) and PBL delivery, which is work-based (placement-based in some cases), with assessment centred on work-based activities and investigations. Such programmes will enable an exploration of theory and practice, but also critical theory for reflection on wider social, as well as personal, values and self-knowledge. Assessment should include investigation and application of learning theories and philosophical traditions of early childhood, also the social policy and sociological processes that enable reflection on personal and cultural meanings in the context outside the nursery door. In some cases, HE departments have been merged to replicate the multi- and trans-agency culture in the infrastructure for governance of Every Child Matters (ECM) (DCSF 2004). Health and Social Care, Early Childhood, Children and Youth, Education and Family Studies are increasingly to be found in new combined faculties enabling the most flexible access to a range of professionally relevant modules.

Many HE institutions have recognised that a work-based investigation can be undertaken by the practitioner in a way that will facilitate knowledge and application of the 'research process', lead to real outcomes in terms of quality improvement in EYFS and enable a depth of personal reflection on theory, expert opinion and the orthodoxy of social policy for children and families. Such investigations may not fit with the traditional quantitative, methodological perspectives but will, crucially, have real meaning for practitioners who can experience the opportunity to make a significant and long-lasting contribution to practice (Callan and Reed 2012). Indeed, where studies such as these are established, some local authorities are 'publishing' student work in their local professional networks and communities of practice.

Such changes will and have had an impact upon the role of the academic tutor who cannot remain that of the 'expert' in the classroom who transmits a defined body of knowledge. Whilst academic tutors still retain a role as guides to academic study skills and application of traditional conventions, the development of new learning strategies requires a different approach, consistent with characteristics of communities of practice (Wenger 1998, 2010). The classroom represents a community of learning and practice, where the course leader will adopt a mentoring role, enabling practitioners to access the benefits of theoretically informed reflective practice. This reflects Canning and Callan's (2010) emphasis on a continual 'pause for thought' in the course process, where practitioners are encouraged to articulate feelings and responses to their learning experience. They are encouraged to express the struggles inherent in learning and share ways of moving towards self-directed, independent study and a paradigm of 'contextual knowing' (Brookfield 1995). The strategy is consistent with Maxine Greene's (1995) notion that only those who know the importance of reflecting on their own thinking are in a position to teach others. In this way the process of reflection can be replicated in course teams, so that response to the student experience is meaningful, taking into account the different dynamics of power represented in the concept of a community of learning and practice. Course design needs to be centred on aligning the needs of learners, the pedagogical values of course staff, all sector requirements (including HEIs) and external policy drivers. As such, there is again the need to utilise reflection to identify ways of developing these strategies for teaching and learning with all undergraduates – whether they are experienced practitioners, or young adults progressing from learning in school or FE colleges.

Of course, as with any movement of change, a prerequisite is the willingness of staff and students alike to engage in respectful, trusting, open and honest relationships. This is a process to be learned, but will surely underpin effective work with children and families in practice. To this extent, it is worth acknowledging that the premise of andragogy (that adults are established, independent, motivated learners) is subject to challenge. We do not find that the needs of adult learners are qualitatively different from the needs of children in the classroom – a point of particular relevance when we recognise that some of our youngest student practitioners will still be under the nurturing umbrella of ECM (DCSF 2004) by dint of their age. This is in addition to the continued support needed to support study skills and academic requirements as they progress through HE:

> being an independent learner, for me was being given the skills, self-belief and self-confidence. I think that the foundation degree is a bridge to higher level study and that when it works well it starts as more tutor intensive, and gradually eases off, leaving autonomous learners – dependent on the individual student's progress.
>
> (Smith 2008: 72)

For staff in further and higher education (FHE), it is worth considering the considerable personal impact of changes in the children's workforce and the steep learning curve for all those involved. We stress that academic expectations are the same as ever; the emphasis now is on different ways of achieving these standards in dialogue with learners. As a result, we seek a process of facilitating emotional literacy, professional dispositions, knowledge and technical skills for practice in a way that enables personal growth and change for all those involved with the children's workforce. In this way we can meet the requirement for a rounded, refined profession.

Conclusion

Many HE establishments have recognised that work-based investigation can be undertaken by the practitioner in a way that will facilitate knowledge and application of the 'research process', and lead to positive outcomes in terms of quality improvement. Some are developing purposeful links with local authorities to enhance quality in the workplace (Solvason 2012). Such investigations may not fit with the traditional methodological perspectives of 'formal research' but will, crucially, have real meaning for practitioners who will use them as the opportunity to make a significant and long-lasting contribution to practice; in effect, modelling the very processes expected of the student with regard to their work with children. This transactional model we see as essential if practitioners are to be encouraged to articulate feelings and responses and self-direct their learning experience (Canning and Callan 2010).

Therefore, course design is evolving so that it starts to be centred on aligning the needs of learners and external policy drivers. Increasingly there are 'new professionals' who are able to forge professional relationships with tutors and play a full part in designing their own learning environments. They are aware of change and how to respond to it, and embrace and use new technologies in their practice and their learning. Tutors are also dealing with change – in the way they perceive teaching and learning and considering a movement from pedagogy to heutagogy. Of course, such approaches should not diminish the academic expectations of engaging in HE and gaining a degree. We only argue for a shift in emphasis towards different pedagogical ways of achieving and improving these standards. We therefore advocate a process of facilitating emotional literacy and professional dispositions alongside the knowledge and technical skills for practice in a way that enables personal growth and change for those most closely involved. In this way we can meet the requirements for rounded, refined new professionals.

QUESTIONS FOR THINKING ABOUT POLICY AND PRACTICE

1. To what extent are there tensions in professional early childhood hierarchies and qualifications? How can such tensions be reconciled by adopting shared pedagogic approaches?

2. We assert that work-based enquiry promotes reflective practice that in turn can change, refine and challenge existing practice. In the increasingly regulated world of early education, and within what may be diminishing resources, how this might be possible?

3. Practitioners are now being asked to borrow significant funds to gain HE qualifications, at least in the English context. Should they be more assertive and question the pedagogic base that will support their studies?

References

Appleby, K. (2010) Reflective thinking; reflective practice, in M. Reed and N. Canning (eds) *Reflective Practice in the Early Years*, London: SAGE.

Ashton, J. and Newman, L. (2006) An unfinished symphony: 21st century teacher education using knowledge creating heutagogies, *British Journal of Educational Technology*, 37(6): 825–840.

Aubrey, C. (2007) *Leading and Managing in the Early Years*, London: SAGE.

Brookfield, S. (1995) *Becoming a Critically Reflective Teacher*, San Francisco, CA: Jossey-Bass

Callan, S. (2007) The Foundation Degree in early years: Students' perception of themselves as learners and the experiences that have contributed to this view: Can an exploration of these issues enhance reflective practice?, Unpublished Dissertation for Postgraduate Modular Scheme Master of Arts (Early Years), University of Worcester.

Callan, S. (2009) From experienced practitioner to reflective professional, in M. Reed and N. Canning (eds) *Reflective Practice in the Early Years*, London: SAGE.

Callan, S. and Reed, M. (eds) (2012) *Work Based Research in the Early Years*, London: SAGE.

Canning, N and Callan S. (2010) Heutagogy: Spirals of reflection to empower learners in higher education, *Reflective Practice*, 11(1): 69–80.

Claxton, G. (2003) *The Intuitive Practitioner: On the Value of Not Always Knowing What One Is Doing*, Maidenhead: Open University Press.

CWDC (2010) *The Common Core of Skills and Knowledge*, Leeds: CWDC.

DCSF (2004) *Every Child Matters: Change for Children*, Nottingham: DCSF.

DCSF (2007) *The Children's Plan: Building Brighter Futures. Summary*, Norwich: TSO.

DCSF (2008) *Early Years Foundation Stage: Setting the Standards for Learning, Development and Care for Children from Birth to Five*, Nottingham: DCFS.

Finlay L. and Gough, B. (2003) *Reflexivity: A Practical Guide for Researchers and Health and Social Sciences*, Oxford: Blackwell.

Greene, M. (1995) *Realising the Imagination: Essays on Education, the Arts and Social Change*, San Francisco, CA: Jossey-Bass.

Hase, S. and Kenyon, C. (2000) *From Andragogy to Heutagogy*, Melbourne: ultiBASE.

Hyland, H. and Merill, B. (2003) *The Changing Face of Further Education: Lifelong Learning, Inclusion and Community Values in Further Education*, London: Routledge.

Littlejohn, A. and Pegler, C. (2007) *Preparing for Blended e-Learning*, London: Routledge.

Knowles, M. S. (1990) *The Adult Learner: A Neglected Species*, Houston, TX: Gulf Publishing Company.

McLinden, M., McCall, S., Hinton, D. and Weston, A. (2006) *Embedding On-Line Problem Based Learning Resources in a Professional Programme for Specialist Teachers of Children with Visual Impairment*, available online at: www.education.bham.ac.uk/research/victar/publicationsx/VICTAR_Publications_List_October_2006.pdf (accessed 11 May 2011).

Miller, L. and Cable, C. (eds) (2011) *Professionalization: Leadership and Management in the Early Years*, London: SAGE.

Moss, P. (2008) Foreword, in A. Paige-Smith and A. Craft (eds) *Developing Reflective Practice in the Early Years*, Maidenhead: Open University Press.

Murray, J. (2009) Value-based leadership and management, in A. Robins and S. Callan (eds) *Managing Early Years Settings*, London: SAGE.

Nurse, A. (2007) *The New Early Years Professional: Dilemmas and Debates*, London: David Fulton.

Pound, L. (2008) Exploring leadership: Roles and responsibilities of the early years professional, in A. Paige-Smith and A. Craft (eds) *Developing Reflective Practice in the Early Years*, Maidenhead: Open University Press.

QAA (2004) *Foundation Degree Qualification Benchmark*, available online at: www.qaa.ac.uk (accessed 11 May 2011).

Reed, M. (2008) Professional development through reflective practice, in A. Paige-Smith and A. Craft (eds) *Developing Reflective Practice in the Early Years*, Maidenhead: Open University Press.

Reed, M. (2009) Children's Centress and Children's Services, in M. Reed and N. Canning (eds) *Reflective Practice in the Early Years*, London: SAGE.

Reed, M. (2011) Reflective practice and professional development, in A. Paige-Smith and A. Craft (eds) *Developing Reflective Practice in the Early Years*, 2nd edn, Milton Keynes: Open University Press.

Rike, C. and Sharp, L.K. (2008) Assessing pre-service teachers' dispositions: A critical dimension of professional preparation, *Childhood Education*, 84(3): 150–153.

Smith, S. L. (2008) Foundation degrees: Further education or highering aspirations? To what extent do further education institutions support transition into higher education?, Unpublished Paper, University of Worcester.

Solvason, C. (2012) Improving quality in the early years, starting with the student experience, in M. Reed and N. Canning (eds) *Implementing Quality Improvement and Change in the Early Years*, London: SAGE.

The Childcare Act (2006) Commencement No.1 Order 2006 S.I 3360, London: H.M Government.

Thompson, N. (1997) *Anti-discriminatory Practice*, 2nd edn, London: Macmillan.

Tyler, L. (2012) Now we've got it, how do we know it's working? Evaluating the quality impact of technology in the early years, in M. Reed and N. Canning (eds) *Implementing Quality Improvement and Change in the Early Years*, London: SAGE.

Wenger, E. (1998) *Communities of Practice: Learning, Meaning and Identity*, Cambridge: Cambridge University Press.

Wenger, E. (2010) *Landscapes of Practice*, a series of workshops held at the practice-based Professional Learning Centre for Excellence in Teaching and Learning, Open University.

Wenger, E., McDermott, R. and Snyder, W. (2002) *Cultivating Communities of Practice*, Cambridge, MA: Harvard Business School Press.

9

THE EARLY CHILDHOOD PEDAGOGICAL DILEMMA IN IRELAND

Florence Dinneen

OVERVIEW

From the introduction of the Child Care Regulations in Ireland in 1996 and their subsequent revision in 2006, no significant legislation has been enacted that stipulates minimum qualifications for all entrants into the early years profession; in fact, its status as a profession is still lacking. Consequently, despite key policy initiatives to progress the early childhood sector over the past decade in particular, a pedagogical dilemma now exists. This chapter is about changing perspectives in education. It initially looks at issues around training within the early childhood sector in the first decade of the twenty-first century in Ireland and then moves on to issues concerning early childhood pedagogy within the same period. It discusses the results from the final phase of a longitudinal study with a two-fold aim: to promote professionalism in all aspects of the training of the educarer; and to devise innovative and supportive methodologies for the training of early years professionals, particularly in the pedagogical area. The results indicate that effecting change in the training of educarers cannot be rushed.

Key words: Ireland; early childhood policy; pedagogical dilemma; training; professionalism; supportive methodologies.

Introduction

The title of this chapter is dealt with both interrogatively and discursively. First, it asks: 'Is there an early childhood pedagogical dilemma in Ireland?' The answer is found to be complex as its investigation reveals that recent policy trends in the provision of pre-schooling, in the year prior to entering junior infants, have surged ahead of the provision of adequately trained staff to meet the newly created demand. Second, through examination and discussion, the answer will demonstrate that current training trends along with early childhood curriculum development cannot be separated from sound policy developments (Department of Education and Science 2009a). Since the author was head of one of the key degree programmes in ECCE in the country (at Mary Immaculate College, University of Limerick), an opportunity arose to conduct a study which aimed to devise innovative and supportive methodologies for the training of educarers, particularly in the pedagogical area. Qualitative and quantitative research methods were used. The results are convincing on two fronts: professionalism in the early childhood sector presupposes quality training; and training for early childhood in Ireland in the twenty-first century sees the pressing need for policy and pedagogy to meet.

National trends: international influences

Within the Irish context historically, while the term 'childcare' was understood to refer to services for children aged from birth to six years, nowadays a wider interpretation applies and the term is interchangeable with early childhood education. At a deeper conceptual level still, there is extensive usage and acceptance throughout the literature of the term early childhood care and education (ECCE) (Coolahan 1998; NCCA 2004, 2009; CECDE 2006; DES 2009b). While the concept of education for many denoted 'schooling' in the past, linkage with the word curriculum would have confirmed further the concept of formalised education. A newer lexicon within early years education gives rise to words like 'educare' (Dinneen 2002a) to encapsulate the notion that care and education are inextricably linked.

Curriculum in the early years in Ireland

The recent launch of *Aistear:* Ireland's first Early Childhood Curriculum Framework (NCCA 2009) is a further point of departure in the care and education debate that is ongoing, not only in Ireland (Department of Education and Science 1999; Douglas 1994), but internationally (Hustedt *et al.* 2008; Frede *et al.* 2007). *Aistear*, a thematic approach to learning, according to its authors, 'describes the types of learning (dispositions, values and attitudes, skills, knowledge and understanding) that are important for children in their early years, and offers suggestions as to how this learning might be nurtured' (NCCA 2009: 6).

Heretofore in Ireland, universal pre-schooling prior to children's entry into the National School system was never really considered and any voluntary initiatives to organise pre-schooling, since the late 1960s, went unrecognised at official levels. However, the voluntary sector, under the banner of the Irish Preschool Playgroup Association (IPPA) (Douglas 1994), became so vocal and widespread throughout the 1980s and 1990s that something had to be done in relation to the regulation of that sector. Since children under school age were then under the remit of the

Department of Health, pre-school regulations were issued by that department in 1996 and revised again in 2006 (Department of Health and Children 1996, 2006). As in many other European countries in relation to pre-school provision, the driving forces for the development of services in early education were the 'disadvantage factor' and the 'equality factor', with the voluntary sector at the forefront as the main instigators of provision closely followed by the social services (David 1998). However, a reversal of the stance on universal pre-schooling has now taken place and from January 2010, a pre-school place is on offer to every three-year-old child in the country.

Consequently, the topics of training and varying standards raise their problematic heads yet again! The training problem has been *tackled* at government level over the past 15 years through several European-funded initiatives – many based on the accreditation of prior learning. The most significant developments in relation to training, however, were the introduction of the National Framework of Qualifications (NFQ) and the setting up of the National Awards Councils comprising the Higher Education and Training Awards Council (HETAC) and the Further Education and Training Awards Council (FETAC) (Department of Education and Science 2009a). Third-level colleges and universities have now entered the frame and, in many respects, the move to the higher education institutions has spearheaded the exponential development of the early years sector in Ireland.

International influences

In 2004, the Organisation for Economic Co-operation and Development (OECD) reported that an over-didactic approach was prevalent in infant classes in Irish schools and that evidence of activity-based learning was wanting. Other reports placed their focus on staffing issues to ensure a quality service: for example, *Starting Strong II* (Organisation for Economic Co-operation and Development 2006). Therefore, it is clear that with the momentum for change outlined in the preceding sections there is concurrently an overarching need for vigilance in terms of monitoring early education and care to ensure system performance. A great volume of international literature sees the research act as meeting this need (Anning *et al.* 2009; David 1998; Frede *et al.* 2007; Hustedt *et al.* 2008). However, the lack of unity and cohesion within the birth to six years sector at the moment in Ireland underpins many of the causes of the 'pedagogical dilemma' even before the issue of monitoring system performance can be contemplated.

Unity, cohesion and the pedagogical dilemma

Ireland can boast of a rich history in terms of educational expertise. We only have to recap on the national trends outlined above over a relatively short period of time to realise that unity and cohesion within the sector are definitely on the agenda. For example, both *Aistear* (NCCA 2009) and *Síolta* – Ireland's National Quality Framework for Early Childhood Education (CECDE 2006) are presented for use with children between birth and six years of age in all settings including the infant classes of primary school. A recently conducted consultative process on the perception of stakeholders within the childcare sector reveals that there is unity of perception around the needs of the workforce for the years ahead coupled with a cohesive understanding that things must improve (Department of Education and Science 2009a). On the standardisation of training course content for participants, it is noteworthy that training in the use of *Síolta* (CECDE 2006) and *Alistear* (NCCA 2009) were prominent needs mentioned, thus showing cohesion and unity of thought. But is there a pedagogical dilemma?

A pedagogical dilemma that is double-edged!

In its own way, the consensus noted above underpins a pedagogical dilemma that is double-edged. One side of the dilemma portrays the felt need by adults for high-quality training while the other side portrays the consequences of not having an adequately trained workforce ready to deliver programmes of a high pedagogical standard.

Another aspect of the pedagogical dilemma that pertains to the Irish scene is the non-recognition of members of the early years sector as a potential *educational force*. Consequently, status is perceived to be low leading to diminished visibility. In spite of many laudable collaborative efforts and much rhetoric, little has been achieved within the last decade to progress the sector to a credible professional standing. The roots of this stem from the historical concept of education as being the preserve of teachers working within the statutory school system along with the lingering notion that younger children have a greater need for care. This thinking, whatever the root cause, obviates the responsibility to consider education and care as a dual developmental need in the nurturing process from birth.

The longitudinal study (Phase 2): methodology

On this ECCE degree programme, the learning focus of each placement is thematic. The theme for Phase 2, 'Towards Professionalism', addressed the full range of professional approaches towards children, other adults and the environment. Students (61 in total) were given eight hours of focused training, spanning a four-week period, covering the following topics:

1. relational pedagogy revisited (focus of Phase 1, see Dinneen 2009);
2. curriculum implementation with the under-threes – *thematic/strand approaches*;
3. professionalism in the workplace;
4. portfolio: ongoing development of pedagogical resources.

On placement, each ECCE student receives a minimum of three visits lasting one hour from a dedicated supervisor. It was the consultant supervisor who directed the research and the training of students and supervisors in the current study. Ethical issues were dealt with in the same successful manner as for Phase 1.

TABLE 9.1 Methods of collecting data (Phase 1 and Phase 2)

Phase 1 – Spring 2007 *1st-year students*	*Phase 2 – Autumn 2008* *3rd-year students*
1 The Caregiver Interaction Scale (Arnett 1989)	1 The Caregiver Interaction Scale (Arnett 1989)
2 Running records (a) researcher as observer of JIEs (b) student as observer of JIEs	2 Running records (a) researcher as observer of JIEs
3 Student reports: Questionnaires – basic-level pedagogy (selected areas)	3 Student reports: Questionnaires – pedagogy at advanced level
	4 Whole-class peer evaluation of videoed learning activities – pedagogical expertise probed

In many respects, the methodology used in Phase 1 was replicated. However, modification of the approach was necessary to capture the students' emerging ability in relation to their pedagogical expertise with the children. Table 9.1 shows the potential for incremental professional development in educarers to be documented while not losing sight of the fundamental rudiments of relational pedagogy that establish the foundation of early childhood care and education.

Finally, the standard method of assessing student performance on placement helped with the triangulation of results by including the assessment given by each participating student's supervisor. This was then aligned with the individual assessment yielded by the research methodology used above. Every detail in research such as this is important and is captured ultimately through thick descriptive accounts, thus aiding the process of triangulation towards validation.

The Caregiver Interaction Scale (CIS, Arnett 1989)

This instrument gauges the sensitivity of carers and was used with 12 students over a period of 30 minutes as they interacted with toddlers. Of the 12 students, eight were follow-on students from Phase 1 and four were new participants. This scale has 26 caregiver characteristic statements and is organised into four subscales: (a) positive, (b) punitive, (c) firm/permissive, (d) detached. While this instrument was applied by the main researcher, an inter-rater reliability of .93 was established by two observers prior to its use in the field (any score above .75 may be considered adequate reliability). Analysis was carried out using the Statistical Package for the Social Sciences (SPSS).

Running records

Another 12 students, located in baby rooms, were observed for a set period of ten minutes by the lead researcher and her assistant to examine their interactions with babies in order to determine what efforts they were making to promote and extend the children's language. The focus in particular was to see if students could identify opportunities to promote Joint Involvement Episodes (JIEs) (Dinneen 2002b).

Student reports (questionnaire)

This marks the participation of the whole class in the research act. For ease of analysis, the questionnaire was organised into three themes as before: (a) the tutorials – this time focused on pedagogy, a thematic approach to learning, curriculum planning, and a professional approach to leadership; (b) students' perception of needs; (c) 'my personal placement supervisor' – no change.

Whole-class peer evaluation

Seven students gave permission to be videoed while on placement in a variety of baby and toddler rooms for the sole purpose of having some of the material evaluated by their peers. Following the placement, the lead researcher, in conjunction with her assistant, made an initial selection of suitable material. The selection was based on the merits of the footage in relation to its perceived ability to motivate the entire group to identify some positive examples of good practice and yet have sufficient scope to allow the viewers to reflect on what *they* might do differently. In consultation with the student involved, permission was granted to have this used for peer evaluation.

The selected vignette depicted *Vera*★ leading an activity-based session featuring play-dough initially and culminating with a group action-song. The children's ages ranged from 18–24 months. There were seven children in the group and the videoing took up to 20 minutes. Finally, a response sheet that detailed student reactions to the selected vignette was prepared (see Figure 9.1).

Positives as you perceive them	What *you* would do differently
Learning and development were fostered when Vera...*	Re: *(a) Organisation of the learning environment* – I would . . .
	Re: *(b) Language development* – I would . . .
	Re: *(c) Holistic development* – I would . . .
	Re: *(d) Teaching methodology* – I would . . .

★ (fictitious name for publication purposes)

FIGURE 9.1 Student response sheet on selected vignette

Findings and analysis

Student caregivers' sensitivity

Table 9.2 (below) demonstrates an increase in the positive characteristics of five of the participants from Phase 1 of the study. Three scores can be rated as showing highly significant increases, two showed marginal increases and one maintained the former rating at 2.3 which is 'somewhat' positive rather than 'quite a bit' on this scale. Two students, however, decreased their scores significantly. The four new participants identified in single letters achieved scores between 3.3 and 3.8 which indicate that a positive approach in their interactions with young children is highly characteristic.

What is most gratifying in this result is that the very low score of 1.9 for positive characteristics by one student in Phase 1 was increased to 2.7 this time. The term 'punitive' for the subscale of the same name can best be understood when the words 'critical', 'threatening', 'authoritarian' and 'harsh' are invoked. Once again it was through the authoritarian interpretation that five students from Phase 2 erred. The term 'permissive' was taken to mean firm rather than the affordance of liberty without limits: therefore, all students except one (1.8) fall within an acceptable range. The term 'detached' is self-explanatory and the results indicate that all of the new entrants to Phase 2 fall within the acceptable range. However, while two of the former participants show an improvement with scores of 1.3 (FF) and 2.0 (KK) respectively, any form of detachment as a characteristic in adults working with young children is not to be desired. What is even more worrying is the level of detachment that this instrument picked up in five of the students, with three demonstrating an increase on the scores obtained in Phase 1.

While deep forensic investigations such as those outlined above are certainly useful at a personal and developmental level for aspiring educarers, it must be said in defence of low scores, that a snapshot on one's mood taken over a particular 20–30 minutes on a given day may not necessarily give a true indication of the measure of the person generally. For this reason, it is necessary to view the results above at group level in an effort to rate the group as a whole in terms of sensitivity. Figure 9.2 (see p. 113) provides the cumulative result.

Overall, the key areas for attention are the Positive and Detached subscales. These must be considered, however, in light of the influence of unacceptable scores in the Punitive and Detached subscales since they may well cause variations in the characteristics under scrutiny in the Positive area. This is aptly illustrated when we compare Figure 9.2 and Figure 9.3 (Phase 1) (see p. 113).

Figure 9.3 allows us to recap on the overview of the CIS caregiver characteristics for the group as a whole in Phase 1. When compared with Figure 9.2, it is clear that an improvement on the positive characteristics is now evident. However, in light of high individual scores within the Detached subscale in Phase 2, the results clearly emphasise the delicate balance that exists between all of these characteristics in one's day-to-day dealings with very young children.

TABLE 9.2 Analysis of student caregivers' sensitivity

	Positive			Punitive			Permissive			Detached		
	Phase 1	Phase 2	Variance	Phase 1	Phase 2	Variance	Phase 1	Phase 2	Var.	Phase 1	Phase 2	Variance
Student A	N/A	3.3	N/A	N/A	1	N/A	N/A	2.5	N/A	N/A	1	N/A
Student BB	2.1	2.4	+0.3	1	1.3	+0.3	2.5	2.8	+0.3	1.5	2.8	+1.3
Student CC	3.1	3.2	+0.1	1	1	=	3	2.8	−0.2	1	1	=
Student D	N/A	3.8	N/A	N/A	1	N/A	N/A	2.5	N/A	N/A	1	N/A
Student EE	3	2.1	−0.9	1.1	1.1	=	3	1.8	−1.2	1	1.5	+0.5
Student FF	1.9	2.7	+0.8	1.3	1.1	−0.2	2.8	2.8	=	1.8	1.3	−0.5
Student G	N/A	3.5	N/A	N/A	1	N/A	N/A	2.5	N/A	N/A	1	N/A
Student H	N/A	3.4	N/A	N/A	1.1	N/A	N/A	2.3	N/A	N/A	1	N/A
Student II	3.2	3.3	+0.1	1	1	=	3	2.8	−0.2	1	1.5	+0.5
Student JJ	2.9	3.3	+0.4	1	1.4	+0.4	3	2.3	−0.7	1	1	=
Student KK	2.3	2.3	=	1	1	=	2.5	2.5	=	2.5	2	−0.5
Student LL	3	2.1	−0.9	1	1	=	2.8	2.8	=	1	1	=

Key: A score of 1 indicates that it is not at all characteristic; 2 indicates that it is somewhat characteristic; 3 indicates that it is quite a bit characteristic; and 4 indicates that it is very much characteristic.

Notes:

1 For the purpose of comparison, a significant difference at the 5% level is equal to 0.2 on any item on the above scale.

2 The four new students listed in this table are entered as N/A for Phase 1 of the study and are identified in single letters.

CIS caregiver characteristics for the group as a whole

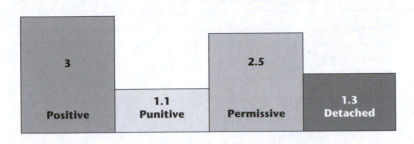

1 = Not at all   2 = Somewhat   3 = Quite a bit   4 = Very much

FIGURE 9.2 Results of Caregiver Interaction Scale (CIS) at group level: Phase 2

CIS caregiver characteristics for the group as a whole

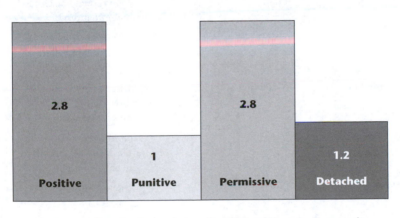

1 = Not at all   2 = Somewhat   3 = Quite a bit   4 = Very much

FIGURE 9.3 Results of Caregiver Interaction Scale (CIS) at group level: Phase 1

Student ability in promoting Joint Involvement Episodes (JIEs)

Running records were carried out for the sole purpose of extracting the evidence of the students' ability in promoting JIEs with babies. The results are outlined in Table 9.3 (see p. 114).

In a set ten-minute period during the consultant supervisor's visit, each of the 12 students was observed for their ability to promote, sustain and develop JIEs. There was a marked improvement in the students' ability in this regard with a total of seven students bringing 22 JIEs to conclusion when compared with four students and 12 JIEs at Phase 1 level. This demonstrates the importance of focused training at

TABLE 9.3 Student ability in promoting Joint Involvement Episodes (JIEs)

Running record analysis – Phase 2				
Student	*Demonstrated ability to promote a JIE type interaction (commence)* ★★★	*Demonstrated ability to sustain a JIE type interaction* ★★★	*Resulting JIEs*	*Observed context Missed/Other*
Student M	Low	Low	0	Child pointing – no adult response
Student N	Medium	Low	0	One-to-one language opportunities at mirror
Student O	High	High	3	Over-stimulation at times
Student PP	High	High	3	None missed
Student Q	High	High	3	None missed
Student RR	High	High	3	None missed – acted on child initiations
Student SS	Low	Low	0	Did not observe the specific interest of the child in one object
Student TT	Medium	Medium	1	Missed many by not following the child's interest in objects
Student U	Very high	Very high	8	Seized every opportunity to lead and also to follow the child's interest
Student VV	Low	Low	0	Missed two pointing gestures
				Offered toys but did not develop attentional focus
Student WW	Medium	Medium	1	Playing with body parts – missed communication opportunities
Student XX	High	Low	0	Adult commenced many through communication but did not sustain.
				Inclined to shift focus
Total JIEs			*22*	

Key: ★★★ Low = None; Medium = 1–2; High = 3–4; Very high = 4+

Note: The five new students listed in this table are indicated through the use of single lettering, e.g. M, N. Double lettering indicates participation in Phase 1 of the study.

foundational level in terms of developing relational pedagogy that can become the normal mode of interacting with young children particularly in the pre-verbal phase.

Focus on pedagogy

The first theme focused on pedagogy, a thematic approach to learning, curriculum planning and holistic development, the importance of assessment, the value of learning stories (Carr 2001), confidence in applying behaviour management techniques and a professional approach to leadership. Figure 9.4 represents the opinions offered by the full complement of students for the 11 statements on this theme. Each statement commenced with verbs that elicited the students' perception of how the tutorials helped their learning outcomes, e.g. 'Introduced me', 'Helped me', 'Confirmed for me', 'Taught me', 'Made direct links with'. The final statement in this questionnaire read: 'The tutorials taught me that professionalism is linked with leadership qualities at a personal level for each student': It elicited the response of 'Strongly agree', 49.2 per cent; 'Agree', 50.8 per cent; and differs little from the whole-class response *to all* of the statements as outlined in Figure 9.4. While almost half of the participants strongly agreed with the benefit of the focused tutorials, the remaining participants indicated to a somewhat lesser degree that the areas of behaviour management and the use of learning stories as an assessment tool would have needed more attention to promote a stronger confidence in their application and use.

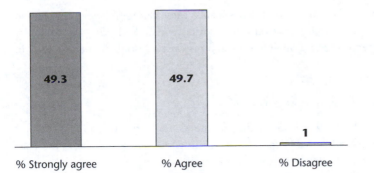

FIGURE 9.4 The extent of student agreement with regard to how tutorials helped them to meet the learning outcomes

Students' perception of needs

No change was made in Phase 2 in the statements in this theme since a clear demonstration of confusion was evident in the responses in Phase 1 (see Table 9.4 on p. 116). One new statement (No. 6) was added, however, and, clearly, the majority of students judged this appropriately. Much less confusion is evident on this occasion with far fewer and much more lightly weighted 'no opinions'. The opinions and the weighting of the 'no opinions' expressed for statements 2, 3 and

TABLE 9.4 Students' perception of needs

Statement	Cumulative agreement	No opinion	Cumulative disagreement
1 Babies and toddlers need time on their own.	**96.7**	**0**	**3.3**
	61.7	*8.5*	*29.8*
2 Babies and toddlers need adult company at all times.	**39.4**	**3.3**	**57.4**
	40.4	*12.8*	*46.8*
3 Toddlers should be taught obedience.	**29.5**	**24.6**	**44.2**
	50.0	*32.6*	*17.4*
4 Toddlers should be sanctioned for anti-social behaviour.	**6.6**	**11.5**	**82.0**
	34.0	*19.1*	*46.8*
5 Freedom is important for babies and toddlers.	**96.7**	**0**	**3.3**
	89.4	*2.1*	*8.6*
6 A child-centred approach is the most effective behaviour management approach for babies and toddlers.	**96.7**	**3.3**	**0**

Notes:
Phase 2 results are in bold; Phase 1 results are in italics.

A variance of up to 1% may occur due to the rounding-off process for cumulative results: allowance must also be made for missing responses.

4 are still worrying and indicate that topics such as these cannot be taken for granted and need to be discussed periodically in tutorials and linked with the topics of freedom, independence and discipline in lectures on philosophical perspectives in education.

'My personal placement supervisor'

Once again, no change was made to the statements under this theme since a good working relationship between supervisor and student is deemed to be at the core of professionalism. The statements were linked with quality guidance, accretion of learning and confidence-building. Figure 9.5 graphically illustrates the results in percentage terms from the 61 respondents.

The feedback to be discussed here has to centre on the disagreement area of the statements. It takes thick description to do this and the questionnaire design facilitated this through the following qualitative statement – 'My supervisor's advice and guidance [were] in tune with the advice and guidance given in the tutorials. . .'.

Only four of the returned questionnaires indicated some form of dissatisfaction with the supervisor. These ranged from a perception that the supervisor failed to understand the exact requirements of placement to supervisors displaying a negative attitude.

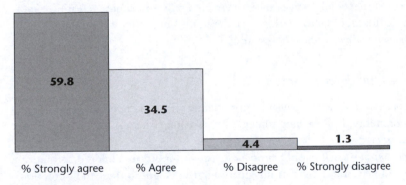

FIGURE 9.5 Students' perception of supervisor

Whole-class peer evaluation

There was wide uniformity in the identification of the more obvious characteristics of learning and development as fostered in the scenario by *Vera*. While the majority mentioned the positive aspects that one would expect to be identified, some negative aspects were, however, hailed as positive, indicating a weakness in the concept of sound pedagogical principles linked with the age-group in question (18–24 months). Some examples are:

- commending the use of 'sharing' as encouraged in the video even though it was only used verbally and without a concrete example of how to do this;
- commending the didactic approach in the naming of colours;
- commending the over-use of the questioning technique.

Regarding the remainder of the exercise where students had to identify how they might 'do things differently', there was wide variation in the frequency of mentions of the more obvious approaches. Some examples include:

Re: (a) Organisation of the learning environment

- *Important and frequently mentioned*: group size; space; freedom; choice; health and safety issues.
- *Important but less frequently mentioned*: giving individual attention; encouraging awareness of peers; encouraging social interaction; motivating children.

Re: (b) Language development

- *Important and frequently mentioned*: use of descriptive commenting; use of open-ended questions; a good model of speech; reflecting back utterances in the correct format; repetition; relevance of songs, poems and rhymes.

- *Important but less frequently mentioned*: encouraging child input – creating opportunities for children to speak; vocabulary build-up; using shorter sentences.
- *Important but not mentioned*: listening.

Re: (c) Holistic development

- *Important and frequently mentioned*: importance of exploration; independence and responsibility; key teaching strategies; turn-taking, sharing; positive behaviour management.
- *Important but less frequently mentioned*: how to motivate children; promoting pretend play and the use of imagination; attunement to the child's emotional needs; meaning-making; labelling/identifying emotions.
- *Important but not mentioned*: sensorial learning.

Re: (d) Teaching methodology

- *Important and frequently mentioned*: many of the usual teaching strategies; allowing the child to lead/following the child's lead.
- *Important but less frequently mentioned*: teaching strategies such as recall, revise, recap, suggest and prompt; praise and encourage; allow the child to set his/her own pace; listen; observe.
- *Important but not mentioned*: the role of assessment for learning; one-to-one as a teaching/learning strategy; age-appropriateness.

Standard method of assessment for a placement module

Correlates were found between high scores on the Positive subscale of the CIS with many of the students receiving grades in the mid- to high Bs and into the A category. Likewise, a correlation was clearly evident between unacceptable ratings on the Detached subscale of the CIS and lower grades being independently awarded by supervisors.

Conclusion

To conclude, the results support the initial statement that *effecting change in the training of educarers cannot be rushed*. The research journey also supports the argument put forward at the outset that a pedagogical dilemma now exists in Ireland. It demonstrates unequivocally that this has occurred as a result of rapid development in the early childhood sector on the structural side, concurrent with insufficient attention being paid, to date, to aspects of unity, cohesion and educational principles. The research results therefore support the argument that effecting change within any aspect of human behaviour *must be gradual* and under the guidance of sound ecological developmental principles that link with the assessment of the process at each juncture. This chapter offers insights into the training methodologies that will enable the sector to offer young children a system of early childhood care and education that is pedagogically sound. It closes with a call for due attention to be paid *now* to this dilemma.

QUESTIONS FOR THINKING ABOUT POLICY AND PRACTICE

1. What steps must occur for policy and pedagogy to meet?
2. If a pedagogical dilemma exists in early childhood within a country, what might the consequences be for children?
3. If education is a continuum from birth, what are its key foundational features?

References

Anning, A., Cullen, J. and Fleer, M. (2009) *Early Childhood Education: Society and Culture*, 2nd edn, Los Angeles, CA: SAGE.

Arnett, J. (1989) Caregivers in day-care centers: Does training matter?, *Journal of Applied Developmental Psychology*, 10: 541–552.

Carr, M. (2001) *Assessment in Early Childhood Settings*, London: Paul Chapman Publishing.

CECDE (2006) *Síolta: The National Quality Framework for Early Childhood Education*, Dublin: Centre for Early Childhood Development and Education.

Coolahan, J. (ed.) (1998) *Report on the National Forum for Early Childhood Education*, Dublin: The Stationery Office.

David, T. (1998) *Researching Early Childhood Education: European Perspectives*, London: Paul Chapman Publishing.

Department of Education and Science (1999) *Ready to Learn: White Paper on Early Childhood Education*, Dublin: The Stationery Office.

Department of Education and Science (2009a) *Developing the Workforce in the Early Childhood Care and Education Sector: Report on the Findings from the Consultative Process*, Dublin: DES.

Department of Education and Science (2009b) Developing the workforce in the early childhood care and education sector, Consultation Document, available online at: www.education.ie (accessed 8 September 2009).

Department of Health and Children (1996) *Child Care (Pre-school Services) (No. 1) Regulations 1996*, Dublin: The Stationery Office.

Department of Health and Children (2006) *Child Care (Pre-school Services) (No. 2) Regulations 2006 and Explanatory Guide to Requirements and Procedures for Notification and Inspection*, Dublin: The Stationery Office.

Dinneen, F.E. (2002a) The concept of educare in public day-care facilities in Ireland and in the Irish psyche at the start of the third millennium, Unpublished Doctoral Thesis, Cork: University College Cork.

Dinneen, F.E. (2002b) Joint involvement episodes with babies: Lessons from research for the new millennium, in M. Horgan and F. Douglas (eds) *Lessons for the 21st Century: Research, Reflection, Renewal*, Proceedings of the Conference held in the D.I.T. Aungier Street, Dublin 2 on Saturday, 20 April 2002, OMEP (Ireland), available online at: http://omepireland.ie/publications.html (accessed 26 February 2012).

Dinneen, F.E. (2009) Does relationship training for caregivers enhance learning and language development in young children?, in T. Papatheodorou and J. Moyles (eds) *Learning Together in the Early Years: Exploring Relational Pedagogy*, London: Routledge.

Douglas, F. (1994) *History of the Irish Pre-school Playgroups Association (IPPA)*, Dublin: IPPA.

Frede, E., Jung, K., Barnett, W.S., Lamy, C.E. and Figueras, A. (2007) *The Abbot Preschool Program Longitudinal Effects Study (Apples)*, Interim Report, June 2007, available online at: www.nieer.org (accessed 10 November 2009).

Hustedt, J.T., Barnett, W.S. and Jung, K. (2008) *Longitudinal Effects of the Arkansas Better Chance Program: Findings from Kindergarten and First Grade*, The National Institute for Early Education Research, Rutgers University, available online at: www.nieer.org (accessed 10 November 2009).

NCCA (2004) *Towards a Framework for Early Learning: A Consultative Document*, Dublin: National Council for Curriculum and Assessment.

NCCA (2009) *Aistear: The Early Childhood Curriculum Framework*, Dublin: National Council for Curriculum and Assessment, available online at: www.ncca.ie (accessed 12 November 2009).

Organisation for Economic Co-operation and Development (2004) *Thematic Review of Early Childhood Education and Care Policy in the Republic of Ireland*, Dublin: The Stationery Office.

Organisation for Economic Co-operation and Development (2006) *Starting Strong II: Early Childhood Education and Care*, Paris: OECD.

PART II

Early childhood practice: enabling pedagogical cultures and encounters

10

THE JAPANESE AND WESTERN VIEWS OF NATURE

Beyond cultural incommensurability

Manabu Sumida

OVERVIEW

Sumida and Kawasaki (2008) established the distinction between the Japanese and Western worldviews of nature. The first emphasises the appearance of the natural phenomenal world; the latter makes a distinction between nature and humans and between 'appearance' and 'what is transcendental' with each component appreciated and studied differently. This chapter focuses on differences in cognition as influenced by different language–culture (L–C) communities and worldviews and on the notion of the 'mode of science education'. It recognises that a Japanese 'linguistic mode of science education' requires kindergartens to offer activities that are based on the Japanese L–C tradition and worldview. Such activities will facilitate and support a Japanese way of thinking and clarify its differences from the Western worldviews.

Key words: Japan; view of nature; Western; science; cultural incommensurability.

Introduction

Sociocultural points of view in science education research around the world maintain that, like any other culture, science has its own history of development and change (Cobern 1998, 2000; Matthews 2009). In general, science is identified as a culture that has emerged from the Western Modern Age, especially modern Western Europe. The European languages, used by the cultivators of Western science (W-science), form the basis for the Western scientific (W-scientific) way of thinking;

they offer a linguistic mode of science education which is referred to as the 'standard average European (SAE)' (Whorf 1956: 138).

On the global scale, some language modes of science education are commensurate with the SAE language mode and others are not. In other words, language modes of science education are incommensurate with the SAE language mode if they are conducted in L–C communities where the W-scientific way of thinking is not integrated in the tradition of the particular L–C community. In these L–C communities, such as Japan for instance, dissimilarity in ways of thinking poses a problem in correctly understanding W-scientific concepts. Therefore, scientific knowledge using the SAE linguistic mode of science appears difficult, threatening, and hermetic to those people who have little or no shared language for it; it is literally foreign to them (Montgomery 2000).

Sumida and Kawasaki (2008) established the distinction between the Japanese worldview and the W-scientific worldview, proposing the notion of a *linguistic mode of science education*, which makes it possible for educators to carry out reflections on science education within the setting or community of their own L–C. This is because a specific L–C community provides an intrinsic setting for science education that, in turn, brings about the effects of L–C on science education; namely, its rationale, content and style of teaching. In addition to these effects, the most significant learning factor is the way of thinking fixed in the respective L–C community. It is these effects that result in the differences among *linguistic modes of science education*.

The notion of the *linguistic mode of science education* is relevant to the activities of kindergartens, where most children experience their first science activities and are introduced to the scientific worldview. This chapter aims to address the reconsideration of science activities in Japanese kindergartens from an L–C understanding of nature, comparing Japanese with Western views. The discussion focuses on the relationship between the *phenomenal world* and the world of *idea*. Finally, implications for science education at the kindergarten level in non-Western L–C communities are briefly discussed.

Kindergartens (*yochien*) in Japan

Japanese *yochien*, usually translated as 'kindergarten' in English, provides pre-primary education to children aged 3 to 5 years old. Since 1956, the Japanese Ministry of Education's 'Course of Study for Japanese *Yochien*' has provided legal educational guidelines for all children aged 3 to 5 attending public and private *yochien*. These guidelines are known for their remarkable child-centred characteristics that emphasise the importance of spontaneous play activities.

The course of study (Japanese Ministry of Education Science, Sports and Culture 2008) consists of five areas: health; human relationships; environment; language; and expression. Science activities are mainly incorporated under the area 'environment'. The course of study for environment mandates the development of a sense of familiarity with natural things or enhancement of emotional sensitivity. For example, the course of study for kindergarten (Table 10.1) requires:

- leading a life in close contact with nature, being aware of its grandeur, beauty and wonder;
- developing and incorporating an interest in things surrounding them, such as nature;
- acknowledging the importance of life, appreciating and respecting it, by becoming familiar with animals and plants living in the surrounding area.

TABLE 10.1 Standards for 'environment' in the kindergarten curriculum in Japan

Aims

1. To develop interest in and curiosity about various kinds of things and experiences around them through a sense of familiarity with their surrounding environment and contact with nature.
2. To initiate interaction with their surrounding environment, and to enjoy making and discovering new things and incorporating them into their lives.
3. To enrich children's understanding of the nature of things, the concepts of quantities, written words, etc. through observing, thinking about and dealing with surrounding things and experiences.

Content

1. Leading a life close to nature, being aware of its grandeur, beauty and wonder.
2. Being in contact with various things in their lives and developing an interest in and curiosity about their nature and organization.
3. Being aware of changes in nature and in people's lives in accordance with the seasons.
4. Developing and incorporating an interest in things surrounding them, such as nature.
5. Acknowledging the importance of life, and appreciating and respecting it by becoming familiar with animals and plants living in the surrounding area.
6. Treating their surroundings with care.
7. Developing an interest in surrounding things and play equipment, and thinking about creative ways to make the best use of them.
8. Developing curiosity about the concepts of quantities and diagrams in everyday life.
9. Developing curiosity about simple signs and written words in everyday life.
10. Developing curiosity about the information and facilities that play an important role in their lives.
11. Being familiar with the national flag and all its functions inside and outside the kindergarten.

Dealing with the content

It is necessary to note the following points with regard to dealing with content related to the environment:

1. Teachers should place importance on processes enabling children to learn to think for themselves, by maintaining a relationship with their surrounding environment during play, and then developing curiosity about their surroundings. This will facilitate an interest in the significance and workings of their surroundings and enable them to recognize rules and codes. In particular, teachers should nurture children's desire to think

TABLE 10.1 continued

for themselves, by encouraging them to listen to other children's ideas and to enjoy generating new ideas.

2. Teachers should devise processes whereby children can deepen their relationship with nature, given that the foundation for rich emotions, curiosity, the ability to think and expressiveness is cultivated through direct contact with the grandeur, beauty and wonder of nature, something which is very important to experience during early childhood.

3. Children should be encouraged to develop a willingness to voluntarily interact with nature through sharing their feelings about things and experiences, and animals and plants living in the surrounding area. This should be done in such a way that these various relationships enable children to foster a sense of attachment and awe toward these things, as well as a respect for life, a spirit of social responsibility and an inquisitive mind.

4. Children should be encouraged to place importance on their experiences based on the necessities of their own lives, so that interest, curiosity and an understanding of the concepts of quantities and the written word can be fostered.

Many activities that involve getting close to nature are currently offered in Japanese *yochien*. For example, growing plants and raising small animals are popular (Koizumi *et al.* 2007). Children are taken on hikes where they explore the area, finding birds, bugs, fish, flowers, grasses, trees, and so on. Above all, in their daily spontaneous play activities, children can learn from working with various materials including water, sand, mud, clay, and blocks (Figure 10.1).

However, these activities do not target the acquisition of scientific understanding. Instead, empirical behaviour, empathy and inspiration are stressed. The purpose of science activities such as collecting and raising insects, which are very popular in Japanese kindergartens, is not to study the body parts and ecology of insects, but to acknowledge the importance of life, and develop an appreciation and respect for it.

Tobin *et al.* (1989) pointed out that all aspects of Japanese kindergartens are structured so as to promote the development of a group identity and group skills in young children and to preclude teachers from interacting with children in intense, emotionally complex, mother-like ways. It is also shown in his research that many

FIGURE 10.1 Science activities on insects in Japanese kindergartens

Japanese pre-school teachers, administrators, parents and child-development special-ists consider sympathy/empathy/concern for others as the most important things for children to learn in kindergarten, compared to those in China and the US (Tobin *et al.* 1989).

In contrast, in the US, according to the National Science Education Standards (American Association for the Advancement of Science 1993), science education officially commences in pre-school. Benchmarks for science literacy for grades K–2 include 12 content topics: the nature of science; the nature of mathematics; the

TABLE 10.2 Benchmarks for the 'living environment' in the curriculum for K–2

Diversity of life

1. Some animals and plants are alike in the way they look and in the things they do, and others are very different from one another.
2. Plants and animals have features that help them live in different environment[s].
3. Stories sometimes give plants and animals attributes they really do not have.

Heredity

1. There is variation among individuals of one kind within a population.
2. Offspring are very much, but not exactly, like their parents and like one another.

Cells

1. Magnifiers help people see things they could not see without them.
2. Most living things need water, food and air.

Interdependence of life

1. Animals eat plants or other animals for food and may also use plants (or even other animals) for shelter and nesting.
2. Living things are found almost everywhere in the world. There are somewhat different kinds in different places.

Flow of matter and energy

1. Plants and animals both need to take in water, and animals need to take in food. In addition, plants need light.
2. Many materials can be recycled and used again, sometimes in different forms.

Evolution of life

1. Different plants and animals have external features that help them thrive in different kinds of places.
2. Some kinds of organisms that once lived on Earth have completely disappeared, although they were something like others that are alive today.

nature of technology; the physical setting; the living environment; the human organism; human society; the designed world; the mathematical world; historical perspectives; common themes; and habits of mind. The benchmarks for the 'living environment' for the K–2 Level is shown in Table 10.2 (above).

Science activities in kindergartens in the US encourage children to inquire about natural events and phenomena. For example, Ritz (2007) proposes 89 science activities for children aged 3 to 7 years old, including observing crickets and discovering that they have no teeth and do not bite or sting. Koralek and Colker (2004) introduced hands-on science activities on butterflies to encourage young children to keep detailed records of their experiences in raising butterflies. In the activities, children also describe the stages of growth that occur in the development of a butterfly and document the growth of the caterpillar in a dated journal. At the Education Development Center in the US, a long-term science programme has been developed, where kindergarten teachers and children are encouraged to take their time and engage in substantial exploratory activities based on their own knowledge, interest and curiosity (Chalufour and Worth 2003)..

Science activities for young American children seem to emphasise more the scientific worldview than those in Japan. This is also reflected in parental expectations about learning in pre-schools. Tobin *et al.* (1989), who surveyed Japanese, Chinese and American kindergarten teachers, administrators, parents and child-development specialists on 'What are the most important things for children to learn in pre-school?', reported that 51 per cent of Americans chose to give children 'a good start academically', while only 2 per cent of Japanese chose this answer.

Japanese and Western worldviews of nature

To understand better the different views and expectations between Japanese and American pre-school standards and practices, it would be helpful to examine the worldviews of nature of these two cultures. For a long period, many prominent Japanese works in literature and art involved the surrounding nature, but nature was not itself the object of scientific research. Ito (1995) demonstrated the contrast between the Japanese and Western views of nature using drawings (shown in Figure 10.2 below). In traditional Japanese drawings of nature, artificial objects, such as small boats and bridges, are integrated into nature implicitly with people; there are not any geometrical lines and structures in the drawings. On the other hand, Western drawings of nature from the same period show logos and senses in a hierarchy, and gardens and buildings are structured geometrically. Inglis *et al.* (2005) point out that the Eastern perspective has been portrayed as asserting a fundamental *oneness*, binding all creation, as opposed to the Western dualism unalterably distinguishing humans from nature.

Nisbett (2003) argues that Easterners believe that the world is a complicated place and it might be right to approach everyday life from this stance, but he also maintains that in science we come closer to the truth by overriding complexity rather than welcoming every conceivably relevant factor. He insists that Easterners are closer to

FIGURE 10.2 Japanese and Western drawings of nature

Source: Ito 1995: 337

the truth than Westerners in the belief that the world is a highly complicated place and Westerners are undoubtedly often too simple-minded in their explicit models of the world. On the other hand, he notices that simple models are the most useful ones – at least in science — because they are easier to disprove and, consequently, to improve upon.

The different worldviews of nature are well illustrated in the following famous poem by Kino Tomonori (translated by McMillan 2008):

ひさかたの　光のどけき　春の日に　しづ心なく　花の散るらむ　（紀友則）

'Cherry blossoms, on this quiet lambent day of spring, why do you scatter with such unquiet hearts?'

Newton might have resolved the light from the sun, which is expressed as 'lambent' in the poem, using a prism and developed the theory about colour and light; and 'cherry blossoms scattering' might have inspired Galileo or Newton to discover the laws of motion and gravity. Japanese people prefer to empathise with nature and natural phenomena and 'lambent' or 'cherry blossom scattering' have produced outstanding poetry and literature on nature. The Japanese view of nature emphasises the appearance of the natural phenomenal world. Therefore the purpose of activities such as collecting and raising insects, very popular in Japanese kindergartens, is not to study the body parts and the ecology of insects or to 'observe' them from an immutable and universal point of view. It is to acknowledge life and develop an appreciation and respect for it.

Language–culture incommensurability

Scientific language had to eschew personal feelings and fancies and aspire to objectivity and universality in conformity with nature (Crosland 2006). It was believed that a language could express all knowledge in a methodical, rational and ordered fashion that would mirror the fabric of nature (Crosland 2006). W-scientific laws are expressed in terms of abstract nouns, namely: force, acceleration, point mass, rigid body, ideal gas, etc., which have generality beyond the data obtained from specific experiments. Every W-scientific concept and law can thus be described as immutable and universal.

Kawasaki (2002) explains that abstract nouns are essential for the W-scientific way of thinking into which the dichotomy is inevitably introduced. On the other hand, Ito (1999) points out that Japanese *shizen* (nature) is difficult to be used as a noun because it was originally used only as an adjective or adverb. Verbs are more salient in East Asian languages than in English and many other European languages.

Ikegami (2006) introduces the 'human subject' and the 'inanimate subject' as typical of the difference between Japanese and English sentences from the cognitive linguistic point of view. In English, the inanimate subject is used commonly whereas the Japanese prefer to consistently use the human subject. Two simple sentences in English and Japanese (with direct translation into English) are shown below:

Example 1: [Seeing unexpectedly a friend]
A: 'Hello, Ken. What brings you here?'
B: 'やぁ，ケン。どうしてこんな所に来ているの' ('Hello, Ken. Why are you here?')

Example 2: [Recommending a specific medicine]
A: 'This medicine will make you feel better.'
B: 'この薬で気分が良くなるでしょう' ('If you take this medicine, you will feel better.')

Sentence A, in both examples, is more natural for English native speakers whereas the Japanese prefer sentence B. Arakawa and Moriyama (2009) suggested that English is the language mode of grasping objectivity, whereas Japanese is the language mode of grasping subjectivity.

These characteristics and understanding of different L–C communities appear even in the language acquisition of the infant. De Boysson-Bardies (2001) pointed out that the Japanese language is often structured around verbs placed at the end of sentences – a position that is particularly salient for all children. She has summarised the differences in language acquisition of infants between Japan and the United States from four points:

1. Use of nouns: The Japanese infants had a more restricted vocabulary than the American infants for personal names (7 per cent and 15 per cent respectively)

and for nouns denoting toys, food, and so on. American children also used three times as many proper nouns in their speech compared to Japanese children.

2. Use of verbs: American children used few adjectives and a total of about 9 per cent of verbs in their early vocabularies.

3. Use of social words: Japanese children frequently used social terms such as *hai* (hi), *dozo* (please), *arigato* (thank you), *akushyu* (let's shake hands) in their every-day lives. Many of the forms recorded revealed the importance attached to communicating with others and mentioning 'states' and impressions such as *atta* (I found it, here it is), *jatta* (I did it), *kawaii* (cute).

4. Use of words for physical sensations: Japanese infants were very fond of saying *ja ja* to express the sound of a water fountain, *za za* for heavy rain, *kon kon* for the bang of a hammer, and *iiko iiko* for a gentle tapping. Even the noise made by people when they sleep – *gu gu* – and the sparkle of light – *kira kira* – have their place in the early vocabulary of Japanese children.

De Boysson-Bardies (2001) noticed that, if the groups are considered independently, 30–40 per cent of the words used are common to at least two children in the same group. Individual preferences are attributed more to membership in the same L–C group than variability. Cultural practices then strongly orient the semantic choice of children's first words.

Language–culture and the way of thinking

Kawasaki (2002) elucidated that the Japanese worldview is basically different from the W-scientific worldview. He argues that the Japanese worldview leads Japanese people to search the *phenomenal world* for what appears to be so. In contrast to the Western worldview, the Japanese worldview does not rely on the world of *idea*. It is not possible to describe the Japanese relationship between 'appearance' and 'what is transcendental' in terms of the dichotomy between 'appearance' and 'reality' expressed in the SAE. The English term 'appearance' implies 'mutable and particular' and the English term 'reality' implies 'immutable and universal'. The dichotomy between them is linked with the value upheld by the mainstream of Western philosophy for what is timeless and immutable (Boas 1973).

In the Japanese L–C tradition, 'reality' allows for a mutable and particular character which is found only within appearance. The Japanese L–C tradition has never valued the timeless and immutable and Japanese people take it for granted that they can appreciate the value associated with the mutable and particular. For example, Nakamura (1964: 359) argues that 'the Japanese esteem the sensible beauties of nature, in which they seek revelations of the absolute world'. Nakamura's argument may perplex Westerners, because there seems to be a Japanese sameness encompassing the *phenomenal world* and the world of *idea*, with no distinction between them. These ideas are reflected diagrammatically in Figure 10.3.

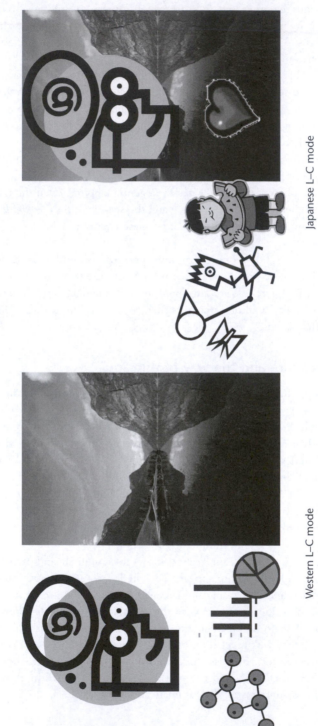

Western L–C mode

Japanese L–C mode

FIGURE 10.3 L–C modes of understanding of nature

Towards L–C appropriate science activities

Since the Japanese L–C community for science education is not prepared with ideas on immutable and universal 'reality', additional considerations are necessary, based on differences in cognition between L–C communities. Kindergarten science activities, however, are rarely examined from this point of view.

Therefore, educators should realise the necessity to distinguish the Japanese language mode of science education from other language modes, especially the SAE mode. Conversely, they should also recognise that the Japanese language mode of science education requires additional teaching based on the Japanese L–C tradition, aesthetics and philosophy in order to clarify the differences between the Western way of thinking about the world and the Japanese way of thinking about *shizen* (natural phenomena). For example, in science activities on butterflies, there are different representations of 'butterfly' in English, such as 'butterfly', 'a butterfly', 'butterflies', 'the butterfly', 'the butterflies', while in Japanese, *cho* includes all these representations in a word. One of the prescriptions for L–C incommensurability is to be sensitive about language and worldview issues in kindergarten science activities. Objective knowledge of insects might reduce the subjective feelings of anxious children to moderate respect for the usefulness and beauty of the small animals around us.

It is also proposed to reconsider science education as second language education. It is suggested that the Japanese have an advantage in studying science as a second language because, as Montgomery (2000) maintains, scientific Japanese language differs from technical languages in Western countries in one very striking aspect. Since it is written in ideograms, known to almost any college-educated person, non-scientists can readily decipher the basic meaning of many of the most complex terms. The layperson can, in a sense, read scientific jargon far more easily in Japanese than his or her counterpart in the West.

Conclusion

The notion of a linguistic mode of science education introduced in this chapter could contribute to debate about preparing kindergarten activities that enrich children's culture and life and contribute to reforming teacher-education programmes in Japan (Sumida *et al.* 2007). These ideas may be also applicable in other countries where science education is carried out in languages incommensurate with the language of W-scientific thought. The concept of science as a second language education could open the door to discussing science in early childhood as a means of meeting diverse needs in a broader and more practical context of the modern industrial, technological and scientifically oriented society.

QUESTIONS FOR THINKING ABOUT POLICY AND PRACTICE

1. What is in your country the language mode of science education for kindergarten?
2. What would be the advantages and disadvantages of introducing science as a second language for kindergarten children in your country?
3. Which experiences would ease the understanding and appreciation of different views of nature in your L–C and SAE?

Acknowledgements

I would like to thank Kawade-Shobo-Shinsya for granting permission to use the drawings for Figure 10.2.

The research discussed is partly supported by Grant-in Aid for Scientific Research (Grant Number: 23402002) supported by the Ministry of Education, Culture, Sports, Science and Technology.

References

American Association for the Advancement of Science (1993) *Benchmarks for Science Literacy*, New York: Oxford University Press.

Arakawa, Y. and Moriyama, S. (2009) *An Introduction to Applied Cognitive Linguistics for Language Teachers*, Tokyo: Bonzinsya (in Japanese).

Boas, G. (1973) Nature, in P. P. Wiener (ed.) *Dictionary of the History of Ideas, Volume III*, New York: Charles Scribner's Sons.

Chalufour, I. and Worth, K. (2003) *Discovering Nature with Young Children*, St Paul, MN: Redleaf Press.

Cobern, W. W. (ed.) (1998) *Socio-cultural Perspectives on Science Education: An International Dialogue*, Dordrecht: Kluwer Academic Publishers.

Cobern, W. W. (2000) *Everyday Thoughts about Nature: A Worldview Investigation of Important Concepts Students Use to Make Sense of Nature with Specific Attention of Science*, Dordrecht: Kluwer Academic Publishers.

Crosland, M. (2006) *The Language of Science: From the Vernacular to the Technical*, Cambridge: The Lutterworth Press.

De Boysson-Bardies, B. (2001) *How Language Comes to Children: From Birth to Two Years*, translated by M. B. DeBevoise, Cambridge, MA: MIT Press.

Ikegami, Y., (2006) *Sense of English and Sense of Japanese*, Tokyo: NHK Books (in Japanese).

Inglis, D., Bone, J. and Wilkie, R. (eds) (2005) *Nature: Critical Concepts in the Social Sciences*, New York: Routledge.

Ito, S. (ed.) (1995) *Japanese View of Nature*, Tokyo: Kawade-Shobo-Shinsya (in Japanese).

Ito, S. (1999) *Shizen*, Tokyo: Sanseido (in Japanese).

Japanese Ministry of Education, Science, Sports and Culture (2008) *Course of Study for Kindergarten*, Tokyo: MEXT, available online at: www.mext.go.jp/a_menu/shotou/ new-cs/youryou/eiyaku/__icsFiles/afieldfile/2011/01/13/1298368_1.pdf (accessed 20 June 2011).

Kawasaki, K. (2002) A cross-cultural comparison of English and Japanese linguistic assumptions influencing pupils' learning of science, *Canadian and International Education*, 31(1): 19–51.

Koizumi, H., Akita, K. and Yamada, T. (eds) (2007) *Developing 'Scientific Mind' in Early Childhood*, Tokyo: Shougakukan (in Japanese).

Koralek, D. and Colker, L. J. (eds) (2004) *Spotlight on Young Children and Science*, Washington, DC: National Association for the Education of Young Children.

McMillan, P. (2008) *One Hundred Poets, One Poem Each: A Translation of the Ogura Hyakunin Isshu*, available online at: www1.ocn.ne.jp/~kobakan/contents/onehundredpoets.html# chap4 (accessed 20 June 2011).

Matthews, M. (ed.) (2009) *Science, Worldviews and Education*, Dordrecht: Springer.

Montgomery, S. L. (2000) *Science in Translation: Movements of Knowledge through Cultures and Time*, Chicago, IL: University of Chicago Press.

Nakamura, H. (1964) *Ways of Thinking of Eastern Peoples*, Honolulu, HI: University of Hawaii Press.

Nisbett, R. E. (2003) *The Geography of Thought: How Asians and Westerners Think Differently . . . and Why*, New York: Free Press.

Ritz, W. C. (ed.) (2007) *A Head Start on Science: Encouraging a Sense of Wonder*, Arlington, VA: National Science Teachers Association.

Sumida, M. and Kawasaki, K. (2008) A language–culture origin understanding of science in Japan, in IOSTE (International Organization for Science and Technology Education), *Proceedings of the XIII IOSTE Symposium on the Use of Science and Technology Education for Peace and Sustainable Development*, Buca-Izmir: Dokuz Eylul University, pp. 689–695.

Sumida, M., Fukada, S., Nakamura, H., Masukagami, M. and Sakata, C. (2007) Developing young children's scientific, technological, and social competency through 'Pendulum' play activities at Japanese kindergarten, *Asia-Pacific Journal of Research in Early Childhood Education*, 1(1): 83–100.

Tobin, J. J., Wu, D. Y. H. and Davidson, D. H. (1989) *Pre-school in Three Cultures: Japan, China, and the United States*, New Haven, CT: Yale University Press.

Whorf, B. L. (1956) *Language, Thought, and Reality*, New York: Technology Press of MIT and John Wiley & Sons.

11

INTEGRATING DANCE AND VISUAL ARTS IN TAIWANESE EARLY CHILDHOOD EDUCATION

Shu-Ying Liu

OVERVIEW

In 2006, the Taiwanese government promoted new approaches to early childhood teaching and learning, quality of provision and kindergarten teachers' professional development. The study discussed in this chapter sought to develop and improve Taiwanese kindergarten teachers' dance teaching through the development of a curriculum that integrated dance with visual arts. The researchers tested concepts and ideas from Davies's (2003) 'movement framework', Matthews' (2003) theory of 'figurative representation' and 'action representation' and Zelazo and Lourenco's (2003) 'transfiguration' model. The project outcomes showed that generalist teachers can use drawing and painting to motivate children to create dance, and remember and express dance learning. The results confirmed that most young children are able to dance and draw in response to visual arts and local cultural themes, and that dance experiences and observations of paintings increase their awareness of shape and stimulate the development of figurative expression.

Key words: early childhood curriculum; creative dance; integrated arts; visual arts; collaborative action research.

Introduction

Mead (2009) identifies that Taiwanese families have long provided significant financial, emotional and moral support for their children's education. While this is often ascribed to entrenched Confucian values, education is also an effective means of upward social mobility, and believed by parents to be the foundation for their offspring's later financial success (Lee and Huang 2001; Chou and Ho 2007). The move to an industrial and high-technology economy since the 1970s has increased further the demand for high-quality education, including excellent early childhood provision.

For many Taiwanese parents, giving their children a head start by enrolling them in a kindergarten is regarded as essential (Government Information Office 2004, para. 10). Public kindergartens, the majority of which are affiliated to primary schools, are often oversubscribed, so many parents decide to send their children to private ones. In both types of kindergarten, there are typically two partner-teachers for a class of 30 children. Although there is no unified curriculum model or teaching style, the timetable usually includes child-led play sessions as well as teacher-led activities, with strong links between spontaneous play and guidance (Jian 1999).

Curriculum development and learning theories in Taiwan

Curriculum development in Taiwan has long been influenced by Western learning theories, including those of John Dewey, Piaget and Vygotsky. Chinese pioneer educators such as Hsueh-Men Zhang, Ho-Chin Chen and Xing-Zhi Tao, who were key figures in establishing the 1929 Kindergarten Curriculum Standards in China, were all influenced by these Western ideas (Lin and Spodek 1992; Weng 1998). These educators particularly advocated Dewey's 'child-centred' educational philosophy and 'learning by doing' (Weng 1998: 363). The 1929 standards were later incorporated into the Taiwanese early childhood curriculum following the fleeing of the Nationalist government to Taiwan after the communist takeover of the Chinese mainland in 1949. Post 1960, Western theories gained even more prominence as increasing numbers of Taiwanese students enrolled on postgraduate early childhood education programmes abroad.

Present-day Taiwanese kindergarten curriculum standards date from 1987, and are based on previous versions from 1975. However, many scholars have long considered that they do not reflect modern-day educational thinking (for example, Cai 2011; Shing 2011). As a result, new early childhood curriculum guidelines, incorporating developmental learning concepts, have been tested at selected kindergartens from 2010.

Obstacles to curriculum reform

Since 1997, the Taiwanese government has introduced some significant educational initiatives, including the promotion and development of arts education. In 2001, a new national curriculum for elementary and junior high schools was introduced that placed dance in a new performing arts domain (Ministry of Education 1998); while in 2002, the *White Paper on Creativity in Education* stressed the importance of facilitating creative projects at all levels of education (Ministry of Education 2002).

In order to facilitate kindergarten teachers' professional development and to enhance the quality of teaching and learning, a five-year government-funded Early Childhood Education Supervising Project was launched in 2006. This was the first time government grants were made available specifically for teacher development. Unlike the existing inspection and evaluation-based system, the project focused on guidance and assistance by subject specialists in curriculum and instruction. Subject specialists visited kindergartens approximately monthly and for up to 60 hours per annum. However, the development of school-based curriculum in Taiwan is rather problematic. The Ministry of Education has introduced new policies very quickly and too frequently without considering their full impact on classroom practice. Although generalist teachers are willing to engage in arts-based curriculum experiments, their lack of specialist knowledge and the absence of support lead them to mistrust their own abilities to innovate.

Dance in Taiwanese kindergartens

Although dance teaching takes place in kindergartens, this tends to be largely product-oriented, involving rote-learning. Specialist and generalist teachers focus on getting children to copy specific movements as a means of achieving of what is often the prime objective: an impressive, error-free, adult-like performance. Although it can help children gain movement skills, and they sometimes appear to enjoy it, such intensive repeated practice fails to address the broader educational goals of developing creativity and appreciation of the arts (Liu 1998; Liu *et al.* 1998). This product-oriented approach led Ni (1993: 8) to refer to Taiwanese kindergarten teachers as 'dance trainers' and to students as 'movement machines'.

While the above issue indicates that the theory and practice of dance education for young children is underdeveloped in Taiwan, there are other problems too. Generally, within society, dance is largely perceived as a performance art. While there are many dance courses at universities, these focus almost exclusively on training for the professional stage. There are few programmes for training teachers of dance, leading to an acute shortage of dance teachers.

My previous research and collaborations with kindergarten teachers indicated that it is possible to develop effective strategies to integrate dance learning and drawing (Liu 2006). Outcomes showed that young children are able to represent their movement experience in drawings that aid their kinaesthetic and visual understanding of specific movement concepts. In many cases, their dance-drawings did not merely represent the shapes and movement they saw, but also the experience of creating them. These findings led me to believe that this approach would be appropriate for the Early Childhood Education Supervising Project. It would improve teachers' abilities to teach dance in a way that would develop young children's abilities to make, perform and appreciate the art form.

Collaborative action research

Collaborative action research was chosen as the methodology in the belief that it would further teachers' professional development and improve their reflective abilities as well as leading to curriculum innovation in real educational settings (Chen and Lee 2001; MacNaughton *et al.* 2001). The methodology is also advocated by the Taiwan Association of Early Childhood Education Reform (2003).

My role in this project was to supervise the development of teachers' knowledge and skills in integrated arts teaching with a focus on dance. For classroom experiments to succeed, generalist kindergarten teachers need to be supported by early childhood educators and dance specialists who provide them with dance knowledge and foster their confidence and abilities to teach dance.

Davies's movement framework in dance teaching and learning

Many Western pioneers in dance education have mapped a conceptual framework for creative dance (H'Doubler 1940; Laban 1948; Russell 1965). Their ideas and work, specifically appropriated for early childhood by Stinson (1988a, 1988b, 1991) and Davies (1995, 2003), provided the theoretical base for the project. These authors highlight three domains of a dance curriculum: making, performance and appreciation. They also stress the importance of interactive relationships in the creative teaching and learning process that allow teachers to facilitate young children's physical, cognitive, emotional and social development.

Davies (1995, 2003) provides a conceptual movement framework which prioritises body, dynamics, space and relationships as the key movement elements of dance learning and teaching in primary education settings (see Table 11.1 below). The framework can be used to develop young children's abilities to make and perform dance by focusing attention on particular movement concepts; for example, what the body does, where it moves, the dynamics involved, and the relationships with oneself, other people and objects. Davies (2003: 158) says that 'dance is dancing and dancing is the dance'. In other words, the moment of children's dance making is dance performing.

Davies identifies four phases of learning that were utilised in this project:

1. free exploration, where teachers encouraged children to develop their own movement vocabulary in response to a given story;
2. guided exploration, where teachers introduced often contrasting movement elements, sometimes without demonstration, to challenge the children's dance making;
3. consolidation, where teachers interpreted and compared children's movements, asking them to imitate each other to help them better understand and increase their personal movement vocabularies;
4. extension, where teachers' and children's movement vocabularies were combined to create dance phrases to accompany nursery rhymes.

TABLE 11.1 Davies's movement framework

Main category	Sub-category	Further divisions
Body (What takes place)	Action	Travelling (e.g. crawling, stepping, running, climbing, sliding, balancing) Weight taking and transference (e.g. rocking, rolling, tumbling, swinging, handstands, cartwheels) Flight (e.g. hopping, jumping, leaping, vaulting) Handling (e.g. kicking, throwing, catching, hitting, rolling)
	Design	Symmetry Asymmetry
	Articulation	Parts leading the movement Parts highlighting the movement Parts limiting the movement
	Shape	Long and stretched Wide and stretched Curved Twisted
	Fluency	Successive Simultaneous
Dynamics (How movement takes place)	Weight	Strong, firm Light, gentle
	Space (qualitative)	Straight, direct Flexible, wavy
	Time	Quick, sudden Slow, sustained
	Flow	Controlled, bound Ongoing, free
Space (The medium in which movement takes place)	Size	Big Little
	Zone	In front Behind To the side Above Below
	Extension	Near Far
	Level	High Low
	Direction	Forwards Backwards Sideways Upwards Downwards

Main category	Sub-category	Further divisions
	Pathways and patterns	Straight Zigzag Curved Twisted
Relationships (The moving body interrelates)	The body relates to itself	One half with the other half Body parts meeting Body parts parting Body parts staying in contact
	The body relates to objects	Handling Manoeuvring Wearing
	The body relates to other people	Alongside Doing the same Copying Leading Following Co-operating Competing against

Source: Davies 2003

The teachers used a 'co-construction concept' (Anning *et al.* 2004: 177); they acted as movement interpreters, explaining children's movements to develop their understanding and introduce further movement elements from which they could choose, add or develop.

Linking dance and visual arts

Davies (2003: 161) says: 'Dances cannot be made from nothing', while Matthews (1994: 54–55), observes that young children explore relationships between their movements in a range of contexts and use different media to produce different drawing results. Matthews (1994) uses the terms 'figurative representation' and 'action representation' to describe how children's drawings and paintings not only capture the shape or structure of an object, but frequently incorporate representations of the movement of an object or the actions within an event (Matthews 2003: 24–26).

My own research supports Matthews' views by showing that drawing can facilitate dance learning at kindergarten level (Liu 2006). More specifically, my findings indicated that:

- getting children to represent body movements in space through drawing helps them to improvise dance;

- collecting and sequencing the drawings helps children compose dance phrases;
- displaying children's drawings of movements helps them memorise dance phrases;
- getting children to observe each other's dance performances and then draw them facilitates their reflection on, and appreciation of, dance.

As previously observed, a dance product or final 'finished' dance, performed for others, is important in the Taiwanese context. Chang (2007), an influential dance scholar in Taiwan, suggests the use of a logical sequence in the dance-making process, referring to seven steps of building a dance, originally set out by McGreevy-Nichols *et al.* (2001). In this project, kindergartens that adopted a performance approach tested this process by: choosing the subject matter; exploring and selecting movements; coordinating music and movement; exploring possibilities; refining and memorising the dance; and adding finishing touches before performing the dance.

The teachers encouraged the children to discuss ideas to develop their imagination, and used peer collaboration and demonstrations of movement ideas to stimulate their expression and consolidate their performance ability. Language was an important scaffolding tool throughout as they guided the children's dance exploration and helped them understand movement elements. The young children performed in their classroom, kindergarten hall, and finally in a graduation ceremony where outcomes were shared with parents. Discussion and appreciation of all performances were an important part of student learning. This included using the children's own drawings to express their impressions of and interpretations about the dance.

The children, teachers and the researcher formed a 'learning group', defined by Krechevsky and Mardell (2001: 285) as '[a] collection of persons who are emotionally, intellectually, and aesthetically engaged in solving problems, creating products, and making meaning – an assemblage in which each person learns autonomously and through the ways of learning of others.' Here, in addition to using movement concepts and paintings as stimuli, the collaborative nature of the teaching enabled the children, teachers and researcher to learn from each other, and the teachers and the researcher to modify, extend, clarify and enrich their dance teaching strategies for formative evaluation.

Connecting with local culture

Bruner (1960) advocates facilitating and structuring curricula around the issues, principles and values that society deems significant and worthy of continual concern, and refers to the idea of revisiting basic ideas over and over, building and elaborating upon them until full understanding and mastery is reached. According to Jeffrey and Woods (2003: 82), using stories, ideas, people and materials helps teachers and children to gain 'ownership of the knowledge'.

Although this project was grounded in Western theories, it was important to link activities to local culture. The Lunar New Year was chosen as a theme for the research because the teachers believed it was rooted in the children's life experiences.

Activities were originally based on a New Year monster story in which villagers scare away a man-eating monster with fire, and from which the traditional use of fire-crackers derives. This is a well-known children's tale. To emphasise friendship and acceptance of others, this was later transformed into a 'happy monster' story in which the villagers shared food with the monster. The children's imagination was further stimulated by other activities inspired by trips to local traditional shops and temples.

The Lunar New Year theme and each different scene of the monster story acted as 'scaffolding'. The scenes gave the teachers and children a structure within which Davies's movement framework could be used to develop their learning of many different kinds. Activities for the children included the following.

Stage 1: Motivating dance images:

- introduction to the original Lunar New Year monster story, in which the children improvised moving like a monster; then they drew how they thought the monster looked;
- visiting local temples and traditional shops to help understanding of cultural symbols and how the Lunar New Year is celebrated;
- painting images of temple guards on huge sheets of paper, based on what they had seen at the temples, to create a New Year atmosphere for their dance;
- painting traditional long red banners that carry messages and that are seen at New Year – these were displayed around the classroom with the images of the guards;
- creating a new 'happy monster' story by discussing and then drawing it.

Stage 2: Facilitating dance creation:

- using light from an overhead projector shone onto a large piece of fabric; the children stood behind the fabric creating 'moving' and 'still' monster-like shadows; the shadows were photographed; the children then drew their version of the 'monsters';
- drawing and making monster masks, based on the Peking opera masks;
- creating movement in which the children acted as human-size firecrackers;
- using fabric or lightweight coloured paper to create images of travelling food smells similar to that often seen in children's cartoons;
- using very long pieces of stretchy material to create movement inspired by traditional sticky rice cakes that signify good luck;
- using the body to create movement and shapes that were based on numbers which represent the amount of money traditionally given in red envelopes as gifts on New Year's Eve;
- using recycled materials to make a large lion body and mask and create a lion dance.

Stage 3: Reflecting on the dance performance:

- drawing a complete monster story as part of their reflection on the complete 'happy monster' dance.

Transfiguration and transformation

Although each stage and activity drew on what went before, the children's dance-drawings and dance-paintings gradually went beyond realistic representation and became increasingly symbolic. Each activity led to the creation of personal symbols used to facilitate dance learning. The use of multiple pictorial systems helped the children to discover and create symbolic representation, which they used to translate and transform their understanding of the dance. The team were amazed by the ways in which the four- and five-year-old children were able to represent the three-dimensional movements or kinetic experiences two dimensionally. Once the children recognised the personal symbols in their drawings or paintings, they could share and dance them again later. Some of the drawings and paintings effectively became self-created dance notation. Bruce (2004: 173) argues: 'If children lose their ability to make personal symbols, they lose the possibility of becoming creative, imaginative symbol users.' The evidence from this project supports the view that personal symbols can play an important role in dance learning.

Zelazo and Lourenco (2003: 74) consider that all internal and external representations are 'intrinsically imitative' and 'interpretative'. They argue that imitation is comprehended and developed subjectively, and is not mere copying or mime. They propose a model to explain the processes of imitation and the dialectic of representation in children's learning. According to the model, the children in the research had taken an initial prefiguration, the initial stimuli (for example, the monster story or temple visits), the configurations of others (for example, dances and drawings) and then transfigured them in their own artworks. The process is circular with each prefiguration leading in turn to a configuration and transfiguration, which leads to the next prefiguration, and so on.

Zelazo and Lourenco (2003) propose that such a transfiguration process allows for feedback that scaffolds the representational process and facilitates critical self-reflection. Moreover, once children master dealing with the continuity of internal and external information and representation, the constraints of external support for their representational learning, such as imitation stimuli, can be gradually diminished. Eventually, imitation becomes less automatic and more deliberate, and the use of advanced schemas allows children to repeat their own stimuli. This implies that teachers do not need to be anxious about imitation; it can be a positive learning strategy that promotes children's transfiguration and advances their dance making, performance and appreciation.

Conclusion

The evidence from the project supports Sahasrabudhe's argument (2005: 19) that visual realism should not be viewed as the end point of children's artistic development. It is more important to consider the ways children use, perceive, respond to and transform abstract aesthetic forms in visual arts and dance. The project outcomes demonstrated that the use of external visual stimuli combined with internal kinetic experiences positively affected children's artistic development in that they are able to transform their experience of dance and communicate it in a visual, symbolic mode. The use of multiple sensory-motor and pictorial systems facilitated the transfiguration of children's representations from realistic to symbolic, or combinations of the two, and involved creation, imitation, re-creation and interpretation. The cyclical learning process and the use of dance-drawings and dance-paintings fostered the development of both symbolic and representational artistic modes.

Although the children in the study used different kinds of visual representational modes and combined or developed realistic figurative representations with symbolic action representations during the transfiguration process, all their drawings were intentional and deliberate responses to the dances they created, saw, felt or knew. Communication of individual visual symbolic representations with the whole class is important because it is only when they are interpreted by others that they become communicative, recognisable and shareable. Such sharing is also important for children's social and emotional development. It was clear that when children imitated symbolic representations, they incorporated their own ideas into them, and transformed them into or combined them with other symbols. Once children master the continuity of internal and external information and representation, they can internalise and combine stimuli to create later representations even if the external support for their representation learning is diminished.

One should never forget that visual art, dance or any art form can and should be studied in its own right. But integration is important and using visual art as stimuli can motivate children to create personal, symbolic representations in their dances, drawings and paintings. Creating, showing, sharing and viewing dance and visual arts are reciprocal learning processes. The children in the project showed an increasing awareness of spatial relationships when their dance making was associated with visual stimuli or objects. Vice versa, the research outcomes confirmed Kapsch and Kruger's (2004) finding that young children's figurative drawings are significantly more dynamic following kinaesthetic learning. They are able to draw 'what they see', 'what they know' and 'what they feel inside their bodies' in one image. These kinds of visual representations of kinetic information tend to distort realistic figurations, making them more dynamic and abstract.

The project outcomes also demonstrated that a Western movement framework and concept of creative dance can be applied to and motivate those in other cultures. However, although the world is becoming increasingly globalised, I consider that we must never forget local themes and if children are to be fully engaged, the learning process needs to be culturally meaningful. Finally, through participation in the research, the teachers became aware of the importance of interactivity and creativity in the teaching and learning process. The project shows that collaboration with researchers in real-life classroom settings can improve teachers' dance pedagogy, and working together can significantly influence their approach to professional development as a whole.

QUESTIONS FOR THINKING ABOUT POLICY AND PRACTICE

1. In what ways could dance specialists and researchers help generalist kindergarten teachers to improve dance teaching in your own context? What local cultural themes could be integrated in dance and visual arts teaching?
2. In what other ways could dance and visual arts be integrated in an early childhood curriculum?
3. What is the best way to analyse young children's dances and drawings to understand more deeply their learning and thinking processes?

References

Anning, A., Cullen, J. and Fleer, M. (eds) (2004) *Early Childhood Education: Society and Culture*, London: Sage.

Bruce, T. (2004) *Developing Learning in Early Childhood*, London: Sage.

Bruner, J. (1960) *The Process of Education*, Cambridge, MA: Harvard University Press.

Cai, M.-L. (2011) The New Curriculum Guidelines for Kindergarten, Unpublished Conference Paper, Kindergarten Teaching Activity and Curriculum Guideline Conference, Taipei Municipal University of Education, 6–7 August.

Chang, C.-S. (2007) *The Treasure Book of Creative Dance for the Grade One through Nine Curriculum*, Taipei: Taipei National University of the Arts.

Chen, H.-B. and Lee, L.-X. (2001) *Ongoing Journey: Collaborative Action Research*, Taipei: Normal University Press.

Chou, C.-I. and Ho, A.-H. (2007) Schooling in Taiwan, in G. Postiglione and J. Tan (eds) *Going to School in East Asia*, Westport, CT: Greenwood Books, pp. 344–375.

Davies, M. (1995) *Helping Children to Learn through a Movement Perspective*, London: Hodder & Stoughton.

Davies, M. (2003) *Movement and Dance in Early Childhood*, 2nd edn, London: Paul Chapman Publishing.

Government Information Office (2004) *Mainstream Education*, Taipei: Government Information Office, available online at: www.gio.gov.tw/ct.asp?xItem=19027&ctNode=2598&mp=607 (accessed 16 November 2006).

H'Doubler, M. (1940) *Dance – A Creative Art Experience*, Madison, WI: University of Wisconsin Press.

Jeffrey, B. and Woods, P. (2003) *The Creative School: A Framework for Success, Quality and Effectiveness*, London: Routledge.

Jian, C.-Y. (ed.) (1999) *Curriculum Models of Early Childhood Education: Theories and Practice*, Taipei: Psychology Books.

Kapsch, L. and Kruger, A. (2004) Change in Figure Drawing Following Kinaesthetic Experience, *Visual Arts Research*, 30(2): 62–74.

Krechevsky, M. and Mardell, B. (2001) Four Features of Learning in Groups, in Project Zero and Reggio Children (eds) *Making Learning Visible: Children as Individual and Group Learners*, Reggio Emilia: Reggio Children.

Laban, R. (1948) *Modern Educational Dance*, London: Macdonald & Evans.

Lee, Y.-T. and Huang, W.-F. (2001) Innovation and Learning Transformation: Taiwan Perspective, Paper presented to the Catching the Knowledge Wave Conference, Auckland, 1–3 August.

Lin, Y.-W. and Spodek, B. (1992) Early Childhood Teacher Preparation in Taiwan, *Early Child Development and Care*, 78(1): 95–109.

Liu, S.-Y. (1998) Reflection on Dance Education in Primary Schools in Taiwan, *Kang Hsuan Educational Magazine*, 34(1): 9.

Liu, S.-Y. (2006) *Developing Generalist Teachers' Understanding of Dance Teaching in Early Childhood Education in Taiwan*, Unpublished PhD thesis, Roehampton University.

Liu, S.-Y., Liao, Y.-Z., Xie, S.-L and Xie, Y.-Y. (1998) *Teachers' Handbook of Arts Education: Dance for Early Childhood Education*, Taipei: National Taiwan Arts Education Institute.

McGreevy-Nichols, S., Scheff, H. and Sprague, M. (2001) *Building More Dances*, Champaign, IL: Human Kinetics.

MacNaughton, G. M., Rolfe, S. A. and Siraj-Blatchford, I. (2001) *Doing Early Childhood Research: International Perspectives on Theory and Practice*, Buckingham: Open University Press.

Matthews, J. (1994) *Helping Children to Draw and Paint in Early Education: Children and Visual Representation*, London: Hodder & Stoughton.

Matthews, J. (2003) *Drawing and Painting: Children and Visual Representation*, 2nd edn, London: Paul Chapman Publishing.

Mead, D. (2009) A creative ethos: Teaching and learning at the Cloud Gate Dance School in Taiwan, Unpublished PhD Thesis, University of Surrey.

Ministry of Education (1998) *The Guidelines for Nine-year Integrated Curricula*. Taipei: Ministry of Education.

Ministry of Education (2002) *White Paper on Creative Education*, Taipei: Ministry of Education.

Ni, M.-X. (1993) Foreword: The Magic of Mind, in H. L. Chiang (ed.) *Creative Movements and Activities*, Taipei: Xinyi, pp. 8–10.

Russell, J. (1965) *Creative Dance in the Primary School*, London: Macdonald & Evans.

Sahasrabudhe, P. (2005) *Transmissions and Transformations: Learning though the Arts in Asia*, Issues Paper, New Delhi: India International Center and UNESCO.

Shing, M.-L. (2011) The 'yes' and 'no' in the new curriculum guidelines, Unpublished Conference Paper, Kindergarten Teaching Activity and Curriculum Guideline Conference, Taipei Municipal University of Education, 6–7 August.

Stinson, S. (1988a) *Dance for Young Children: Finding the Magic in Movement*, Reston, VA: American Alliance for Health, Physical Education, Recreation, and Dance.

Stinson, S. (1988b) Creative Dance for Preschool Children, *Journal of Physical Education, Recreation and Dance*, 59(7): 52–56.

Stinson, S. (1991) Transforming Movement into Dance for Young Children, in L. Y. Overby (ed.) *Early Childhood Creative Arts*, Reston, VA: American Alliance for Health, Physical Education, Recreation and Dance, pp. 134–139.

Taiwan Association of Early Childhood Education Reform (ed.) (2003) *Come! Telling Our Story: Kindergarten Teachers' Professional Development*, Taipei: Psychology Books.

Weng, L.-F. (1998) *The History of Early Childhood Education in Taiwan*, Taipei: Psychology Books.

Zelazo, P. and Lourenco, S. (2003) Imitation and the Dialectic of Representation, *Developmental Reviews*, 23(1): 55–78.

12

WORKING THEORIES AND LEARNING DISPOSITIONS IN EARLY CHILDHOOD EDUCATION

Perspectives from New Zealand

Sally Peters and Keryn Davis

OVERVIEW

New Zealand has a diverse early childhood sector and a flexible curriculum *Te Whāriki* (Ministry of Education 1996). The curriculum outcomes are indicative rather than definitive with a focus on children's working theories and learning dispositions. Over the last decade, teachers have been working to explore what this means in practice, resulting in interesting developments in pedagogy and approaches to assessment. This chapter outlines some of the key features of early childhood education in New Zealand and discusses some of the pedagogical challenges of fostering children's working theories and dispositions. Examples will be drawn from two projects: *Kimihia te ara tōtika, hei oranga mō tō ao: Key learning competencies across place and time* (2005–2008); and *Moments of wonder, everyday events: How are young children theorising and making sense of their world?* (2009–2010). The first project looked at learning dispositions and key competencies in early childhood and school settings. The second project involved working with practitioners and families in Playcentre settings to explore children's working theories in action.

Key words: Curriculum; pedagogy; learning dispositions; working theories.

Introduction

Early childhood education (ECE) in New Zealand is non-compulsory, and includes a diverse range of services (Ministry of Education 2009). There are teacher-led settings such as kindergartens, education and care settings (some of which have a particular language or cultural base or follow specific philosophies such as Steiner or Montessori) and home-based settings with qualified and registered coordinators. The sector also includes a range of parent-led services such as Playcentre settings which offer sessional ECE to children, and parents are trained 'to become educators of their own children' while also undertaking responsibility for 'administering and managing centres and running sessions' (Hill *et al*. 2003: 30).

The diversity of ECE provision, and the complexity of family arrangements, mean that children may attend more than one early childhood service. This makes it difficult to determine precisely the percentage of children that are enrolled as the system double counts children who are enrolled at more than one service. Data collected from parents on the child's entry to school placed total participation at 94.8 per cent in 2011 (Education Counts 2011c). While the overall participation figures are high, this does not indicate the length of time a child has attended ECE or how many hours were attended per week. In addition, it appears that attendance rates are linked to family income. Mitchell and Hodgen (2008) found that although overall participation in ECE was 94.5 per cent in 2006, participation rates were only 74 per cent and 78 per cent in the two areas in their study with the lowest median income levels.

Participation rates also vary for age and ethnicity. There appears to have been a steady increase in enrolments in early childhood education, especially for children under three (for whom enrolment rates in 2009 were double those in 1990) (Education Counts 2011a). Recent figures indicate that the majority of enrolments in 2010 (nearly 62 per cent of total enrolments) were for three- and four-year-old children. The figure for children under one year was 4.6 per cent of the total, with one- and two-year-olds representing 33 per cent (a very small proportion of five-year-olds accounted for the remainder of the total) (Education Counts 2011b). Within these groups, Mitchell and Hodgen (2008) found that European/Pākehā new entrants had the highest rate of participation in ECE services (98.3 per cent), compared with 90.4 per cent for Māori. Ten per cent of all new entrants were Pasifika; of these, only 84.8 per cent had prior participation in early childhood education. These figures were reiterated on a recent Ministry of Education (2010) website, which also noted that the figures vary according to the region, with some areas reporting only 75 per cent attendance for Māori children. Increasing participation, especially for children from low socio-economic backgrounds, is part of the government's agenda for early childhood (Ministry of Education 2010).

The early childhood curriculum *Te Whāriki*

New Zealand has a centralised curriculum and regulatory framework under the control of the Ministry of Education. This is combined with a holistic inclusive curriculum that promotes diversity (Cullen 2008). As noted earlier, ECE provision in New Zealand covers a range of settings and includes children from birth until school entry. Stover (2003: 10) reflected that the writers of the early childhood curriculum *Te Whāriki* achieved 'what was regarded as a near-impossibility – a curriculum that had been developed within the industry and could be applied throughout the industry'. Diversity is addressed by settings weaving their own curriculum *whāriki* (woven mat) from a framework of principles and strands, to develop and emphasise their own priorities (Ministry of Education 1996).

Curriculum documents reflect the aspirations of their developers. Often there are tensions between competing ideas even at this stage. *Te Whāriki* drew on a liberal progressive/socially critical discourse, which went against the economically driven agenda at the time that it was developed (Mutch 2001). Carr and May (1993), described the influential support and commitment of Māori working-group members during the development process. The nature of the resulting bi-cultural early childhood curriculum document reflected the emphasis on holistic development that is evident in Māori developmental theory (Macfarlane 2000; Pere 1988). The four principles at the centre of the curriculum are: empowerment; holistic development; family and community; relationships.

Te Whāriki states that 'the outcomes of a curriculum are knowledge, skills, and attitudes' and notes that these are closely linked. 'These three aspects combine together to form a child's "working theory" and help the child develop dispositions that encourage learning' (Ministry of Education 1996: 44). The learning outcomes therefore emphasise children's development of working theories and learning dispositions.

Learning dispositions and identity as a learner

The dispositional outcome in *Te Whāriki* has been explained as children developing positive learning dispositions so that they are 'ready, willing and able' to engage with learning and utilise the knowledge and skills that develop (Carr 2001; Claxton and Carr 2004). Carr *et al.* (2009: 15) noted that dispositions

> act as an affective and cultural filter for trajectories of learning in the making. They can turn knowledge and skill into action . . . [they] are strengthened, adapted, transformed or interrupted by circumstances and experience. They are the source of the recognition (or misrecognition) of learning opportunities and provide strategy and motivation for the inevitable improvisation that is learning.

Dispositions should be viewed as verbs rather than nouns (things to be acquired) as a learner becomes more or less disposed to respond in particular ways (Claxton and Carr 2004): 'Dispositions to learn develop when children are immersed in an environment that is characterised by well-being, trust, belonging and purposeful activity, contributing and collaborating, communicating and representing, and exploring and guided participation' (Ministry of Education 1996: 45).

In our first project we explored the development of dispositions (and key competencies) over time. The following example, from a case study of Cameron described in Carr *et al.* (2008: 67–68), illustrated this in practice. It is based on an analysis of narrative assessments written by Cameron's teachers over a two-year period. The stories illustrated the following developments:

> Cameron took more *initiative* in communication and relating to others, and the *range* of people he related to expanded. Initially he stood and observed children before playing alongside them. Teachers recorded several instances of his willingness to join unfamiliar children and his circle of peers widened. He also welcomed play initiated by peers, and later took the first steps to inviting play (a ritualised sequence of the haka leading to rugby play was an interesting example of this), opening conversations ('That's where my Dad buys beer' when out on a walk to the mall) and discussing artefacts such as books or portfolios. Gradually his confidence in relating to others seemed to increase, although most of the documented examples were of interactions with adults. In the beginning teachers supported and encouraged his learning, and invited him to help with activities. In his second year at the centre Cameron's stories recorded him asking for help and in the final year he was questioning adults and offering his help and advice.

This example of 'relating to others' illustrates the four-track framework of the ways in which dispositions are strengthened that was developed by Professor Margaret Carr:

> These tracks can be called: *mindfulness* (as learners begin to "make these prac-tices part of their own identity and expertise"), *breadth* (more wide-ranging contexts, as connections are made beyond any one setting or community), *frequency* (over time), and *complexity* (across mediating resources—including people). These dimensions overlap and intertwine.
>
> (Carr *et al.* 2008: 72)

Over time, as successive writers have expanded on the descriptions of learning dispositions, we can see some consistency in their views about the kinds of learners and learning that are desirable in the twenty-first century. In England, Siraj-Blatchford (2007) noted the importance of communication, collaboration and creativity. Claxton (2008) writes about the 'learning muscles' of courage, curiosity, investigation, experimentation, imagination, reasoning, sociability and reflection and encourages parents and teachers to foster children's resilience and resourcefulness. Carr *et al.* (2009) focus on reciprocity, resilience and imagination. However, learning dispositions are only one aspect of the key learning outcomes for early childhood education; the other is working theories. In the years since *Te Whāriki* was published, working theories as a curriculum outcome have received less attention than the focus on learning dispositions. When reviewing research needs in the New Zealand early childhood sector, Meade (2008: 3) noted that: 'We've ended up a bit out of balance, with little focus on working theories, except where they cross over with dispositions. We need to know what is happening in centres to give children more of a stretch with their thinking, their theorising.' Working theories were the focus of our second 'Moments of wonder. . .' research project.

Working theories

Children's working theories, as described in *Te Whāriki*, are derived from Claxton's (1990) work on 'minitheories' (Ministry of Education 1993). Claxton (1990) used three simple analogies to describe mini–theories – islands, amoebae and computer files. It is Claxton's island analogy that first resonated with us as we searched for ways to frame our thinking about what was being noticed and documented by the project team, and other parents, about children's behaviours and ideas as examples of children's working theories in action. Claxton (1990) referred to what we know as being like islands in a sea of what we do not know. When we experience something new we are either 'on firm ground', because we relate it easily to what we know – our island of knowledge – or we are 'at sea' and are uncertain and unsure how to take this experience or how to behave. Islands may eventually connect as we come to realise they are not dissimilar. Likewise, what was once thought of as one island could, with greater experience, become two.

Claxton (1990: 66) described one's knowledge as consisting of

> a large number of purpose-built, situation-specific packages called 'minitheories', and . . . our basic method of learning – our natural learning ability, as I call it – involves a gradual process of editing these minitheories so that they become (1) to contain better-quality knowledge and skill, and (2) to be better 'located' with respect to the area of experience for which they are suitable.

In *Te Whāriki*, children's working theories as learning outcomes in early childhood are described as follows:

> Children develop working theories through observing, listening, doing, participating, discussing, and representing within the topics and activities provided in the programme. As children gain greater experience, knowledge, and skills, the theories they develop become more widely applicable and have more connecting links between them. Working theories become increasingly useful for making sense of the world, for giving the child control over what happens, for problem solving, and for further learning. Many of these theories retain a magical and creative quality, and for many communities, theories about the world are infused with a spiritual dimension.
>
> (Ministry of Education 1996: 44)

We found many examples of unspoken theories that could be inferred from children's behaviour; for example, every time Timmy (22 months) went past the water trough, he checked underneath to see whether the water was flowing out of the plug hole or not. On occasion a look of puzzlement or surprise suggested a theory may have been disrupted.

Other theories are expressed and fostered through interactions with others. In England, the Effective Provision of Pre-school Education (EPPE) project identified high cognitive outcomes for children as associated with sustained adult–child interactions. The term 'sustained shared thinking' was used to define 'instances where two or more individuals "work together" in an intellectual way to solve a problem, clarify a concept, evaluate activities, or extend a narrative' (Siraj-Blatchford 2010: 157). This was a key feature of pedagogy in quality early years settings and was especially powerful when encouraged in the home by family members too. We found this was supported when the adult was genuinely interested in the child's theories. This is illustrated in the following example where Eleanor strives to understand Jake's explanation of how his bike is powered:

E: Sorry Jake tell me that again.

J: My car doesn't need petrol.

E: Why not?

J: Because it has electric.

E: Wow . . . so it's got electric and it doesn't need petrol.

J: Yeah – and it has more electric if I put another cable in.

E: Ah, so the electricity gets in by a . . . um . . .

J: By the cable.

E: By the cable . . . And what does the cable plug into at the other end that's not in the car?

J: It plugs into . . . I'll show you which end it goes into . . .

E: OK.

J: This is where it plugs in.

E: That's where the electricity plugs in. So the cable plugs in at one end into the car and then where does your cable go after that?

J: It goes inside this trailer.

E: Inside the trailer?

J: Yes.

E: But how does the electricity get into the cable?

J: It goes in here and then the electricity goes wooop [shows with his hands].

E: Mmm hmmm.

J: Yeah – that's where it goes.

Te Whāriki recognises the importance of environments where children have opportunities to engage in complex thinking with others, observe, listen, participate and discuss within the context of topics and activities (Ministry of Education 1996). Carr *et al.* (2009) conclude that if learning dispositions are to become robust, both curriculum and pedagogy should focus more deliberately on their enhancement. We found that the same applied to working theories.

Implementing *Te Whāriki*

This section explores some of the pedagogical issues and challenges involved in implementing the outcomes of *Te Whāriki*.

The outcomes in Te Whāriki *are not easy to define*

In our first project (Carr *et al.* 2008) we found learning dispositions were rather 'fuzzy' outcomes, and concluded that it was important that shared meanings were co-constructed by teachers and learners and reified in some way (made available and transparent in documentation and wall charts, for instance). Unless this happens, the key principle behind the development of these dispositional outcomes – that learners will become able to take responsibility for their learning and will be able to navigate their way across boundaries of content and culture – will be threatened.

Similarly, initial data collection using observations of children led the practitioner researchers in the second project to question exactly what might be considered a working theory as there were so many instances of language or behaviour which implied theorising. We found many 'spontaneous wonderings' (Donaldson, cited in Siraj-Blatchford 2009) and what the practitioners came to think of as 'throw away theories'. For example, 'Don't touch the spider, they pinch'; 'The rain will make a waterfall'.

Faced with the dilemma of what exactly constituted a working theory, and what to prioritise when responding, the team decided to focus largely on the theorising that appeared to be more than a fleeting interest or 'throw away theory'. Crowley and Jacobs (2002) described the ways in which knowledge deepens and becomes more complex over time as children find and develop areas of interest that can become 'islands of expertise' through reciprocal engagement with others. This resonated with Claxton's (1990) islands analogy for the mini-theories that under-pinned the working theories outcomes in *Te Whāriki*. Documentation played a crucial role in identifying patterns of interest, as it was only in retrospect that the significance of some comments or behaviours became apparent. In other cases, reflecting on documentation led the practitioners to reflect that they may have initially misunderstood the child's main focus and responded to a superficial aspect of the child's theory.

Having one curriculum from birth to school entry requires skilful, flexible teachers

The principles and strands of *Te Whāriki* apply to all children from birth to school entry, but settings may need to weave these slightly differently depending on the children's age. This was illustrated in Carr *et al.* (2008), where two of the teachers in an infants and toddlers programme began to think about the particular framework of learning dispositions that they had been using, drawn from the Learning Story framework set out in Carr (2001). They felt that it needed some alterations to align more with the actions, behaviours and special characteristics of infants and toddlers:

It wasn't the notion of dispositions we had a problem with, rather it was the language of the framework that didn't seem to correspond to the learning we wanted to describe, but neither of us felt we were qualified to alter the framework to make it fit. . .

With encouragement from the research team the teachers began to draft their thoughts and ideas into a new framework. They returned to *Te Whāriki*, and after 'many, many hours of discussion', often linking their ideas back to the children for whom they had been writing learning stories, they developed some cues and examples that they felt better recognised the dispositions in their setting. These included: courage and curiosity; to trust; making sense of self, people, places and things; to communicate; and to contribute (Carr *et al*. 2008). Degotardi and Davis (2008: 232) describe the potential value of early childhood practitioners reflecting on the ways in which they interpret infants in their day-to-day practice, suggesting that 'this may bring about the emergence of new or more complex interpretive ideas which will deepen their understanding of infants in their care, and thus contribute towards the enhancement of professional early childhood practices'. The flexibility of centres weaving their own *whāriki* allows such development, but how this is implemented will depend on the qualities of the staff.

The adults' role

A number of dilemmas have arisen in our working theories project in relation to the adults' role in working with children. We have explored some of these, including when to disrupt a child's working theory, and the dangers of unintentionally hijacking the focus of an interaction in an earlier paper (Peters and Davis 2011). Other dilemmas centred on adults creating opportunities for actively listening to children and engaging in episodes of sustained shared thinking. Valuable debates surfaced within some of the Playcentre communities about the philosophical approach underpinning pedagogy in the setting. Some parents noted that they felt that the Playcentre should be 'a place to play' and were unsure about the practitioner researchers' attempts to take a more active role in working with children in order to develop a culture of inquiry and foster children's thinking. This was interesting, given that there was an unquestioned culture of engaging in children's play in ways that were generally considered to be child-centred, but in fact reflected adult power and decision making regarding the direction of the play; for example, initiating 'volcano' eruptions in the sandpit in response to a child's interest in volcanoes or planning for opportunities to make wool-and-stick webs after a child noted that the 'gloop' she was playing with looked like spider webs when pulled out into thin strips.

Using the working theories lens the team came to see such approaches as only loosely connected to the child's thinking. The child's interest in volcanoes began with an interest in them as a defining feature of place (after visiting Auckland and observing some of the volcanic features of the landscape there). Over several days it progressed to questioning whether volcanoes have conscious will and can choose when to erupt. This was a much more sophisticated topic for consideration than the practical activity in the sandpit. Over time, other observations of the child with the 'gloop' suggested an interest in analogies, as other comparisons and similes were documented in her descriptive language.

There was an interesting tension therefore regarding what was seen as an appropriate role for the adult. Mitchell's (2006) report on research into Playcentre suggested that adults in other settings may face similar dilemmas and hesitancy regarding taking an active role in engaging with children's thinking.

Conclusion

Early childhood education in New Zealand is provided by a diverse range of settings. *Te Whāriki*, a flexible curriculum based on the principles of holistic development, empowerment, relationships and family and community, allows for local interpretation within settings. The key learning outcomes of learning dispositions and working theories offer rich scope for the development of 'competent and confident' learners (Ministry of Education 1996: 9). However, its implementation is not without challenges and dilemmas. This chapter has discussed some of the pedagogical challenges of fostering children's working theories and dispositions. The findings from the two studies underpinning these discussions highlighted the importance of careful, skilled practitioners who can respond thoughtfully and flexibly to children in order to support their learning in these important 'fuzzy' domains. When practitioners are challenged to strive to understand and are mindful of children's learning intentions they can encourage learning in rich and complex ways. We need to strengthen and nurture these outcomes. In New Zealand, a strong foundation for early childhood education was laid with the development of *Te Whāriki*. This set the sector on a sound path to supporting learners for a rich and unknown future. However, while there have been many valuable developments in pedagogy and approaches to assessment in recent years, there is still much to be learned about ways to live this curriculum. This will require a continued emphasis on educators in both parent-led and teacher-led settings being well prepared for, and well supported in, their role.

QUESTIONS FOR THINKING ABOUT POLICY AND PRACTICE

1. In what ways do adults working with children ensure that the children's theories and ideas are understood and nurtured in ways that encourage them to develop over time?
2. What opportunities do learners in your educational setting have to develop positive learning dispositions?
3. What learning outcomes are privileged over others in your educational setting?

Acknowledgements

We are grateful to the Teaching and Learning Research Initiative (TLRI: www.tlri. org.nz) for the funding of the two projects described in this chapter. We are also grateful to our colleagues (especially Professor Margaret Carr, co-director of the first project), and the teachers, practitioners, families and children in those projects for allowing us to share their work.

References

Carr, M. (2001) *Assessment in Early Childhood Settings: Learning Stories*, London: Paul Chapman Publishing.

Carr, M. and May, H. (1993) Choosing a model: Reflecting on the development process of *Te Whāriki*: National early childhood curriculum guidelines in New Zealand, *Journal of Early Years Education*, 1(3): 7–21.

Carr, M., Smith, A.B., Duncan, J., Jones, C., Lee, W. and Marshall, K. (2009) *Learning in the Making: Disposition and Design in the Early Years*, Rotterdam: Sense.

Carr, M., Peters, S., Davis, K., Bartlett, C., Bashford, N., Berry, P., Greenslade, S., Molloy, S., O'Connor, N., Simpson, M., Smith, Y., Williams, T. and Wilson-Tukaki, A. (2008) *Key Learning Competencies across Place and Time: Kimihia te ara tōtika, hei oranga mō tō ao*, Teaching and Learning Research Initiative Final Report, available online at: http://www.tlri.org.nz/sites/default/files/projects/9216_summaryreport_0.pdf (accessed 27 February 2012).

Claxton, G. (1990) *Teaching to Learn: A Direction for Education*, London: Cassell.

Claxton, G. (2008) *What's the Point of School? Rediscovering the Heart of Education*, Oxford: Oneworld.

Claxton, G. and Carr, M. (2004) A framework for teaching learning: The dynamics of disposition, *Early Years: Journal of International Research and Development*, 24(1): 87–98.

Crowley, K. and Jacobs, M. (2002) Building islands of expertise in everyday family activity, in G. Leinhardt, K. Crowley and K. Knutson (eds) *Learning Conversations in Museums*, Mahwah, NJ: Lawrence Erlbaum.

Cullen, J. (2008) Outcomes of early childhood education: Do we know, can we tell, and does it matter?, Jean Herbison Lecture, presented at the NZARE Annual Conference, Palmerston North NZ, December.

Degotardi, S. and Davis, B. (2008) Understanding infants: Characteristics of early childhood practitioners' interpretations of infants and their behaviours, *Early Years: International Journal of Research and Development*, 28(3): 221–234.

Education Counts (2011a) *Participation in Early Childhood Education*, available online at: www.educationcounts.govt.nz/indicators/main/student-engagement-participation/1923 (accessed 13 June 2011).

Education Counts (2011b) *Statistics: Early Childhood Education*, available online at: www. educationcounts.govt.nz/statistics/ece/55414 (accessed13 June 2011).

Education Counts (2011c) *Statistics: Prior Participation in ECE*, available online at: www. educationcounts.govt.nz/statistics/ece/prior-participation-in-ece (accessed 13 June 2011).

Education Counts (2011d) *Statistics: Student Numbers*, available online at: www.education counts.govt.nz/statistics/schooling/july_school_roll_returns/6028 (accessed 2 May 2011).

Hill, D., Reid, R. and Stover, S. (2003) More than educating children: The evolutionary nature of Playcentre's philosophy of education, in S. Stover (ed.) *Good Clean Fun: New Zealand's Playcentre Movement*, Wellington: New Zealand Playcentre Federation.

Macfarlane, A. H. (2000) The value of Māori ecologies in the study of human development, in L. Bird and W. Drewery (eds) *Human Development in Aotearoa: A Journey through Life*, Auckland: McGraw-Hill.

Meade, A. (2008) *Research Needs in the Early Childhood Sector*, Teaching and Learning Research Initiative, available online at: www.tlri.org.nz/proposals.html (accessed 3 March 2008).

Ministry of Education (1993) *Te Whāriki: Draft Guidelines for Developmentally Appropriate Programmes in Early Childhood Services*, Wellington: Learning Media.

Ministry of Education (1996) *Te Whāriki. He Whāriki Mātauranga mō ngā Mokopuna o Aotearoa: Early Childhood Curriculum*, Wellington: Learning Media.

Ministry of Education (2009) *Types of ECE Service*, available online at: www.minedu.govt.nz/Parents/EarlyYears/HowECEWorks/TypesOfECEService.aspx (accessed 14 January 2010).

Ministry of Education (2010) *ECE Participation*, available online at: www.minedu.govt.nz/theMinistry/Budget/Budget2010/Factsheets/ECEParticipation.aspx (accessed 16 September 2010).

Mitchell, L. (2006) Playcentre: Highlights and challenges from recent research, Keynote Address to the New Zealand Playcentre Federation Annual Conference, May, Living Springs, Christchurch.

Mitchell, L. and Hodgen, E. (2008) *Locality-based Evaluation of Pathways to the Future: Ngā Huarahi Arataki Stage 1 Report*, Wellington: Ministry of Education, available online at: www.educationcounts.govt.nz/publications/ece/28948/28949 (accesssed 15 August 2011).

Mutch, C. (2001) Contesting forces: The political and economic context of curriculum development in New Zealand, *Asia Pacific Education Review*, 2(1): 74–84.

Pere, R. R. (1988) Te Wheke: Whaia te maramatanga me aroha, in S. Middleton (ed.) *Women and Education in Aotearoa*, Wellington: Allen & Unwin.

Peters, S. and Davis, K. (2011) Fostering children's working theories: Pedagogic issues and dilemmas in New Zealand, *Early Years: International Journal of Research and Development*, 31(1): 5–17.

Siraj-Blatchford, I. (2007) Creativity, communication and collaboration: The identification of pedagogic progression in sustained shared thinking, *Asia-Pacific Journal of Research in Early Childhood Education*, 1(2): 3–23.

Siraj-Blatchford, I. (2009) Conceptualising progression in the pedagogy of play and sustained shared thinking in early childhood education: A Vygotskian perspective, *Educational and Child Psychology*, 26(2): 77–89.

Siraj-Blatchford, I. (2010) A focus on pedagogy: Case studies of effective practice, in K. Sylva, E. Melhuish, P. Sammons, I. Siraj-Blatchford and B. Taggart (eds) *Early Childhood Matters: Evidence from the Effective Pre-school and Primary Education Project*, London: Routledge.

Stover, S. (2003) The history and significance of the Playcentre movement, in S. Stover (ed.) *Good Clean Fun: New Zealand's Playcentre Movement*, Wellington: New Zealand Playcentre Federation.

13

EARLY CHILDHOOD INCLUSION INITIATIVES IN GREECE

Athina Kammenou

OVERVIEW

This chapter discusses a case study which focused on the integration of young children with special needs in mainstream nursery schools. Based on early intervention theories, an Individualized Education Programme (IEP) was developed to be implanted in the conditions of the Greek educational system. The Programme was implemented for three years in five nursery schools and included five children with various educational, cognitive and/or psychological problems. The Programme aimed to: support the presence of children with special needs in mainstreaming classes; respond to targeted needs of the educators in relation to children's integration; support the families in assisting their children to accomplish their educational tasks; and enhance the collaboration between the educators and the families. The study showed that educators require more information and support on techniques and methods related to the integration of young children with special needs in mainstream nursery schools. The study also revealed the importance of collaboration between educators and families and some of the difficulties which exist in such collaboration and in co-operation with other specialist professionals.

Key words: Greece; mainstream; integration; early intervention; partnership; interdisciplinary.

Introduction

During recent years, the number of children requiring additional educational support and/or special intervention, in the short and long term, has increased considerably in both kindergartens and day care settings. However, current levels of support and provision do not match the actual demand, despite the legislative measures taken, especially during the last three decades. The first significant step in the evolution of special education in Greece appeared in 1981 with the introduction of the Public Law 1143/81 for equality and mutual acceptance of persons with special needs (Greek Public Law/Νόμος 1143/1981). In 2000, a new law supported the integration of children with special needs in mainstream educational settings, reserving special schools only for children with severe disabilities and complex special educational needs (Greek Public Law/Νόμος 2817/2000). At the same time, the government legislated the introduction of IEPs and instituted interdisciplinary services for assessing and monitoring of children's progress and providing family support. This law offered equal chances for all children to be educated in mainstream educational settings and achieve their social integration, taking into account their special educational needs as well as their potentialities (Zoniou-Sideri 2004).

The result of such legislation was the introduction of the so-called 'parallel' or 'mainstreaming classes' (τάξη ένταξης), where children with special educational needs are taught by a special educator in a separate classroom in mainstream settings. Following a categorical model of special educational needs, initially the placement of young children with disabilities in 'mainstreaming' classes depended on the type of disability and its particular characteristics (e.g. visual or hearing impairment; physical disabilities, etc.). Currently, the placement of children in mainstreaming classes is based on the assessment of their special educational needs rather than the causes of those needs (Greek Public Law/Νόμος 3194/2003).

In spite of the evolution of legal provisions, the evolution of the everyday practices has moved very slowly at different levels – that is, the training of the early years educators; satisfactory operation of mainstreaming classes; collaboration of special needs educator and the mainstream class teacher; parental involvement; and co-operation with other specialist professionals. These challenges are due to the lack of both an adequate operational framework and appropriate human resources (Zoniou-Sideri 2004). The collaboration between the main class educator and the special educator is almost non-existent and it is not supported by the school organisation. For example, there is no provision for any additional time for meetings between the class teacher and the special educational needs teacher.

Internationally, research regarding the education of children with special educational needs and support for families has evolved considerably and new approaches, practices and intervention strategies have been highlighted in order to address children's special educational needs (Bailey *et al.* 1991; Beckman *et al.* 1996; Bouchard 1997; Guralnick 2001). In many countries, relevant legislation has mandated the entitlement of children and their families for early intervention and appropriate support (e.g. in the USA, the Education for All Handicapped Children Act (Pub.

L. 94-142) of 1975 and the Individuals with Disabilities Education Improvement Act (Pub. L. 108-446) (IDEIA) of 2004; in France, Loi n° 75-534 du 30 juin 1975 annexé en 1989; Loi n° 2007-293 du 5 mars 2007 *réformant la protection de l'enfance*).

A common characteristic of relevant legislation is the introduction of an IEP which offers structured and continuous educational intervention to meet children's special educational needs. The IEP allows the designation of educational priorities for the children according to their needs, their potential and in direct and close relationship with the challenges experienced by the family. It also defines the procedure, rights and obligations for each participant (parents, educators, special educators, therapists, etc.). In a way, it 'imposes' collaboration between the family and all professionals who are responsible for the education of the children.

In different countries, IEPs are used in different ways and for different purposes. In the USA, the law requires professionals to offer appropriate and free education to all children with special educational needs who have an annual IEP (US Department of Education, Office of Special Education Programs 2006). In France, IEPs are used for professionals to define the necessary and specialised needs of each child and to suggest her/his placement in the least restricted and specialised educational environment possible. Special nursery schools no longer constitute parents or educators' priority choice (in USA: IDEIA 2004; in France: Loi n°2007-293 du 5 mars 2007).

In general, IEPs are written by a team which usually consists of (Beckman *et al.* 1993):

- the parents of the child with disabilities;
- specialists involved in the child's life (educators, doctors, psychologists, etc.);
- the child her/himself (if possible).

After an initial assessment and evaluation of the child's special educational needs, all participants agree on their role and obligations in the implementation and monitoring of the IEP. The success of the Programme lies on two key words: partnership and interdisciplinarity (Beckman *et al.* 1993; Pugach 1982). The first term determines the kind of collaboration between parents/carers (the family) and 'specialists', imposing bidirectional understanding, communication, decision making and distribution of responsibilities. The second term determines the level of participation for each 'specialist' participating in the programme and aims at the coordination of all involved services; and in particular, at the exchange of knowledge between the involved persons.

The Greek educational system faces two main challenges in this context: (a) the partnership is not yet a usual practice, the status of 'expert' is still dominant among professionals and most meetings for the assessment of children's needs take place without the parent's presence; and (b) the existing laws concern only mandatory pre-school education offered in kindergartens, it does not cover daycare settings which are supervised by the local administration and subordinated to directives issued by each municipality. As each municipality has its own legislative regulations concerning the operation of daycare settings, the arrival of a child with special educational needs may be dealt with in different ways.

In this context, the educator with a child with special needs in her/his classroom is often confronted with an unknown territory. Confronted with challenges and difficulties, s/he may quickly resign her/himself to feelings of inadequacy, leading to a denial of personal investment or refusal to continue working with the child. Often, an unrealistic appreciation of the situation and/or overestimation of the educator's personal capacities may have the same impact. The fear of eventually appearing as 'incompetent', the lack of a specialised training and the need to implement changes in the classroom in the long term have created among early years educators the need for more information and a demand for support and collaboration with specialists (Kamménou 1994).

In the light of these needs and demands, the present study was conducted, aiming to:

- support the inclusion of children with special educational needs in mainstream pre-school institutions;
- respond to educators' everyday needs created by the inclusion of children with special needs in their classes;
- include and reinforce parental involvement in the accomplishment of their children's educational needs;
- enhance the collaboration between educators and parents.

IEPs: our approach to supporting children's integration

In order to address the aims of our study, we developed IEPs for five children (four the boys and one girl) during a four-year period. At the beginning of the programme, the children's ages ranged from two years and eight months to six years and eight months. All children, with the exception of one boy, attended private or public daycare settings. For three of the children, the request for support was initiated by the educators of the daycare settings. For the other two children, the request came from parents as, at the time, their children were not enrolled in any pre-school institution.

The children's assessment was conducted by public assessment services (KE.D.D.Y) and by paediatric or psychiatric clinics for infants (introduced with the Ministerial decree/Απόφαση Γ6/4494, 2001). There was not always a clear diagnosis and identification of children's special educational needs, but in general all children exhibited mild or moderate behaviour difficulties, which triggered parental and/or educators' concerns. Table 13.1 presents the characteristics of the participating children.

Two children participated in the programme for one year as, in the following year, they were moved on to other educational structures: KK went on to a state school for children with special educational needs; HM was enrolled in a mainstream state kindergarten. The girl (GA) followed the programme for two years and then she was admitted to a state mainstream kindergarten receiving individual support.

TABLE 13.1 Profile of children who participated in the study

Children	Sex	Age	Duration of the project (years)	Request made by	Diagnostic
NX	Boy	2.8	3	Family	Williams syndrome
KK	Boy	6.8	1	Nursery school	Autism
PKS	Boy	3.2	2	Nursery school	Autistic spectrum disorders (ASD)
HM	Boy	4.1	1	Nursery school	Autism
GA	Girl	4.5	2	Family	Downs syndrome

The last two children (NX and PKS) were integrated in a mainstream state school and continued to receive support from our programme for a third year.

Developing and implementing IEPs

The first contact between the team conducting this study and the daycare staff and the family was established by telephone. A first meeting was organised with the participation of our team, the educators and the family, in order to explain to all participants the IEP procedures and to get everybody's formal agreement. The IEPs were shaped to fit the structures of the Greek educational system and the resources available in the settings in order to respond to the unique needs of each child. A four steps procedure was proposed in all five cases as follows:

1. *Collection of baseline data* which included:

    *   initial evaluation of the child's needs using a combination of the PORTAGE (Bluma and Cooperative Educational Service Agency 12, Portage 1976) and the Vineland adaptive behaviour scales (Cicchetti 1984);
    *   present level of educational performance which came from educators and observations made by parents – additional information was collected on the possibilities of the school (environment, everyday programme and the human resources);
    *   information about previous interventions provided by other specialist professionals.

    In its totality, this information constituted the basis on which the IEP was built upon and updated.

2. *Definition of needs*: The needs of each interested and participating party (includ-ing the child, parents, educators and early years setting) were defined during meetings organised in the daycare settings or in the child's family. Parents, early childhood educators and one special educator from our team were present.

3. *Definition of annual goals*: This included the long-term goals for the child, family and educators.
4. *Definition of short-term measurable objectives with clearly defined criteria*: Short-term precise objectives were defined for each of the developmental domains: autonomy, socialisation, cognition and motor. Specific strategies and estimated time for their achievement were also identified in the IEP (see Table 13.2).

TABLE 13.2 Example of an IEP

	Objectives	*Method*	*Duration*	*Evaluation* 17.9.07
Autonomy	• To put on/off a jacket by her/himself and to hang it on the hook • To wash hands by her/himself in the bathroom	Put adult's hand on child's hand and guide it	Three weeks	
Socialisation	• To be sited together with other children at least five minutes every day • To be sited at the table for structured activities with peers, at least for five minutes	Limit the space where the child could wander, while not seated with other children	Four weeks	
Cognition	• Shapes: to recognise and name three basic shapes (circle, square, triangle) • To turn her/his head whenever hearing her/his name	Same exercises that are proposed to all children Educator holds the child's head and looks for eye contact	Four weeks	
Motor	Fine motor: • To hold the pencil in an appropriate way so that s/he can draw • To hold the spoon so that s/he can bring the food in her/his mouth (at home)	During the drawing sessions of the rest of the class, the child plays with sand, gravel and modelling clay, in order to exercise her/his fine motor capabilities	Four weeks	

Regular meetings, every six to seven weeks, were organised during the academic year. The meetings took place in the pre-school settings, after the end of the educators' scheduled working hours, and lasted from one hour and 30 minutes to two hours. One goal of the meetings was to give the opportunity to every participant to express their opinion about the child's progress and the observed difficulties. A second goal was the definition of new objectives or the redefinition of the previous objectives that were not achieved (for a timeline of the process, see Figure 13.1 below). Parents, mainstream educators and the special needs coordinator made separate evaluations of the situation. Each time collated information was distributed to all members in advance of the meeting.

In order to encourage parental participation in the meetings, a list of the issues and/or questions for discussion was sent in advance of the meeting. It was arranged that the special needs educator would first ask questions to the educators. This encouraged parents to ask questions in their turn on the progress of their children (Goldstein and Turnbull 1982; Goldstein *et al.* 1980; Wolfendale 1984). Later on the intervention timeline, parents also gave information about their children's doings at home that was useful for updating the IEPs. This approach is generally supported in literature about partnership between family and educators and experts, as well as on the empowerment and enablement of parents (Beckman *et al.* 1996; Bouchard 1997; Vincent 1994).

The introduction of IEPs was evaluated at the end of the first year of their implementation, taking an ethnographic approach (Glesne 1999). The collection of the data was done by means of participatory observation and individual interviews with participants. The results of the study were based on the description and the interpretation of what participants did and said. This chapter deals only with the discussion of data collected during the first year of the study.

Findings

The findings of our analysis were structured at three different levels. The first level concerned the children with special educational needs. All five children demonstrated significant progress, especially in the social and autonomy domains, which were targeted by the majority of the defined objectives. The number of social interactions with peers increased and a certain level of autonomy and self-help skills was reached (e.g. getting dressed/undressed, eating alone, washing hands). The frequency and intensity of disproportionate emotional reactions were reduced, resulting in children's longer stay in the mainstream classroom.

The second level related to parents' role in the education process of their children. Our IEPS specifically aimed at encouraging parents to express their own opinions, to make propositions and especially to consider themselves as equal members of the intervention team. Before the introduction of the IEPs, the parents did not have the opportunity to participate in multidisciplinary meetings and/or to express their wishes and their observations. As a result, the intervention team met significant difficulties when it asked parents to complete the goal definition and evaluation forms. During interviews parents said that:

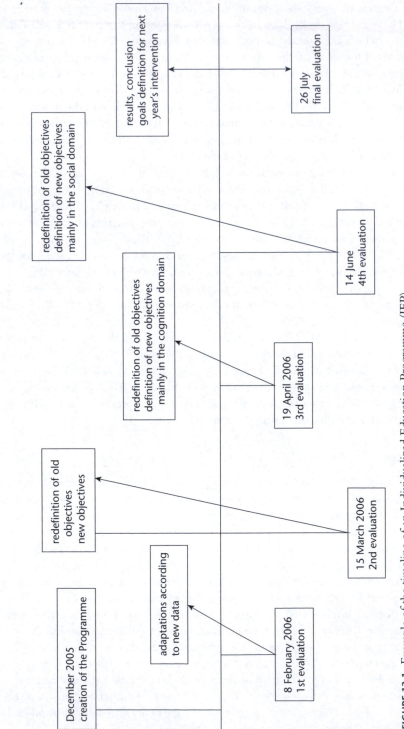

FIGURE 13.1 Example of the timeline of an Individualized Education Programme (IEP)

- It was the first time that their opinion was asked with regard to the implementation of an intervention or a teaching programme that concerned their child.
- This time, they have had the feeling that their thoughts and opinions mattered and were taken into consideration.
- They had great difficulty to express their views, when they were asked to do so. They explained: *you are the experts, you know better than us . . . whatever you think is better; we can't answer because we don't know the programme; I don't know what my child should be able to do at this age.*

The evaluation of the programme helped parents to realise the potential of their child and the support they can offer, and at the same time to understand better the inherent difficulties of the task at hand. A major problem was the lack of presence of both parents during meetings. Even when meetings were accommodated according to the availability of the whole family, only one couple was always present. For the other four families, the father's presence was occasional (once or twice).

The third level of analysis concerned the educators who were involved in this programme. In three cases the children were accompanied on a permanent basis by a non-qualified person (being paid for this support), who nevertheless had a long experience of working with young children. In the two other cases the mainstream educator of the early years setting was additionally in charge of the child with special educational needs; a special educator of the study team supported the mainstream educator once a week. In these two last cases, an indirect goal was the training of staff involved with the children. The special educator visited the classroom weekly during the whole year, and during her/his visits s/he was participating in the daily programme. The objective was to adapt the regular activities of the class to the special needs and capacities of the child, including small groups of peer interaction.

With time, our team tried to modify the role of the 'non-qualified' person, from exclusively supporting the child with special educational needs, to sharing the responsibility for the activities of a small group together with the class teacher. Sometimes, a slight modification of the activities of the class was suggested, by introducing more frequent pauses to accommodate specific needs of the child. This approach, however, proved difficult to implement. The analysis of the interviews showed that at the beginning of the programme the special educator, who had a mediator role between all involved parties, was considered as an 'external specialist'. S/he was expected to be involved with extremely precise and targeted intervention tasks that were exclusively directed to the child with special educational needs, without having an active role in the whole class. By the end of the year, however, the special educator was totally integrated and considered part of the team of the pre-school. The collaboration between adults was established and the competences of all staff were strengthened through exchanges of opinion. In interviews, the mainstream class educators indicated:

> Now, I'm not afraid to face the child's crises.
> I can explain and answer queries of other children.

> *If I can be assured of having effective help, I would like to try this experience again . . . I learned so much.*
>
> *Actually, I don't hesitate now to ask questions and share my thoughts and belief[s] . . . also about other children in the same group.*
>
> *It has been an opportunity for me to speak and share thoughts with somebody who understands the real situation.*

What have we learned?

First, we learned that the implementation of policy with regard to the integration of young children with disabilities in the actual structures of the Greek pre-school institutions is possible and feasible. To achieve this goal certain conditions must be present: the existence of a structured environment; the availability of in-service training for the educators and the accompanying persons; and the possibility to implement a flexible class programme. The educational support offered should include: the child's choice of activities among those implemented in the classroom; appropriate and realistic modifications to the daily class programme; the use of continuous evaluation of the progress made; and the child's equal membership and participation in the everyday life of the micro-system of the pre-school institutions (Bronfenbrenner 1979).

Second, we found informal ways of responding to children's targeted needs within the everyday work of the educators in mainstream settings. This became possible when the special needs educator of our team was present in the classroom and was collaborating with the class staff. During formal meetings, educators were hesitant to ask questions regarding the class management or other educational issues. With the presence of the special educator informal training took place; the class members had an immediate source of information for any kind of questions that arose at any time in the class. This motivated them to develop an interest in the goals of the prevention and intervention programme.

Sometimes the study team proposed small modifications to the daily programme of the class. However, even if these modifications did not affect the operation of the main programme of the nursery school, some resistance occurred, mainly from the managing director. The only plausible explanation for this might be the fear of those in charge that they might lose the status of the 'expert in their own territories'.

Third, we noticed a significant change in the perception of educators with regard to parental role, as active collaborators and participants in the IEP. Through the discussions they had with the parents during the IEP meetings, the educators felt that they were sharing with them responsibilities for the resolution of many problems concerning the children. Parents, too, passed from the 'faulty', 'responsible' and 'guilty' feelings (Witt *et al.* 1984: 27–32), to that of active participants in the intervention programmes. The educators' need to obtain all available information on the children, beyond medical and other experts' reports, allowed parents to see themselves as being on an equal level with other professionals.

Fourth, we were able to support families in the accomplishment of their children's educational tasks. We experienced uncomfortable scenes of despairing parents, crying and feeling guilty for the 'vague diagnostic' or, even in one case, for the lack of a clear medical evaluation. In four cases, parents were unable to realise what their children were able to do and what not, and they often underestimated their abilities. In the beginning the parents demonstrated enormous difficulties in filling in documents about their own expectations for their children. We tried to direct their attention to objectives and goals for their children. After the first meetings and lots of discussions, little by little they started expressing their wishes.

None of the five couples had ever received psychological support and it was unclear when and how they were initially informed about the difficulties of their child. It seemed that the child's difficulties were acknowledged when s/he was admitted in the pre-school setting. This might also explain parents' initial hostile attitude towards the educators. Psychological support for families is particularly important, because without it, families do not have the psychological courage and the necessary resources to participate in an intervention programme (Bronfenbrenner 1979).

Finally, despite our efforts, we were not able to include in our programme other specialist professionals (e.g. psychologist, logotherapist, pediatrician) who were involved with the children or their families. Several professionals claimed that they were not familiar with such practices and they did not wish to participate. The implementation of our programme relied only on resources available without input from interdisciplinary teams and meetings. Evidently, there is a need for wider awareness among all professionals involved with children with special needs and their families of the importance of working together for the best interest of the child.

A note of caution is due here. This was a small-scale study and as a result, the interpretation of its findings should be treated with caution. Families with different characteristics and educators with different levels of training could be encountered in different settings, resulting in different practices. However, the value of the study lies in the transferability of practices that are adaptable and balance well the needs and potential of the child, the family and the pre-school institution.

Conclusion

Our study has shown that the inclusion of children with special educational needs is possible in pre-school institutions when support is well organised and offered by a trained team, despite the lack of any 'official organisation'. Parents, from initially being merely observers, became decision makers in the implementation of IEPs. The educators found new ways of dealing with children's and their families' needs. They changed their views in respect of the role of parents in the education of their children and admitted that, in the past, they were never taught how to work with parents. This study could be used to generate awareness of the need for continuous efforts both at political and educational levels, if the educational system is to achieve its goal for the educational and social inclusion of young children with special educational needs in pre-school institutions.

QUESTIONS FOR THINKING ABOUT POLICY AND PRACTICE

1. What is the role of specialist professionals (psychologists, logotherapists/ speech therapists, ergotherapists, etc.) in the development of IEPs in the context of your own country and/or setting?
2. How can early childhood educators become more competent in early intervention or prevention of special educational needs?
3. How can early childhood educators support and promote parental involvement in the assessment and intervention process?

References

Bailey, D.B., Palsha, S.A. and Simeonsson, R.J. (1991) Professional skills, concerns, and perceived importance of work with families in early intervention, *Exceptional Children*, 58: 156–165.

Beckman, P.J., Boyes, G.B. and Herres, A. (1993). The IEP and IFSP meetings, in P.J. Beckman and G.B. Boyes (eds) *Deciphering the System: A Guide for Families of Young Children with Disabilities*, Cambridge, MA: Brookline Books.

Beckman, P.J., Frank, N. and Newcomb, S. (1996) Qualities and skills for communicating with families, in P.J. Beckman (ed.) *Strategies for Working with Families of Young Children with Disabilities*, Baltimore, MD: Paul H. Brooks Publishing Co.

Bluma, S. and Cooperative Educational Service Agency 12, Portage (1976) *Portage Guide to Early Education, Manual [and] Checklist, Revised Edition*, Washington, DC: ERIC Clearinghouse.

Bouchard, J.M. (1997) Famille et compétence éthique: de l'expert au partenaire chercheur, *Pages Romandes*, 2, 5–8.

Bronfenbrenner, U. (1979) *The Ecology of Human Development*, Cambridge, MA: Harvard University Press.

Cicchetti, D.V. (1984) Diagnostic uses of the Vineland adaptive behavior scales, *Journal of Pediatric Psychology*, 10(2): 215–225.

Education for All Handicapped Children Act, Pub. L. 94-142, 89 Stat. 773 (1975).

Glesne, C. (1999) *Becoming Qualitative Researchers*, Chicago, IL: Addison Wesley Longman.

Goldstein, S. and Turnbull, A. (1982) Strategies to increase parent participation in IEP conferences, *Exceptional Children*, 48(4): 115–125.

Goldstein, S., Strickland, B., Turnbull, A. and Curry, L. (1980) An observational analysis of the IEP conference, *Exceptional Children*, 46(4):278–285.

Greek Public Law/Νόμος 1143 (1981) *Περί ειδικής αγωγής, ειδικής επαγγελματικής εκπαιδεύσεως, απασχολήσεως και κοινωνικής μερίμνης των αποκλινόντων εκ του φυσιολογικού τόμων και άλλων τινών εκπαιδευτικών διατάξεων*, ΦΕΚ 80, 27 Μαρτίου 1981.

Greek Public Law/Νόμος 2817 (2000) *Εκπαίδευση των Ατόμων με ειδικές εκπωδεντικές ανάγκες και άλλες διατάξεις*, ΦΕΚ 78, 14 Μαρτίου 2000.

Greek Public Law/Νόμος 3194 (2003) *Ρύθμιση εκπαιδευτικών θεμάτων και λοιπές διατάξεις*, ΦΕΚ 276/Α, 20 Νοεμβρίου 2003.

Guralnick, M.J. (1990) Major accomplishment and future directions in early childhood mainstreaming, *Topics in Early Childhood Special Education*, 10(2): 1–17.

Guralnick, M.J. (ed.) (2001) *Early Childhood Inclusion: Focus on Change,* Baltimore, MD: Paul H. Brookes Publishing Company.

Individuals with Disabilities Education Improvement Act, Pub. L. 108-446, 118 Stat. 2647 (2004).

Kamménou, A. (1994) *Formation pour une intégration au préscolaire*, Lucerne, CH: SZH.

Loi n°75-534 du 30 juin (1975) *d'orientation en faveur des personnes handicapées*, Décret n°89-798 du 27 octobre 1989.

Loi n°2007-293 du 5 mars (2007) *réformant la protection de l'enfance*.

Ministerial decree/Υπ. Απόφαση Γ6/4494 (2001) *Κανονισμός λειτουργίας των Κέντρων Διάγνωσης, Αξιολόγησης και Υποστήριξης (Κ.Δ.Α.Υ.) των ατόμων με ειδικές ανάγκες και καθορισμός των καθηκόντων και υποχρεώσεων του προσωπικού αυτού.* ΦΕΚ 1503, τ.Β', 8 Νοεμβρίου 2001.

Pugach, M.C. (1982) Regular classroom teacher involvement in the development and utilization of IEPs, *Exceptional Children*, 48(4): 371–374.

US Department of Education, Office of Special Education program (2006) Individualized Education Program (IEP), available online at: www.ideapartnership.org/index.php?option=com_content&view=article&id=846&oseppage=1 (accessed 16 August 2011).

Vincent J.L. (1994) Dix stratégies pour renforcer la famille dans son rôle de preneur de decisions, *Facilitating IFSP Meetings*, video: code d20477.

Witt, J., Miller, C., Mcintyre, R. and Smith, D. (1984) Effects of variables on parental perceptions of staffing, *Exceptional Children*, 51(1): 27–32.

Wolfendale, S. (1984) Special educational needs and the place of parents, *Early Child Development and Care*, 14(3–4): 269–298.

Zoniou-Sideri, A. (2004) The necessity of inclusion: current questions and perspectives, in A. Zoniou-Sideri (ed.) *Current Inclusive Perspectives*, Athens: Ellinika Grammata [in Greek].

14

PROMOTING EMOTIONAL WELL-BEING OR MENTAL HEALTH IN ENGLAND?

What's the difference?

Anita Soni

OVERVIEW

This chapter seeks to show how the early years curricula, and in particular the Early Years Foundation Stage (EYFS), can be used as a vehicle for promoting mental health in the early years. The effectiveness of pre-school has been demonstrated by the Effective Provision of Pre-school Education (EPPE) project which also emphasised the importance of practitioners' understanding of the curriculum and child development. Therefore it would be valuable to state explicitly how the curriculum itself can promote mental health in young children, rather than being hinted in the principles and commitments for personal, social and emotional development (PSED). The development of the EYFS offers a golden opportunity to make explicit how mental health can be promoted in our youngest children. Whilst based essentially in the English context, this paper should be of interest to all those concerned with the mental and emotional health of young children in international contexts. Based on a literature review of English policy documents, I consider different ways of describing mental health in young children, provoking a discussion on how a common language can help practitioners to build upon their current understanding and practice.

Key words: Mental health; emotional well-being; emotional health; early years.

Introduction

The promotion of mental health is an important area for young children; however, there is a desire to not use such a term with young children. Research has been conducted reflecting the place of mental health in English curricula documents for young children over the last ten years. This research demonstrates that the term mental health is often not used within curricula documents, but a number of other terms are used such as: social and emotional development; emotional well-being; emotional health; personal, social and emotional development. This confusion regarding terminology results in many practitioners in the early years workforce being unaware of the potential for promoting mental health using the universal guidance that exists, e.g. *Promoting Children's Mental Health within Early Years and School Settings* (DfES 2001); *Social and Emotional Aspects of Development* (SEAD) (DCSF 2008); *The Early Years Foundation Stage* (DfES 2007) as they are unaware of the links.

Definitions of mental health

According to the British Medical Association (BMA), the term 'mental health' implies a focus on the absence of mental health and on 'mental health problems' which in turn covers a wide range of issues, from the worries and concerns of everyday life, to severe and debilitating disorders such as depression (BMA 2006). Indeed the BMA itself also recognises the tendency of professionals in different disciplines to use different terms, which may in turn increase confusion.

The DfES (2001: 1) *Promoting Chidren's Mental Health within Early Years and School Settings* defines children who are mentally healthy as those who:

• develop psychologically, emotionally, intellectually and spiritually;
• initiate, develop and sustain mutually satisfying personal relationships;
• use and enjoy solitude;
• become aware of others and empathise with them;
• play and learn;
• develop a sense of right and wrong; and
• resolve (face) problems and setbacks and learn from them.

This definition draws upon Kay's (1999) report for the Mental Health Foundation that examined the factors affecting the mental health and emotional development of children in the United Kingdom. The inquiry collated the views of a range of experts across disciplines, and included the views of parents and children. The DfES definition expands on the earlier NHS definition to include solitude, playing and learning and understanding right and wrong (NHS Health Advisory Service 1995), showing there is increased understanding of what terms mean across health and education. However, within early years curriculum, the term 'mental health' is rarely used.

A curriculum-based approach to mental health promotion

Citing the work of Weissberg *et al.* (1991), the document *Promoting Children's Mental Health within Early Years and School Settings* (DfES 2001: 8) makes explicit the link between the curriculum and promotion of mental health by stating that 'Early childhood education may be viewed as an innovative mental health strategy that affects many risk and protective factors'. Weissberg *et al.*'s (1991) views were based on American research such as the High/Scope Perry Pre-school Study (Schweinhart and Weikart 1989) and the Consortium for Longitudinal Studies report (Lazar *et al.* 1982). Woodhead (1988) notes that to understand the characteristics of successful early childhood education programmes, it is important to know the political, social and economic context in which they occurred. He points out that the ideas of successful early childhood education in the US stem from the liberal political philosophy of the 1960s that tried to counterbalance the social pressure for democracy and equality with the economic pressure of a capitalist philosophy. Therefore, can Weissberg *et al.*'s (1991) ideas, which were expressed in the American context and over 20 years ago, be seen to be relevant and applicable in the current English political, social and economic context?

In the UK, the EPPE longitudinal English research has examined the impact of attending pre-school education, and the characteristics that make pre-school education more effective (Sylva *et al.* 2003). Whilst this study has not conducted any research on mental health promotion through curriculum approaches, it has examined the impact of pre-school on children's social and behavioural development over the pre-school period (Sammons *et al.* 2002). The authors state that pre-school in itself can help to combat social exclusion and promote inclusion by offering disadvantaged young children a better start at school. In addition, pre-school experience compared to none enhances children's development, and an earlier start in a good-quality early years setting relates to better intellectual development, improved independence, concentration and sociability (Sylva *et al.* 2003). However, the focus in the EPPE project is on identifying the characteristics of good-quality settings rather than evaluating the impact of the curriculum in itself on children's personal, social and emotional development. Nevertheless, it is useful to see that good-quality early years settings are viewed as those with practitioners with good knowledge of the curriculum and how children learn. This information is useful to consider when one considers the task of mental health promotion in early years settings.

The Good Childhood Inquiry, launched in 2006, also recognises that schools and curriculum approaches can work preventatively to reduce the amount of mental disturbance and promote mental health (The Children's Society 2009). Layard and Dunn (2009) recognise the value of social and emotional learning and highlight Weissberg's (2007) research as an evidence base to show that there is no conflict for schools between helping children manage their emotions and improving their school work. They state that personal, social and health education (PSHE) is the subject area where the systematic development of self-understanding and pro-social behaviour is covered. Social and emotional aspects of learning (SEAL) offer a range of dedicated materials that can be used within this subject area. It is interesting that these authors recommend that social and emotional learning should be covered in all teacher training and that PSHE should be taught by specialist teachers in secondary school. This again highlights how the curriculum, in this case in schools, is seen as an intervention to promote mental health.

Conceptualisation of mental health in curricula for young children

A statutory national curriculum for children under five is a relatively recent innovation in England. In 1996, the School Curriculum and Assessment Authority (SCAA) published *Nursery Education: Desirable Outcomes for Children's Learning on Entering Compulsory Education* with guidance on educational activities (SCAA/DFEE 1996). All children, in publicly funded pre-school education, were expected to follow a curriculum to enable them to make maximum progress towards these desirable learning outcomes. The SCAA/DfEE desirable learning outcomes were explicitly linked to the National Curriculum levels in Key Stage 1 and 'emphasized early literacy, numeracy, and the development of personal and social skills and contributed to children's knowledge, understanding and skills in other areas . . . to provide a foundation for later achievement' (SCAA/DfEE 1996: 1).

This quote illustrates the government's view of young children as pre-schoolers and the primary function of the early years education was to prepare children for school and the National Curriculum. The SCAA/DfEE desirable learning outcomes made no direct and explicit reference to mental health although 'personal and social development' was included as an area of learning, intended to cover personal, social, moral and spiritual development, and the development of personal values and an understanding of the self and others.

The Qualifications and Curriculum Authority (which replaced SCAA) went on to establish a foundation stage for the education of children aged three to the end of the Reception year. This resulted in the *Curriculum Guidance for the Foundation Stage* (CGFS) (QCA/DfEE 2000) which became statutory guidance in 2002. The CGFS built upon the six areas of the SCAA/DfEE desirable learning outcomes and the area of personal and social development was expanded to become 'personal, social and emotional development' (PSED). Within this guidance, PSED was noted to be 'critical for very young children in all aspects of their lives and gives them the best opportunity for success in all other areas of learning.' (QCA/DfEE 2000: 28).

In *Curriculum Guidance for the Foundation Stage*, PSED was placed more centrally and critically in comparison to the preceding SCAA/DfEE desirable learning outcomes framework. In addition it was presented as the first area of learning, aiming 'for each child to become a valued member of that group and community so that a strong self-image and self-esteem are promoted' (QCA/DfEE 2000: 8). This illustrates a rise in the importance of PSED as an area of learning. In addition, concepts such as self-image and self-esteem were included in curriculum guidance; however, no theoretical base or research was drawn upon to support these key ideas.

At the same time, the guidance for *Promoting Children's Mental Health in Early Years and School Settings* does signpost readers to the *Curriculum Guidance for the Foundation Stage* and in particular to PSED. It recommends that practitioners (DfES 2001: 8):

* plan activities that promote emotional, moral, spiritual and social development alongside intellectual development;

- provid[e] support and a structured approach to achieve the successful social and
emotional development of vulnerable children and those with particular
behavioural and communication difficulties.

It would appear that the link between the curriculum and mental health promotion
was already in existence within DfES guidance, but it is unlikely that many practitioners following the *Curriculum Guidance for the Foundation Stage* were aware of
this. Although the *Curriculum Guidance for the Foundation Stage* gave more detailed
guidance for practitioners working with young children, it still maintained the focus
from the *Desirable Learning Outcomes* of the young child as a pre-schooler working
steadily through the developmental stages necessary for starting formal education at
school. Bruce (1987: 3) drawing upon Steiner, Montessori, Froebel and Bruner in
arguing against this, stated as her first principle that 'Childhood is valid in itself, not
simply a preparation for adulthood'. Whilst Bruce refers to preparation for
adulthood, Duffy (2006) argues that the Foundation Stage is seen by many practitioners as a time of preparation for later schooling.

In 2003, the *Birth to Three Matters* framework was introduced and provided
information for practitioners working with children under three on child development and effective practice to promote play and learning (Sure Start 2002). Whilst
this was not statutory guidance, early years settings had to show regard for it when
inspected by OFSTED. The *Birth to Three Matters* framework signalled a different
approach to mental health, and whilst no direct reference was made to mental health,
there was explicit use of the term 'emotional well-being'. David and her colleagues,
who conducted the literature review for the *Birth to Three Matters* framework,
drawing upon Meggitt's model of health (2001), argue that 'Mental health involves
our ability to organise our thoughts logically, and is closely linked to social and
emotional health' (David *et al.* 2002: 105). This is the first explicit link between
mental health and social and emotional development within curricula frameworks.
Up to this point, early years curricula have avoided using the term 'mental health'.

In addition, David *et al.* (2002) drew upon the work of the NICHD Early
Childhood Research Network (1996) which sought to identify the characteristics of
positive care-giving in different types of early childhood education and care (ECEC)
settings. These characteristics were compared to Galinsky *et al.*'s (1994) research on
home-based care and Howes and Hamilton's (1993) study of children in group care.
The literature review also identified risk factors for emotional well-being, including
low birth weight, parental separation and divorce, poverty and emotional abuse.

Whilst this is a more rigorous, evidence-based approach to developing a framework for practitioners, it is important to note that this research is largely American.
David *et al.* (2002) acknowledge the dominance of the theories from the industrial
and post-industrial countries within the review, and note that researchers and
policy makers are likely to be influenced by the assumptions and understandings
about babies and young children in their own context. This shows awareness and
consideration of the epistemological assumptions underpinning the research studies
that have been incorporated within the *Birth to Three Matters* framework. However,

it also highlights the use of the terms emotional well-being and mental health in both curricula documents and the supporting literature.

Mental health in the English Early Years Foundation Stage Curriculum

The Early Years Foundation Stage (EYFS), introduced in 2008 (DfES 2007), builds on the earlier approaches in the *Curriculum Guidance for the Foundation Stage* and, in particular, the *Birth to Three Matters* framework. In a similar approach to the *Birth to Three Matters* framework, the EYFS implicitly addresses mental health definition within its four principles, with one being 'Positive relationships – children learn to be strong and independent from [a] base of loving and secure relationships with parents and/or a key person' (DfES 2007: 5).

Each of the four principles (a unique child; positive relationships; enabling environments; and learning and development) of the EYFS is further broken down into four commitments describing how the principles can be put into practice. Many of the 16 commitments do make reference to parts of the DCSF (2008: 1) definition of mental health as shown by the following:

> Young children are vulnerable. They develop resilience when their physical and psychological well-being is protected by adults.
>
> (1.3 Keeping Safe)

> Children's health is an integral part of their emotional, mental, social, environmental and spiritual well-being and is supported by attention to these aspects.
>
> (1.4 Health and Well-being)

> A key person has special responsibilities for working with a small number of children, giving them the reassurance to feel safe and cared for and building relationships with their parents.
>
> (2.4 Key Person)

The EYFS makes research links for the principles and commitments in the curriculum through a CD-Rom (DCSF 2008). This includes links to the EPPE Project, the guidance on what works in promoting children's mental health and a review of international evidence of success in the area of parenting support (see Sylva *et al.* 2003; DfES 2004; Moran *et al.* 2004). There is also reference to supporting documentation and linked guidance such as the social and emotional aspects of learning (SEAL) materials, and a review of inspections by OFSTED (2005). The EYFS is currently under review (2012) and Tickell (2011) has recommended the development of a high-quality and interactive online version of the revised EYFS, with clear navigation to help people find what they are looking for .

The EYFS also addresses mental health promotion within the area of learning and development – personal, social and emotional development (PSED). The DfES

TABLE 14.1 Links between early learning goals for PSED and definition of mental health in the DfES (2001) document

Aspect of PSED	Early Learning Goals (Early Years Foundation Stage) (DfES 2007)	Definition of mental health in Promoting Children's Mental Health within Early Years and School Settings (DfES 2001)
Dispositions and attitudes	Be confident to try new activities, initiate ideas and speak in a familiar group Maintain attention, concentrate and sit quietly when appropriate	Resolve (face) problems and setbacks and learn from them
Self-confidence and self-esteem	Respond to significant experiences, showing a range of feelings when appropriate Have a developing awareness of their own needs, views and feelings, and be sensitive to the needs, views and feelings of others Have a developing respect for their own cultures and beliefs and those of other people	Develop psychologically, emotionally, intellectually and spiritually
Making relationships	Form good relationships with adults and peers Work as part of a class, taking turns and sharing fairly, understanding that there needs to be agreed values and codes of behaviour for groups of people, including adults and children, to work together harmoniously	Initiate, develop and sustain mutually satisfying personal relationships
Behaviour and self-control	Understand what is right, what is wrong, and why Consider the consequences of their words and actions for themselves and others	Develop a sense of right and wrong, become aware of others and empathise with them
Self-care	Dress and undress independently and manage their own personal hygiene Select and use activities and resources independently	Play and learn
Sense of community	Understand that people have different needs, views, cultures and beliefs that need to be treated with respect Understand that they can expect others to treat their needs, views, cultures and beliefs with respect	Become aware of others and empathise with them; initiate, develop and sustain mutually satisfying personal relationships

(2004: 1) review of what works in promoting children's mental health explicitly links mental health promotion to PSED by stating that the key Sure Start performance target for mental health promotion is 'an increase in the proportion of young children achieving normal levels of personal, social and emotional development'.

The Early Learning Goals (ELG) for PSED in the *Early Years Foundation Stage* (DfES 2007) do have a direct overlap with the definition of mental health promotion in the document *Promoting Children's Mental Health within Early Years and School Settings* (DfES 2001), as shown in Table 14.1 (above). The seven parts of the DfES (2001) definition for mental health are directly addressed by the ELG for PSED with the exception of 'using and enjoying solitude', and therefore can be seen to be a useful approach to promoting mental health in young children.

Indeed the independent review of the EYFS has recommended that personal, social and emotional development alongside communication and language and physical development are identified as prime areas of learning in the EYFS (Tickell 2011). The suggested changes to the six aspects of PSED within the EYFS to three: self-confidence and self-awareness; managing feelings and behaviour; and making relationships are closely aligned to the DfES (2001) definition of mental health. The social and emotional aspects of development (SEAD) guidance (DCSF 2008) utilises the materials within the EYFS to offer greater detail on how to promote PSED in all children. It does make brief reference to mental health but also uses terms such as 'health and well-being' and does not differentiate between the terms or show the links between them.

Emotional health and well-being

The term 'emotional health and well-being' (EHWB) is defined by the National Healthy Schools Programme guidance (DCSF/NHS 2007: 4) as incorporating:

- emotional well-being (including happiness, confidence and the opposite of depression);
- psychological well-being (including autonomy, problem solving, resilience and attentiveness/involvement);
- social well-being (good relationships with others, and the opposite of conduct disorder, delinquency, interpersonal violence and bullying).

There is recognition within this healthy schools guidance that EHWB is known by a variety of terms including emotional literacy and mental well-being and that EHWB is considered as a continuum that includes the range of mental health from mental well-being to mental ill health. The guidance also does include terms such as mental health, but this tends to be with regards to liaison with CAMHS showing a leaning towards mental health problems as discussed previously. The guidance also does incorporate key messages about the value of SEAL (social and emotional aspects of learning) and whilst it does differentiate between the SEAL and EHWB, it does clearly state that the two are closely linked and that:

It is not possible to successfully promote EHWB without helping children and young people to develop social and emotional skills, and it is not possible to teach these skills effectively unless it is in an environment which is designed to support the EHWB of all learners involved.

(DSCF and NHS 2007: 11)

The National Healthy Schools Programme guidance on EHWB has a section on early years and how the guidance links with the EYFS. Whilst this section does make reference to the educational programme for PSED, the links to mental health are again implicit rather than explicitly stated.

Why is mental health indirectly referred to in the Early Years Foundation Stage curriculum?

Whilst there are limited explicit references to mental health in the EYFS, the principles and commitments of the EYFS reflect similarities to the definitions by the NHS Health Advisory Service (1995) and DfES (2001). This can be interpreted in a number of ways:

* mental health promotion was overlooked as a specific item;
* mental health promotion is implicit in the EYFS documentation and as a result does not need to be explicitly included; or
* mental health promotion is not considered an appropriate term to use in the curriculum.

The way mental health is conceptualised in the EYFS would appear to reflect a view that mental health promotion should not be explicitly linked to young children and their practitioners in these terms, but instead should be referred to using other terms such as emotional well-being and through the underpinning philosophical approach. The principles are stated in the EYFS Statutory Framework to guide the work of all early years practitioners (DfES 2007) and the commitments demonstrate how the principles can link to practice. However, this indirect approach would appear to conflict with the EPPE findings that practitioners in high-quality settings need to have good knowledge of the curriculum and how children learn. A practitioner can have good knowledge of the curriculum but yet may be unaware, given the implicit nature of the message, that they can and should play a vital role in promoting children's mental health.

Conclusion

The EYFS presents a golden opportunity for practitioners to link together information, provided via the media, research and the government, concerning the increased incidence of mental health problems and the value practitioners can offer in supporting children under five in promoting children's mental health. This opportunity is not altogether lost if those supporting the implementation of the EYFS realise this link, and support practitioners in both their practice and understanding of the central importance of their role in promoting young children's mental health, and how this directly links to supporting young children's development in personal, social and emotional development.

QUESTIONS FOR THINKING ABOUT POLICY AND PRACTICE

1. Are the terms emotional well-being and mental health the same or different?
2. What can be done to promote children's mental health in the early years?
3. Can the curriculum be used as a universal tool to promote children's mental health? Or is it the responsibility of the family alone?

References

British Medical Association (BMA) (2006) *Child and Adolescent Mental Health: A Guide for Healthcare Professionals*, available online at: www.bma.org.uk (accessed 10 April 2011).

Bruce, T. (1987) *Early Childhood Education*, London: Hodder & Stoughton.

David, T., Goouch, K., Powell, S. and Abbott, L. (2002) *Birth to Three Matters: A Review of the Literature Compiled to Inform the Framework to Support Children in their Earliest Years*, Nottingham: DfES Publications, available online at: www.education.gov.uk/publications/eOrderingDownload/RR444.pdf (accessed 16 August 2011).

DCSF (2008) *Social and Emotional Aspects of Development*, Nottingham: DCSF Publications.

DCSF and NHS (2007) *Guidance for Schools on Developing Emotional Health and Well-Being*, Wetherby, Yorkshire: National Healthy Schools Programme.

DfES (2001) *Promoting Children's Mental Health within Early Years and School Settings*, Nottingham: DfES Publications.

DfES (2004) *What Works in Promoting Children's Mental Health*, Nottingham: DfES Publications.

DfES (2007) *The Early Years Foundation Stage: Setting the Standards for Learning, Development and Care for Children from Birth to Five*, Nottingham: DfES Publications.

Duffy, B. (2006) The curriculum from birth to six, in G. Pugh and B. Duffy (eds) *Contemporary Issues in the Early Years*, 4th edn, London: Sage Publications.

Galinsky, E., Howes, C., Kontos, S. and Shinn, M. (1994) *The Study of Children in Family Child Care and Relative Care*, New York: Families and Work Institute.

Howes, C. and Hamilton, C.E. (1993) Child care for young children, in B. Spodek and O. Saracho (eds) *Yearbook in Early Childhood Education, Vol. 3, Issues in Child Care*, New York: Teachers College Press.

Kay, H. (1999) *Bright Futures: Promoting Children and Young People's Mental Health*, London: Mental Health Foundation.

Layard, R. and Dunn, J. (2009) *A Good Childhood: Searching for Values in a Competitive Age*, London: Penguin Books.

Lazar, I., Darlington, R., Murray, H., Royce, J. and Snipper, A. (1982) *Lasting Effects of Early Education: A Report from the Consortium for Longitudinal Studies*, Monographs of the Society for Research in Child Development, 47 (2–3, serial number 195).

Meggitt, C. (2001) *Baby and Child Health*, Oxford: Heinemann Educational Publishers.

Moran, P., Ghate, D. and van der Merwe, A. (2004) *What Works in Parenting Support: A Review of the International Evidence*, Nottingham: DfES Publications.

NHS Health Advisory Service (1995) *Together We Stand: The Commissioning, Role and Management of Child and Adolescent Mental Health Services*, London: HMSO.

NICHD Early Childhood Research Network (1996) Characteristics of infant child care: factors contributing to positive care giving, *Early Childhood Research Quarterly*, 11(3): 296–306.

OFSTED (2005) *Firm Foundations*, available online at: www.ofsted.gov.uk (accessed 11 April 2011).

QCA/DfEE (2000) *Curriculum Guidance for the Foundation Stage*, London: QCA/DfEE.

Sammons, P., Sylva, K., Melhuish, E. C., Siraj-Blatchford, I., Taggart, B. and Elliot, K. (2002) *The Effective Provision of Pre-school Education (EPPE) Project: Technical Paper 8b – Measuring the Impact of Pre-school on Children's Social/Behavioural Development over the Pre-school Period*, London: DfES/Institute of Education, University of London.

SCAA/DfEE (1996) *Nursery Education: Desirable Outcomes for Children's Learning on Entering Compulsory Education*, London: HMSO

Schweinhart, L.J. and Weikart, D.P. (1989) The High/Scope Perry Pre-school Study: Implications for early childhood care and education, *Prevention in Human Services*, 7: 109–132.

Sure Start (2002) *Birth to Three Matters: A Framework to Support Children in their Earliest Years*, Nottingham: DfES Publications.

Sylva, K., Melhuish, E., Sammons, P., Siraj-Blatchford, I., Taggart, B. and Elliot, K. (2003) *The Effective Provision of Pre-school Education (EPPE) Project: Findings from the Pre-school Period, Summary of Findings*, London: EPPE Publications.

The Children's Society (2009) *The Good Childhood Inquiry*, available online at: www.childrenssociety.org.uk/what-we-do/research/good-childhood-inquiry (accessed 16 August 2011).

Tickell, C. (2011) *The Early Years: Foundations for Life, Health and Learning: An Independent Report on the Early Years Foundation Stage to Her Majesty's Government*, available online at: www.education.gov.uk (accessed 11 April 2011).

Weissberg, R. (2007) Social and emotional learning for student success, Paper presented at the CASEL Forum: Educating All Children for Social, Emotional, and Academic Excellence: From Knowledge to Action, 10 December.

Weissberg, R., Caplan, M. and Harwood, R. (1991) Promoting competent young people in competence enhancing environments: a systems-based perspective on primary prevention, *Journal of Consulting and Clinical Psychology*, 59(6): 830–841

Woodhead, M. (1988) When psychology informs public policy: the case for early childhood intervention, *American Psychologist*, 43(6): 443–454

15

ENGAGING 'HARD-TO-REACH' FAMILIES

A view from the literature

Gill Boag-Munroe

OVERVIEW

This chapter discusses findings from a systematic review of the literature on engaging hard-to-reach families, and suggests areas which might fruitfully be explored in order to make settings more attractive to those who currently feel inhibited or deterred from accessing the facilities they offer. In the course of conducting the review, it was noted that comparatively little work appears to have been done to try to understand how curriculum, setting, pedagogy and policy direction in the field of early childhood care and education (ECCE) might invite, inhibit or deter families from accessing educational facilities which may often have been established with the intention of supporting hard-to-reach families. Drawing on findings from the National Evaluation of the Early Learning Partnership Project (NEELPP) and on a nascent project by Georgeson and Boag-Munroe (see Chapter 17), I point to ways that services working with families understand how they might be hard-to-reach, and how they have gone about attracting families into service provision.

Key words: Hard-to-engage families; early childhood care and education; 'architexture'.

Introduction: policy context

From 1997, under the New Labour government, there was a steady shift in UK policy direction in early childhood care and education (ECCE), with a convergence of two stated aims: the need to improve the life chances of children perceived to be disadvantaged by their family circumstances and the desire to lift families out of poverty. Citing the National Audit Office (2007), Lewis (2011: 75) stated that:

> The greatest emphasis was put on the need to provide integrated childcare and early years education, and to reach the most disadvantaged, hard-to-reach parents – both aims being strongly associated with the concern to promote adult employment and to address the issue of workless families, which are disproportionately numerous in the UK compared to other EU Member States.

Both these agendas are premised on the desirability of ensuring the employability of mothers and future generations in order to reduce dependence on state benefits: hence the increasing influence on local policy agendas from international organisations such as the Organisation for Economic Co-operation and Development (OECD) and the World Bank, which has loaned over £1bn for the support of childcare programmes (Dahlberg and Moss 2005).

Dahlberg and Moss (2005: 5) additionally argue that the purpose of investment in childcare is to 'secure both social order and economic success', by drawing very young children into straitjackets of assessment and standardisation, and enculturating them in regimes of truth and governmentality; that is, understandings about how society works to ensure that those children will accept and perpetuate the dominant culture and ideology of capitalism. What appears to be lacking in current education policy (2012) is an ethical dimension (Dahlberg and Moss 2005), or an idea of the 'common good and public morality' found in the concepts of the French *l'éducation* or the Russian *vospitanie* (Alexander 2009), which understand family and school to be jointly responsible for the upbringing and education of children, rather than creating a division of labour in which families focus on upbringing and schools focus on education.

These government agendas appear to be structured on seemingly incompatible or contradictory ideas. Three in particular stand out, as Pugh and Duffy (2006) point out: first, there is a dichotomy of the perceived need to get parents back to work, and the understanding of parents as the main educators of children in their early years; second, the personalised learning agenda in schools may be in tension with the universalistic, technicist 'what works' agenda, which suggests that what works for one person or group can be universally applied; third, the apparent desire of policy makers to offer choice and create flexible, open-minded and life-long learners appears to conflict with the same 'what works' agenda, which applies prescribed codes and aims for closure and reduction of choice. The consequences of these agendas for those working in the ECCE sector have been not only an emphasis on increasing professionalism, but also on increased regulation, and its concomitant compliance.

Further, these policies presuppose a parental desire to participate in programmes for families with children in the early years. Whilst this may be true for many families, there are nonetheless those who remain on the margins of participation, or completely outside the services offered. Such families may be understood as 'hard-to-reach' or 'hard-to-engage'. Both groups have been discussed in the full literature review (Boag-Munroe and Evangelou 2010). For the purposes of this chapter, I focus only on those we designated 'hard-to-engage' families.

Reaching the 'hard-to-engage'

There are two broad categories of families who might be understood as 'hard-to-engage': those who might be isolated; and those who are disengaged from service intervention for reasons of lack of knowledge or interest, wariness, disenchantment, or lack of will to engage. How organisations are structured, organised and operate might also be erecting barriers which inhibit the engagement of these groups (Boag-Munroe and Evangelou 2010).

Families who are physically isolated, such as those living in rural areas and others who are culturally or socially isolated, such as refugees, asylum seekers and travellers are dealt with at some length in the literature (Katz *et al.* 2007; Barrett 2008). Similarly, peripatetic families – who may be isolated less by stigma or fear than by the nature of their lifestyle which inhibits prolonged engagement with services – have also been the focus of considerable research. These families tend to be well targeted by services and evidence from other work shows an awareness of the availability of these services with which the early childhood practitioners and family services are willing to liaise (Evangelou *et al.* 2008).

Other families isolated by their lifestyle are dealt with in limited ways in the literature; for example, faith-based families and families with a gambling addiction (Brackertz 2007b). Additional groups who may prefer to remain invisible include those where there is drug, alcohol or substance abuse, as they may fear the stigma attached to what they do, or be unwilling to acknowledge their behaviours. Similarly, sex workers are understood to be particularly hard-to-reach because acknowledgement of belonging to this group is seen as threatening; 'outsiders' are mistrusted for fear that they will reveal identities of workers. The lifestyle of children from such families may be so different from that of other children in their setting that they find it difficult to access the discourses and models or social conventions used in the setting.

Brackertz (2007b) and Crowley (2005) draw attention to gay and lesbian parents as a minority, potentially isolated group who may choose to hide if they are afraid of drawing attention to themselves and their needs. Although no specific strategies are offered for reaching such families, clearly many of those used to reach and engage other isolated families might be successful. For example, services need to become conscious of the language and family modelling that they use, so that children from less conventional families feel included.

A range of means by which services become aware of the existence of these groups and how they might reach and engage them is pointed to in the literature. The snowball or chain referral technique as a means to make the families visible is suggested by many researchers (Faugier and Sargeant 1997; Heckathorn 1997; Atkinson and Flint 2001; Penrod *et al.* 2003; Sheldon 2003; Brackertz 2007a; Emmel *et al.* 2007; Coe *et al.* 2008); the use of interpreters and designated workers for outreach is recommended by others (Garbers *et al.* 2006; Coe *et al.* 2008); and the need for integrated, holistic, tailored and consistent services for these families is highlighted by Statham (2004).

Statham (2004) believes that there is no simple way to engage such families. Agencies and services need to work together in sophisticated ways to provide a sustained, holistic service that families want and which is non-stigmatising and practical. Parents need to be able to discuss their own problems with practitioners who are willing to listen and respond to individuals rather than generic issues. Repeated attempts to reach and then sustain involvement with all these families are emphasised by Faugier and Sargeant (1997) and Benoit *et al.* (2005). Linked services in reaching the hard-to-reach and the provision of appropriate buildings in which families might engage are supported by NESS (2005). Buildings should be in the local community and, if not specially built for working with families, at least familiar and comfortable to them. Multi-agency communication and cohesion of approach are understood to be vital for these families (Evangelou *et al.* 2008).

There are, though, families who, even when they know about services, for a variety of reasons fear involvement because their lives may be unconventional and socially stigmatised. Families might also be unaware of the service because it is invisible to them or because they have insufficient information about it to fully understand what it does. Korfmacher *et al.* (2008) point out that families will not be involved with programmes which are unresponsive to their needs, interests or beliefs. Engaging these groups requires time, initiative and sensitivity on the part of the service aiming to reach them. Landy and Menna (2006: 180) suggest that 'working effectively with families who might be labelled 'hard-to-reach' involves a shift from perceiving the family as being hard-to-reach to thinking about what makes the service that is being offered hard to accept for a particular family'. Working with such families 'involves a shift from providing information to listening and knowing how to respond to particular behaviours' (Landy and Menna 2006: 180). Crozier and Davies (2007) point to how schools render parents invisible by their inaccurate conceptualisation of their needs, suggesting that engagement may, in fact, be inhibited by the quality of the service or with the service's regime of truth – that is, with the design or ethos of the setting or the curriculum on offer – rather than with the families. This issue is one which researchers frequently point to in their recommendations for improved engagement. Many suggest that it is relatively easy for services to raise their profile in the community and improve dissemination of information about themselves by distributing leaflets door to door in appropriately targeted communities, in libraries and in GP surgeries. Statham (2004) suggests that agencies might co-operate with each other to make better use of the data they hold in order to ensure that families know of the services' existence, have adequate information about the work they do, and are prevented from slipping through the net. Several authors suggest going out into communities as a means of increasing awareness of the services' work (Sheldon 2003; Hourihan and Hoban 2004; Statham 2004; Glennie *et al.* 2005; NESS 2005; Bryant *et al.* 2006; Garbers *et al.* 2006, Coe *et al.* 2008).

Some authors emphasise the importance of paraprofessionals, or community gatekeepers; that is, voluntary community services (VCS), statutory services and those in the community who have no formal role but who nonetheless assist in engaging families (Jack *et al.* 2002; Curtis *et al.* 2004; Emmel *et al.* 2007). Although many services have already understood how useful health visitors are in referring families to them, it may be that other services and agencies view their relationships anew through the lens of the marketplace to find people or routes they could successfully exploit as conduits for contact between family and service (De la Cuesta 1994).

Families who are disengaged for lack of motivation may present more of a challenge, as they will not be involved with programmes which are unresponsive to their interests, needs or beliefs (Korfmacher *et al.* 2008). As with other families, therefore, services need time to give careful attention to the needs of those who are disinterested in order to match the service to the requirements of the family. Such families may need to be gradually drawn in to the service through informal contact such as fun days, or by offering inducements such as transport, crèche facilities; or befrienders, who effectively act as parent ambassadors (Avis *et al.* 2006; Garbers *et al.* 2006). It is additionally recommended that parents are drawn into networks so that they feel part of something and are more motivated to engage (Avis *et al.* 2006). This may be particularly important in the case of early childhood settings so that parents and children feel that they 'belong' there. The NESS study (2005) found that families wanted friendly and relaxed staff that they could trust, located in appropriate buildings which met the needs of the family. In particular, certain aspects of the setting may need to be considered in order to create an environment which makes potential users feel comfortable (Boag-Munroe and Georgeson 2008).

There are families who lack the will to engage with services through passive disengagement, service resistance, refusal to co-operate or incompatibility with the service or staff (Doherty *et al.* 2003, 2004). It is recommended that practitioners increase visibility, perhaps, by shifting the locus of provision to reduce spatial distance between provider and user in order to identify what makes the families unwilling to engage and develop new strategies to overcome that unwillingness (Doherty *et al.* 2003, 2004). The site of delivery of the service and configuration of the service team are considered important factors in engaging the hard-to-reach, though services and agencies might overcome resistance to services by blurring agency identities and agency specific roles (Doherty *et al.* 2003). Practitioners might overcome resistance by addressing the fears and negativity of the families and aiming to resolve differences in opinion between service and user (Barnes *et al.* 2006).

In the same way, engagement with families who are disenchanted with services – for reasons which might include expectations not being met in the past; non-materialisation of anticipated services; negative prior experience of being involved with services; or weariness of new initiatives – might be made through time-intensive relationship-building approaches (Statham 2004; Landy and Menna 2006). Services which may already be aware of the needs of these families but are experiencing difficulty in meeting these needs, are cautioned to avoid promising what they cannot offer. Barnes *et al.* (2006) make the seemingly obvious point that in order to engage these families, those issues which turned them off the service need to be addressed before further work with them can take place. Statham (2004) and NESS (2005) suggest that initial contact might be made with these families through outreach work or referrals from other agencies to draw them in to a one-stop service which is holistic, meets the practical needs of the family and allows them space to discuss their concerns (Landy et al. 2006).

Organisational barriers to access

Dissonances of cultural and language understandings may inhibit contact between families and service. In addition to awareness of ways that families and communities engage with services that may be perceived to have power, status and authority, sensitivity to how cultural messages are conveyed not only in words, but also in dress, etiquette, scripts and routines is important, particularly in work with refugees and asylum seekers, who may need vital help from services but fear the consequences of being formally engaged with them (Milbourne 2002; Statham 2004; Glennie et al. 2005; NESS 2005; Landy and Menna 2006).

Several authors suggest innovation in contacting parents who are isolated by their limited English or low literacy skills (Avis et al. 2006; Landy and Menna 2006), while others draw attention to the alienating effect of professional jargon with families who may not understand it, pointing to the need for a language which families and services share (Milbourne 2002; Avis et al. 2006; Landy and Menna 2006; Devaney 2008). The importance of shared language among the services, alongside shared understandings and practices, cannot be underestimated (Doherty et al. 2003, 2004).

Ethos and regimes of truth within early childhood settings may also be alienating factors for families. These may be evidenced in the discourses in use, or in the design and presentation of the setting, or in the programmes and curricula in use in the service. Barnes et al. (2006) and Landy and Menna (2006) draw attention to how some settings seem to create an unwelcoming atmosphere for families, though they do not offer any strategies for overcoming this. They do, however, suggest consideration of how welcoming the setting is by being culturally aware and by avoiding officialdom in the early stages of contact. If practitioners adopt a non-judgmental, friendly and relaxed stance, families may feel more comfortable in settings and trust staff (Landy and Menna 2006; NESS 2005). Reception staff, who help to create the first impression that families have of a service, are particularly important (Chand and Thoburn 2005).

If a service is located in an inappropriate venue, families are unlikely to use it (Avis et al. 2006). Services need to be located where families can access them (Glennie et al. 2005) and in appropriate purpose-built buildings meeting families' needs (NESS 2005). The design and atmosphere of the building can affect families' response to a service (Ball and Niven 2005) or alienate potential users through their choices of colour, contents, layout and signing (discussed further in Chapter 17). The importance of the cleanliness of the setting and the alienating effect of perceived 'cliquiness' in a setting are highlighted by Avis et al. (2006).

Some writers draw attention to how settings or services might be understood as stigmatised, or stigmatising, though none offers suggestions for overcoming the problem (Doherty *et al.* 2003; Glennie *et al.* 2005; Avis *et al.* 2006 and Barnes *et al.* 2006). Appropriate location of services might contribute to their success. For example, an early childhood group which is located on a busy high street, below a women's shelter and next door to a brothel might expect to be stigmatised, but the courage of selecting this location is, perhaps, the reason behind its success (Boag-Munroe and Georgeson 2008).

A final cluster of organisational barriers to access relates to the quality of service offered. In some cases, these barriers might be overcome through self-reflection which leads to change; in other cases, the service may be unable to remedy the situation itself. Barriers noted include lack of effort (Barnes *et al.* 2006), inconsistency of approach (Devaney 2008), perceived lack of resources (Barnes *et al.* 2006), poor quality of service (NESS 2005; Barnes *et al.* 2006); and high staff turnover for some services (Devaney 2008). Once again, this may be an issue for some introspection on the part of the service to identify reasons for the high turnover, but where funding is the problem, the service may have limited options for action.

Lack of common understandings or practices among linked organisations is a further barrier for some parents who become weary of repeatedly explaining themselves and their problems. If services are to make holistic provision for families, it is essential that they develop common practices and shared scripts (Doherty *et al.* 2003, 2004; Statham 2004; Barrett 2008; Evangelou *et al.* 2008).

Conclusion

Many of the factors which appear to impede engagement can be relatively quickly and inexpensively addressed. Others such as problems caused by alienating attitudes or unwelcoming buildings take time and money to remedy. The key is to be aware of what the problems are in the first place. Careful consideration of language use – including multi-modal signs and symbols taken for granted in settings – and its effect on target families is important. Early childhood professionals need also to frequently re-evaluate the social values, cultures and ways of being that are expressed and afforded in their setting and curriculum to ensure that they are matching their offer to the needs and aspirations of those they wish to reach. The development of a shared language not just between agencies, but with the families with whom they are working, is vital, but takes time.

Time is the most vital resource that a setting needs for working with families. Unless policy makers acknowledge this, and allocate both space and time for work with the hard-to-reach, few of the policy initiative programmes are likely to have the success that all within the community of practice of early childhood care and education desire.

QUESTIONS FOR THINKING ABOUT POLICY AND PRACTICE

1. What steps is your institution taking to align its offer with those it most wishes to engage?
2. What arrangements are in place within your organisation for cycles of review of practice to ensure that you continue to make the best contact with families?
3. How far is your organisation attuned to, and working in alignment with, other organisations who are reaching out to the same families?

References

Alexander, R. (2009) Pedagogy, culture and the power of comparison, in H. Daniels, H. Lauder and J. Porter (eds) *Educational Theories, Cultures and Learning: A Critical Perspective*, London: Routledge.

Atkinson, R. and Flint, J. (2001) Accessing hidden and hard to reach populations: Snowball research strategies, *Social Research Update*, Issue 33, available online at: http://sru.soc.surrey.ac.uk/SRU33.html (accessed 26 May 2011).

Avis, M., Bulman, D. and Leighton, P. (2006) Factors affecting participation in Sure Start programmes: A qualitative investigation of parents' views, *Health and Social Care in the Community*, 15(3): 203–211.

Ball, M. and Niven, L. (2005) *Buildings in Sure Start Local Programmes*, Nottingham: DfES Publications.

Barnes, J., McPherson, K. and Senior, R. (2006) Factors influencing the acceptance of volunteer home-visiting support to families with new babies, *Child and Family Social Work*, 11(2): 107–117.

Barrett, H. (2008) *'Hard-to-Reach' Families: Engagement in the Voluntary and Community Sector*, London: Family And Parenting Institute.

Benoit, C., Jansson, M., Millar, A. and Phillips, R. (2005) Community academic research on hard to reach populations: Benefits and challenges, *Qualitative Health Research*, 15(2): 263–282.

Boag-Munroe, G. and Evangelou, M. (2010) From hard to reach to how to reach: A systematic review of the literature on hard-to-reach families, *Research Papers in Education*, September (iFirst), available online at: http://dx.doi.org/10.1080/02671522.2010.509515 (accessed 29 August 2011).

Boag-Munroe, G. and Georgeson, J. (2008) Spatial semiotics of early years settings and the kinds of identity they might construct, Paper to accompany poster presented at the First UK and Ireland ISCAR Conference, Bath, July; and at ISCAR, San Diego, September.

Brackertz, N. (2007a) Who is Hard-to-Reach and why? ISR Working Paper, available online at: http://hdl.handle.net/1959.3/23213 (accessed 11 April 2011).

Brackertz, N. (2007b) *Community Consultation and the 'Hard to Reach': City of Maribyrnong Case Study Report*, Delivered Meals Consultation, available online at: http://sisr.net/flagships/democracy/projects/community.htm (accessed 23 February 2012).

Bryant, W.K., Ompad, D.C., Sisco, S., Blaney, S., Gidden, K., Phillips, E., Vlahov, D. and Galea, S. (2006) Determinants of influenza vaccination in hard-to-reach urban populations, *Preventive Medicine*, 43(1): 60–70.

Chand, A. and Thoburn, J. (2005) Research review: Child and family support services with minority ethnic families: What can we learn from research?, *Child and Family Social Work*, 10(2): 169–178.

Coe, C., Gibson, A., Spencer, N. and Stuttaford, M. (2008) Sure Start: Voices of the hard-to-reach, *Child: Care, Health and Development*, 34(4): 447–453.

Crowley, M. (2005) Working with parents, in R. Chambers and K. Licence (eds) *Looking after Children in Primary Care: A Companion to the Children's NSF*, Oxford: Radcliffe Publishing.

Crozier, G. and Davies, J. (2007) 'Hard-to-reach parents or hard-to-reach schools? A discussion of home-school relations with particular reference to Bangladeshi and Pakistani parents, *British Educational Research Journal*, 33(3): 295–313.

Curtis, K., Roberts, H., Copperman, J., Downie, A. and Liabo, K. (2004) 'How come I don't get asked no questions?' Researching 'hard to reach' children and teenagers, *Children and Family Social Work*, 9(2): 167–175.

Dahlberg, G. and Moss, P. (2005) *Ethics and Politics in Early Childhood*, London: RoutledgeFalmer.

De la Cuesta, C. (1994) Relationships in health visiting: Enabling and mediating, *International Journal of Nursing Studies*, 31(5): 451–459.

Devaney, J. (2008) Interprofessional working in child protection with families with long term and complex needs, *Child Abuse Review*, 17(4): 242–261.

Doherty, P., Hall, M. and Kinder, K. (2003) *On Track Thematic Report: Assessment, Referral and Hard to Reach Groups*, London: DfES.

Doherty, P., Stott, A. and Kinder, K. (2004) *Delivering Services to Hard-to-Reach Families in the On Track Areas: Definition, Consultation and Needs Assessment*, London: Home Office.

Emmel, N., Hughes, K., Greenhalgh, J. and Sales, A. (2007) Accessing socially excluded people: Trust and the gatekeeper in the researcher participant relationship, *Sociological Research On Line*, available online at: www.socresonline.org.uk/12/2/emmel.html (accessed 23 February 2012).

Evangelou, M. and Boag-Munroe, G. (2009) 'A systematic review of the literature on how hard-to-reach families might be engaged to reduce social exclusion, *British Educational Research Association (BERA) Research Intelligence*, 108 (August).

Evangelou, M., Sylva, K., Edwards, A. and Smith, T. (2008) *Supporting Parents in Promoting Early Learning: The Evaluation of the Early Learning Partnership Project*, Report Number DCSF-RR039, Nottingham: DCSF, available online at: www.dcsf.gov.uk/research (accessed 26 May 2011).

Faugier, J. and Sargeant, M. (1997) Sampling hard to reach populations, *Journal of Advanced Nursing*, 26(4): 790–797.

Garbers, C., Tunstill, J., Allnock, D. and Akhurst, S. (2006) Facilitating access to services for children and families: Lessons from Sure Start local programmes, *Child and Family Social Work*, 11(4): 287–296.

Glennie, S., Treseder, G., Williams, J. and Williams, M. (2005) *Mini Sure Start Local Programmes: An Overview of their Early Implementation*, London: DfES.

Heckathorn, B.D. (1997) Respondent-driven sampling: A new approach to the study of hidden populations, *Social Problems*, 44(2): 174–199.

Hourihan, F. and Hoban, D. (2004) Learning, enjoying, growing, support model: An innovative collaborative approach to the prevention of conduct disorder in pre-schoolers in hard to reach rural families, *Australian Journal of Rural Health*, 12(6): 269–276.

Jack, S., Dicenso, A. and Lonfeld, L. (2002) Opening doors: Factors influencing the establishment of a working relationship between paraprofessional home visitors and at risk families, *Canadian Journal of Nursing Research*, 34(4): 59–69.

Katz, I., La Placa, V. and Hunter, S. (2007) *Barriers to Inclusion and Successful Engagement of Parents in Mainstream Services*, York: Joseph Rowntree Foundation.

Korfmacher, J., Gree, B., Staerkel, F., Peterson, C., Cook, G., Roggman, L., Faldowski, R.A. and Schiffman, R. (2008) Parental involvement in early childhood home visiting, *Child Youth Care Forum*, 37(4): 171–196.

Landy, S. and Menna, R. (2006) *Early Intervention with Multi-Risk Families: An Integrative Approach*, Baltimore, MD: Paul H. Brookes Publishing Company.

Lewis, J. (2011) From Sure Start to Children's Centres: An analysis of policy change in English early years programmes, *Journal of Social Policy*, 40(1): 71–88.

Milbourne, L. (2002) Unspoken exclusion: Experiences of continued marginalisation from education among 'Hard to Reach' adults and children in the UK, *British Journal of Sociology of Education*, 23(2): 287–305.

NAO (National Audit Office) (2007) *Helping People from Workless Households into Work*, HC609, London: The Stationery Office.

National Evaluation of Sure Start Programmes (NESS) (2005) *Implementing Sure Start Local Programmes: An In-Depth Study*, Nottingham: DfES.

Penrod, J., Preston, D.B., Cain, R.E. and Starks, M.T. (2003) A discussion of chain referral as a method of sampling Hard-to-Reach populations, *Journal of Transcultural Nursing*, 14(2): 100–107.

Pugh, G. and Duffy, B. (eds) (2006) *Contemporary Issues in the Early Years*, 4th edn, London: Sage Publications.

Sheldon, S.B. (2003) Linking school–family–community partnerships in urban elementary schools to student achievement on state tests, *The Urban Review*, 35(2): 149–165.

Statham, J. (2004) Effective services to support children in special circumstances, *Child: Care, Health and Development*, 30(6): 589–598.

16

A RELATIONAL PEDAGOGY IN COMMUNITY-BASED EARLY CHILDHOOD DEVELOPMENT IN SOUTH AFRICA

Peter Rule

OVERVIEW

The community-based model of early childhood development (ECD) pays attention to the family and the child through active involvement of the community. Family facilitators are responsible for interventions with poor and vulnerable young children and their families in their lived context. The chapter sheds light on such an intervention developed by the Little Elephant Training Centre for Early Education (LETCEE). A relational pedagogy is illuminated through the practices of the family facilitators *with* and *for* the children. This involves family facilitators mediating the boundary between school, on the one hand, and family and community, on the other. The chapter draws on notions of dialogue and boundary learning from Mikhail Bakhtin and Paulo Freire.

Key words: Community-based; family facilitators; relational pedagogy.

Introduction

The notion of relational pedagogy within early childhood development is at the heart of this chapter. More specifically, the place of dialogue and dialogic space within relational pedagogy is developed with reference to a South African case. My particular interest is a community-based pedagogy for poor and vulnerable young children who do not have access to early education centres. The chapter begins by outlining the organisational, socio–economic and policy contexts of the research. It then provides a conceptual framework, drawing on notions of relational pedagogy, dialogue and dialogic space. These ideas frame the chapter's exploration of pedagogic practices within the *Siyabathanda Abantwana* programme.

The *Siyabathanda Abantwana* (We Cherish the Children) programme is run by the Little Elephant Training Centre for Early Education (LETCEE) in partnership with the community of Matimatolo. The LETCEE is a non-governmental organisation (NGO) based in Greytown in the KwaZulu-Natal Midlands. It specialises in the training of ECD educators and ECD community work with poor and vulnerable young children in several of the surrounding rural communities.

Matimatolo is a rural community approximately 20km from Greytown (Figure 16.1). It is characterised by subsistence agriculture, high levels of poverty, the absence of young men and women who work in the cities, and dependence on government pensions and child-support grants. These characteristics make it typical of rural communities in KwaZulu-Natal. It is governed locally by elected ward councillors who sit on the Greytown municipal council as well as by traditional authority structures, including a chief *induna* (chief headman) and a traditional council of *izinduna* (headmen).

Although there is some evidence that HIV prevalence in South Africa is stabilising at around 10.9 per cent and incidence declining somewhat from levels in the early 2000s, KwaZulu-Natal remains the province with highest prevalence (15.8 per cent) with a particularly high prevalence among women attending ante-natal clinics (38.7 per cent) (Department of Health 2009). In KwaZulu-Natal, prevalence among children 2–14 years old is 2.8 per cent and among young people 15–24 years old it is 15.3 per cent. Whereas HIV prevalence in most provinces has stabilised or declined, it has increased in KwaZulu-Natal in the 25+ age group from 14.9 per cent in 2002 to 23.5 per cent in 2008 (HSRC 2009). What this means for early childhood development in the province is that a significant number of young children are infected with HIV, and an even greater number are affected through

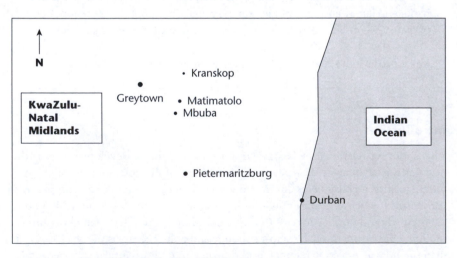

FIGURE 16.1 Map of KwaZulu-Natal Midlands

the illness or mortality of their caregivers, resulting in an increase in the number of AIDS orphans and child-headed households.

A number of additional factors exacerbate the position of young children in KwaZulu-Natal, particularly in rural areas. The national unemployment rate stands officially at 24.3 per cent, but in KwaZulu-Natal, only 36.7 per cent of the working-age population are actually employed (Statistics South Africa 2009), with others described as 'economically inactive'. Poverty is another debilitating factor: approximately 26 per cent of the South African population lives on less than US$2 per day, with 11 per cent living on less than US$1 per day (UNESCO 2010). Pre-school educational provision reaches only 16.9 per cent of children in the age group 0–4 (Statistics South Africa 2008).

The following extracts from interviews and focus groups in Matimatolo and the neighbouring Mbuba area illustrate some of the key contextual issues that confront children growing up in the area (Rule *et al.* 2008: 2):

> Some parents go to the city and never come back. Most of the time they come back when they are sick; the grandmother is the one who does everything for that person.
>
> (Project co-ordinator A)

> The main thing that this community needs is education and there are so many guys here that do not work, they do not even finish Std 10 [equivalent to year 12 in the English system], so they do not have an education. Many, many people here die of AIDS and so more children are not getting an education so things might get a lot worse.
>
> (Clinic support officer)

> Close to where I live there are children who head their own household. I usually go there to keep an eye on them. Most of the time there is no food. I help them with some food. I am unemployed. My husband passed away. Sometimes I also have a problem with food.
>
> (Focus group: Caregivers A)

> My son made another girl pregnant and she dropped the child Amanda at my home. I can't get a birth certificate and get a child-support grant.
>
> (Focus group: Caregivers B)

> Some of the children are physically challenged, locked up inside for the whole day, do not even get any fresh air, don't ever go outside for fresh air, the parents are embarrassed about their having disabled children.
>
> (Focus group: Sikhulakahle Intervention Committee)

Over the last few years in South Africa, there has been an increase in interest concerning policy for poor and vulnerable young children, and the development of appropriate models to meet the needs of children who are not reached by centre-based provision. This has taken the form, *inter alia*, of *White Paper Five on Early Childhood Education* (Department of Education 2001), which sets up a national system of Grade R (Reception year) provision for five-year-olds; a National Integrated Plan for Early Childhood Development (UNICEF 2005) which articulates the government's intention to develop an integrated system of service delivery. There is recognition that all children cannot access centre-based provisioning, and that interventions at the level of family and community are crucial (Ebrahim 2010). Recent research commissioned by UNICEF explored a number of models of provision for poor and vulnerable young children in the 0–4 age group (see Ebrahim *et al.* 2010), including the *Siyabathanda Abantwana* project which is the focus of this chapter.

Purpose of the *Siyabathanda Abantwana* project

The overall purpose of the *Siyabathanda Abantwana* project is to provide poor and vulnerable young children with a springboard to education and development opportunities (LETCEE Director 2008). This evolved from an initial purpose of taking ECD opportunities to vulnerable children in their communities, to a more holistic conception of changing the lives of vulnerable children within those communities, including not only early education but also care, documentation, nutrition, health, protection, and emotional well-being.

The model fully appreciates the reality that a child is a part of a larger system and if the family system is in distress, or is rendered vulnerable due to a complex set of circumstances, real help to the child is only possible if the caregivers become more empowered, participate more and are supported and affirmed in their caregiving roles: in such cases 'help for the child needs to include some form of help for his parents' (Campion 1992: 5).

Thus a key purpose of the project is to build the resilience of poor and vulnerable young children by working to empower both them and their caregivers: 'To build resilience among children building on what they have, strengthening relationships in the home by being there and being available' (LETCEE Director 2008). An important aspect of this approach is 'building on what they have', rather than adopting a deficit model which sees children and caregivers as 'having nothing'. The programme recognises that even poor homes have cultural, human and material resources which, if supported, can play a crucial role in the development of the child. This understanding is crucial to the attitude of the family facilitator, who develops a relationship of support and reciprocity with the caregiver.

A final purpose arising from those above is to mobilise the community for early childhood development and to develop the awareness of the community of children's needs and rights. Again, this purpose reflects the understanding that children grow up within the wider context of the community, and their upbringing is crucially informed by attitudes and practices towards children in the community.

Family facilitators: key actors in the *Siyabathanda Abantwana* model

Family facilitators are women who are selected within the local community by the community itself at a community meeting. They typically volunteer or are nominated, and then are screened at a community meeting in a very public and transparent process on the basis of criteria such as commitment, love of children, responsibility and trustworthiness. Their role is to work with vulnerable children and their caregivers, also identified by the community, in order to build their resilience and prepare them for schooling. Each family facilitator is responsible for 8–10 children. Her support for the child takes the form of weekly visits to the family home where she plays with and stimulates the child, converses with and supports the caregiver, and develops a relationship of trust and support with them. Support might extend to areas such as helping the caregiver obtain a child-support grant and helping with the child's enrolment at a local school for the coming year. Family facilitators receive on-the-job training in the areas of community development and early childhood education. They are supported by a project co-ordinator and have access to resources such as a toy library and appropriate reading and writing materials.

Theoretical framing: relational pedagogy

Relational pedagogy sees relationality as the core element of pedagogy (Papatheodorou 2009). This includes the dialectical learning relation between learner and teacher, but also the relations between and among learners, between teacher and caregiver, and between the learning environment and the wider community in which it is situated. A relational pedagogy is underpinned by values of trust, interdependence, community, reciprocity and mutual respect encompassed by the African notion of *ubuntu*.

The ontological basis of relational pedagogy comprises an understanding of human existence as being-with-others and being-in-the-world. We are constituted through our relationships with others. This is not only in the crucial early years when the child's relationship with the primary caregiver is so formative of their identity, but throughout life. Similarly, relational pedagogy understands the situatedness of learning within particular cultural and socio-economic contexts. Learning is thus a situated and experiential activity which involves others in particular environments.

According to Brownlee and Berthelsen (2006: 24), relational pedagogy values the student's knowledge and processes of knowing, connects learning experiences with students' experiences, and promotes a constructivist perspective of knowing and learning. A key to this perspective is the relationship between the learner and the learner's knowledge and experiences, on the one hand; and the learning environment, on the other. Relational pedagogy stands in contrast to transmission-based pedagogies which see the teacher as the fount of all knowledge and learners as empty receptacles, pedagogy as a technical process of transmitting information from teacher to learner, and knowledge as a commodity which is consumed. A relational perspective on pedagogy is important in a world which reduces education to sets of measurable outcomes and abstracts content and process from the relationships which underpin them.

Dialogue, dialogic space and relationality

Relational pedagogy is also characterised in spatial terms as an 'in-between space occupied by all those involved in the learning process' (Papatheodorou 2009: 5). The Russian literary theorist Mikhail Bakhtin (1895–1975) and the Brazilian adult educator Paulo Freire (1921–1997) view dialogue as more than just a conversation between two people. For both, it is an ontological notion embracing the nature of human beings and the way that they learn (Rule 2010). Bakhtin and Freire share a profound ethical concern regarding the relationship between the self and the other. For Bakhtin, dialogue involves the whole of a person's being as it interacts with the other (Bakhtin 1981, 1984, 1986). He contrasts dialogue with monologue, which he sees as an authoritarian and inauthentic way of being which denies the other and treats him or her as an object. Freire views dialogue as central to learning. It involves a dialectic between teacher and learner in which they interact with each other as teacher-learners and learner-teachers. Through exploring generative themes that arise from their worlds, they learn to know not only 'the word' but also 'the world' (Freire 1972, 1998).

Drawing on Bakhtin, Freire and Martin Buber (1958), I bring the notions of dialogue and space together in the concept of 'dialogic space' (Rule 2004). Here 'space' is understood not as an empty place-holder but as socially, culturally and cognitively constructed (Lefebre 1991; Shields 1997). The 'space' is thus shaped by the human, cultural and material resources that participants bring to it, such as their particular personalities, the languages that they speak, and the furniture and artefacts that they use, and the assumptions and experiences they have.

Dialogic space refers to a learning space that involves the interaction between teachers and learners and their worlds through the exchange of codes, including language, movement and visual symbols. The learning space could be an actual place, such as a rural compound, or a virtual place, such as an electronic chat room.

Dialogic space is a normative notion in that it is underpinned by values of love, respect and trust, and provides a safe and supportive as well as challenging environment for learning. It involves dialogue at a number of levels, including dialogue between, among and within participants, dialogue across cultures and languages, and dialogue between discourses in which participants are situated. Dialogic learning spaces allow for movement, growth and change among participants, all of whom are learners at some level and who cross learning boundaries through their interaction with one another.

Dialogic space and boundary learning

Drawing on Bakhtin, Freire and Lev Vygotsky (1978), I see children as occupying a dialogic learning space which is characterised by a porous, shifting boundary between their own words and worlds and the words and worlds of others. Acts of learning take them across this boundary into the territory of the unfamiliar, from which they return with new ideas, concepts and experiences. The teacher, in turn, crosses the boundary into the learners' worlds as she learns about them, their experiences, words, games, songs and dances, their hopes and dreams for the future, their uncertainties and trepidations. The teacher's world is thus challenged and enlarged by her engagement with the children.

Boundary learning within a relational pedagogy framework eschews the traditional Western dichotomies of teacher/learner, home/school and body/mind by locating these within a relational learning space in which movement is the norm. The boundary is not some kind of permanent and fixed line of division between teacher and learner, but is rather a permeable and shifting threshold of contact and communication which is present both between teacher and learner, and within each teacher-learner and learner-teacher (Rule 2010). Within a dialogic approach to learning, both teacher and learner operate on and across this boundary in a zone of potentiality. As teacher-learner and learner-teacher, to use Freire's expression, they learn each other's words and worlds as they widen and deepen their respective understandings, and the boundary between them becomes a boundary within the self that they cross, transgress, redefine. Bakhtin understands this process as one of ideological becoming: 'the process of selecting and assimilating the words of others' (Bakhtin 1981: 341).

In this chapter I would like to develop the dialogic and spatial aspects of relational pedagogy by linking it to the notion of dialogic space and illustrating it with a South African example of ECD in a community context involving family facilitators and poor and vulnerable young children.

Methodology

This study adopted a case study approach which is characterised by an intensive focus on an instance in order to illuminate a broader set of cases (Bassey 1999; Yin 2009) that comprise community-based early childhood development initiatives. More specifically, it develops theory from a case with the hope that it may illuminate other cases that deal with poor and vulnerable young children in community contexts.

Case studies often make use of multiple methods and sources of information (Graham 2000; Simons 2009). The methods used here included observation of family facilitators' home visits and interactions with children and caregivers, as well as interviews of family facilitators and community members, and focus-group discussions with family facilitators and caregivers. The data were analysed thematically through a process of content analysis, while observational data were also analysed spatially to explore the relation between spatial and pedagogical dynamics.

Findings

Family facilitators as boundary mediators

For the children in the *Siyabathanda Abantwana* programme, the boundary between school and family often becomes a barrier. Given the lack of financial resources and educational support at home, children might either never attend school or drop out at an early stage. Interviews with and observations of family facilitators revealed that they mediate this boundary in their visits to the children by drawing on indigenous knowledge such as stories, songs and games in the local language, IsiZulu. The family facilitator also introduces school-type activities such as drawing, counting and group work. She develops a supportive relationship with the caregiver, encouraging him or her to engage in similar activities with the children. This support can extend to assisting the caregiver to make arrangements for the child to register for primary school; and accessing official documents for the child in order, for example, to secure a child–support grant or to visit the local clinic. Figure 16.2 below attempts to depict the mediating role of the family facilitator in her engagement with the child and caregiver/s.

Dialogue between home and school

The family facilitator creates a dialogue between the world of family and community and the world of school so that these two worlds do not exist as polar opposites for the child but rather in a dialogic relationship. She affirms the world of the home and the world of the caregiver, by drawing on the spatial, material and cultural

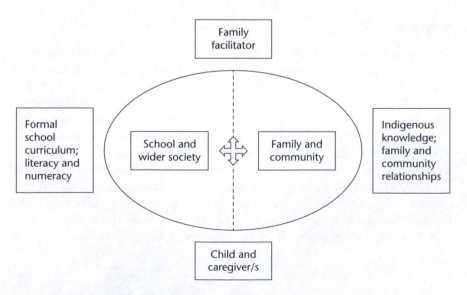

FIGURE 16.2 The *Siyabathanda Abantwana* project and boundary learning

resources of the home for learning purposes. These include the words, games, songs, dances, artefacts and relationships that come from the world of the home. At the same time, the family facilitator brings in new ideas, artefacts and practices from the world of the school – books, drawing, writing, counting and words – into the domestic learning space. The caregiver and her/his family admit this learning culture into their home, affirming and welcoming it, thus showing a hospitality to the world of learning that the family facilitator brings. This hospitality and openness create the conditions which transform the domestic space into a dialogic learning space.

At the same time, the family facilitator practises a 'learning hospitality' by inviting the caregiver's children into a learning space in which she is host, and modelling the role of educator-in-the-home for the caregiver. One example of this occurred when the family facilitator moved indoors into the rondavel from the hot sun with her group of children (Figure 16.3). She spread out a grass mat on the floor and sat with the seven children in a circle around her. She was thus drawing on the physical and spatial resources of the homestead (the mat, the rondavel). She took a book out of her toy bag and read it to the children, thus bringing the resources of the school into the home space. She allowed the children to handle and manipulate the book and to examine the pictures. She then sang a lullaby '*Thula mntwana*' ('Be still, my child') related to one of the pictures in the book, and the children joined in. She was drawing on the cultural resources, in the form of a lullaby, with which the children were familiar and brought with them from the home environment.

The small two-year-old child, who was sitting on the sofa with the caregiver, the grandmother, became interested in the group's activities, especially when the family facilitator found some paper and crayons in her bag and asked the children to draw a picture of what they wanted to be when they grew up. The small child left her grandmother on the sofa and joined the children in the circle, receiving a sheet of paper and crayons from the family facilitator and settling down to draw a picture. When she completed her drawing, the family facilitator lifted it and showed it to the grandmother. 'She is learning to draw today', remarked the grandmother in IsiZulu. The family facilitator and the grandmother both affirmed the child's new venture and encouraged her risk-taking, and her self-concept as a learner, as she crossed and recrossed the boundary of learning.

The self-concept of the child consists in the child's relationship with himself or herself (De Witt 2009). Relationships with others play a crucial role in informing the child's self-concept, particularly relationships with significant others such as parents, teachers and siblings. This child's understanding of herself as a learner – 'I can learn'; 'I am valued as a learner' – was affirmed through her interactions within the dialogic space of the group. Both the family facilitator and the caregiver affirmed the child's learner role by providing opportunities for her to learn, encouraging and supporting her in the process of learning. The child found it safe to move across the boundary of learning, from the known to the unknown and back again, each time expanding the range of words and practices that she can call her own.

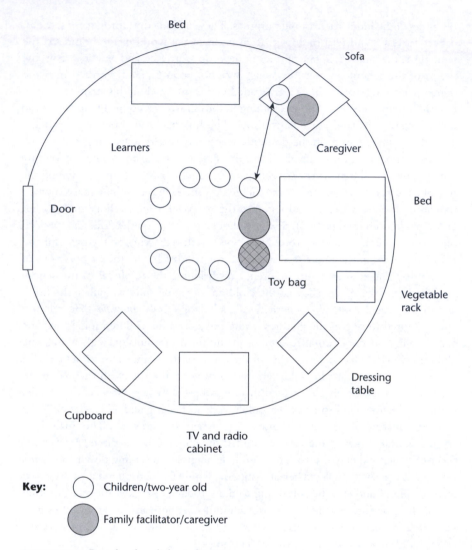

Bed

Sofa

Learners

Caregiver

Bed

Door

Toy bag

Vegetable
rack

Dressing
table

Cupboard

TV and radio
cabinet

Key: ◯ Children/two-year old

⬤ Family facilitator/caregiver

FIGURE 16.3 Rondavel as dialogic learning space

Adult–adult and adult–child dialogue

Another interesting dialogic aspect of the programme became evident through observing home visits undertaken by family facilitators. This was the two levels of communication in which the family facilitator engages within the caregiver's family home (in rural areas this typically consists of a compound with several huts, a yard and a garden). The first is a learning–caring dialogue with the children in which she structures activities, asks questions, listens to the children's stories, recognises individual contributions and provides affirmation. This typically happens within a learning circle in the compound yard or in one of the compound buildings, as

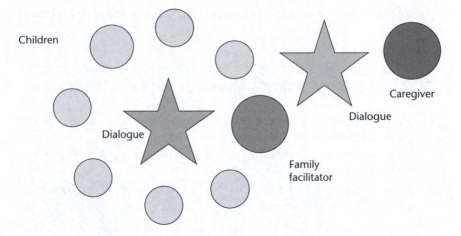

FIGURE 16.4 Adult–child and adult–adult dialogue in the *Siyabathanda Abantwana* programme

illustrated above. The second is a conversive–supportive dialogue with the caregiver which might include discussions about individual children, household problems, family relations and neighbourhood gossip. Through these interactions, the family facilitator builds relationships both with the children and with the caregiver, who often comes to view the family facilitator as a friend and confidant (Figure 16.4). Dialogue is thus essential to the relational pedagogy which the family facilitator adopts.

The learning–caring dialogue with the children and the conversive–supportive dialogue with the caregiver/s enable the family facilitator to establish and engage a porous learning boundary within the dialogic space of the compound. Her words provide pathways for both the children and caregiver to cross the boundary into her world, while their words give her access to their worlds. This kind of interaction is evidence of a relational pedagogy at work within the home and family context. There is emerging anecdotal evidence from schools (although this requires further research) that children who participate in the *Siyabathanda Abantwana* adapt well to the school environment and cope confidently with its demands.

Conclusion

In this chapter, I have tried to develop and exemplify the dialogic aspects of relational pedagogy (Brownlee and Berthelsen 2006; Papatheodorou 2009) with reference to the role of family facilitators in the *Siyabathanda Abantwana* programme. It has shown how dialogue is key to building relationships between family facilitators and both the children and the caregivers. Dialogue also plays an important role in enabling participants to cross the boundaries between the world of the home and the community, on the one hand, and the world of the school, on the other, within a dialogic learning space. A relational pedagogy within the context of the home and family can play a crucial role in providing vulnerable children with pathways to the wider world.

QUESTIONS FOR THINKING ABOUT POLICY AND PRACTICE

1. How can relational pedagogy link centre-based and family- and community-based early education?
2. What barriers might relational pedagogy encounter within family and community contexts?
3. What are the implications for policy of a community-based approach to early childhood development?

References

Bakhtin, M. (1981) *The Dialogic Imagination*, trans. C. Emerson and M. Holquist, Austin, TX: University of Texas Press.

Bakhtin, M. (1984) *Problems of Dostoevsky's Poetics*, trans. and ed. C. Emerson, Minneapolis, MN: University of Minnesota Press.

Bakhtin, M. (1986) *Speech Genres and Other Late Essays*, trans. V. McGee, Austin, TX: University of Texas Press.

Bassey, M. (1999) *Case Study Research in Educational Settings*, Buckingham: Open University Press.

Brownlee, J. and Berthelsen, D. (2006) Personal epistemology and relational pedagogy in early childhood teacher education programs, *Early Years*, 26(1): 17–29.

Buber, M. (1958) *I and Thou*, 2nd edn, New York: Scribners.

Campion, J. (1992) *Working with Vulnerable Young Children: Early Intervention*, London: Cassell.

Department of Education (2001) *White Paper Five on Early Childhood Education*, Pretoria: Government Printers.

Department of Health (2009) *2008 National Antenatal Sentinel HIV & Syphilis Prevalence Survey*, Pretoria: Department of Health.

De Witt, Marika (2009) *The Young Child in Context: A Thematic Approach*, Pretoria: Van Schaik.

Ebrahim, H. (2010) Tracing historical shifts in early care and education in South Africa, *Journal of Education*, 48: 119–136.

Ebrahim, H., Killian, B. and Rule, P. (2010) Practices of early childhood development practitioners for poor and vulnerable children from birth to four years in South Africa, *Early Childhood Development and Care*, 181(3): 387–396.

Freire, P. (1972) *Pedagogy of the Oppressed*, Harmondsworth: Penguin.

Freire, P. (1998) *Pedagogy of Hope: Reliving Pedagogy of the Oppressed*, New York: Continuum.

Graham, B. (2000) *Case Study Research Methods*, London: Continuum.

Human Sciences Research Council (2009) *South African National HIV Prevalence, Incidence, Behaviour and Communication Survey, 2008*, Pretoria: HSRC.

Lefebre, H. (1991) *The Production of Space*, Oxford: Blackwell.

LETCEE Director (2008) Personal communication on *Siyabathanda Abantwana* project, 15 July.

Papatheodorou, T. (2009) Exploring relational pedagogy, in T. Papatheodorou and J. Moyles (eds) *Learning Together in the Early Years: Exploring Relational Pedagogy*, London and New York: Routledge, pp. 3–18.

Rule, P. (2004) Dialogic spaces: adult education projects and social engagement, *International Journal of Lifelong Education*, 23(3): 319–334.

Rule, P. (2010) Bakhtin and Freire: Dialogue, dialectic and boundary learning, *Educational Philosophy and Theory*, 43(9): 924–942.

Rule, P., Ebrahim, H. and Killian, B. (2008) *Report on the Practice, Principles, Cost Drivers, Interventions, Methodologies and Stakeholder Analysis of the Project Based on the Concept of ECD Programmes as Resources for the Care and Support of Poor and Vulnerable Young Children: LETCEE* – Siyabathanda Abantwana *and Sikhulakahle Interventions*, Report submitted to UNICEF, 30 September, Pietermaritzburg: University of KwaZulu-Natal.

Shields, R. (1997) Spatial stress and resistance: social meanings of spatialization, in G. Benko and U. Strohmayer (eds) *Space and Social Theory: Interpreting Modernity and Postmodernity*, Oxford: Blackwell.

Simons, H. (2009) *Case Study Research in Practice*, Los Angeles, CA: Sage.

Statistics South Africa (2008) *General Household Survey*, available online at: www.statssa.gov.za (accessed 14 March 2010).

Statistics South Africa (2009) *Quarterly Labour Force Survey*, available online at: www.statssa.gov.za (accessed 14 March 2010).

UNESCO (2010) *Reaching the Marginalized: EFA Global Monitoring Report 2010*, Paris: UNESCO.

UNICEF (2005) *National Integrated Plan for Early Childhood Development in South Africa 2005–2010*, Pretoria: UNICEF.

Vygotsky, L.S. (1978) *Mind and Society: The Development of Higher Psychological Processes*, Cambridge, MA: Harvard University Press.

Yin, R.K. (2009) *Case Study Research*, 4th edn, Los Angeles, CA: Sage.

17

'ARCHITEXTURE'

Reading the early years environment

Jan Georgeson and Gill Boag-Munroe

OVERVIEW

This chapter presents the findings from an ongoing project to develop under-standing about how the physical environment of early years settings might influence the staff and families who use them. The co-occurrence of particular features of buildings with particular activities develops our expectations of the kinds of activity that might take place in different kinds of building; we therefore learn to 'read' buildings as texts – hence our adoption of the term 'architexture' – and while this may not be something that we can readily articulate, the combinations of sensory, social and cultural affordances of a building can affect how comfortable we feel when approaching, entering and using that building. We describe here what happened when we shared these ideas with early years practitioners to support them in thinking about their settings' build-ings and wider environment. This analysis enabled staff to evaluate the extent to which their buildings were 'hard to read' or 'easy to read'. We argue that such an analysis is particularly important when settings are trying to reach those participants or users who might be reluctant or uncertain users of the space.

Key words: Early years buildings; parental engagement; enabling environ-ments.

Introduction: places for children

The issue of place has emerged as significant at various points in the history of edu-cation outside the family for very young children; Montessori advocated miniature furniture and fittings in the 'Children's House', Margaret McMillan championed the open air nursery school and Reggio Emilia's famous pre-schools cite the environment as the 'Third Teacher'. However, while there are many countries where there has been a strong tradition of architectural design for children, this has not been the case in the UK and many settings here have operated in buildings designed for other purposes and adapted, more or less successfully, for use with young children (Penn 2000). Even in the process of adaptation, we appear not to adhere to the aesthetic standards we set when assembling our own lifestyle interiors, and fill nurseries with garish images, plastic kitsch and 'ugliness and clutter . . . colours and textures we would not tolerate in our own homes' (Goldschmeid and Jackson 1994: 17).

The wide range of buildings offering pre-school provision in England reflects over a century of different motivations for caring for and educating young children. Garland and White (1980), reviewing provision in the late 1970s, thought that they could detect echoes of the nineteenth-century and early twentieth-century traditions in some of the day nurseries in their study. They stated:

> However, looking back at some of the day nurseries we visited, it is hard not to feel that there existed a continuity of tradition between the dame schools . . . [where] the children were felt to be primitive and irrational creatures to be kept carefully and constantly controlled by the adult world.
>
> We can perceive a similar continuity of tradition between early nursery education [that is, the Froebelian tradition], in which the importance of the child itself was the rationale for the nursery's activities.
>
> (Garland and White 1980: 112)

In recent times, however, there was a sudden increase in new publicly funded buildings for children's services through the Sure Start initiative and subsequent rollout of Children's Centres that provide a range of services locally for children and their families, including childcare and early learning. The Children's Centre project has proceeded in three phases, and while many buildings in the first phase were architect-designed and purpose-built, in the third phase, Children's Centres were more likely to be found in existing buildings, often shared with schools or other services (DCSF 2007). Karen Buck (MP) (cited in *Children & Young People Now* 2010: n.p.) noted: 'The expansion has been driven at least as much in the later stages by what buildings were available rather than whether centres were being developed in exactly the right place and with the right facilities.'

Later in this chapter we will describe the experiences of two practitioners working in centres established in early and later phases of the Children's Centres project, but first we want to share our own experiences of this diversity of provision.

Origins of 'architexture'

While carrying out the fieldwork for the National Evaluation of the Early Learning Partnership Project (NEELPP) (Evangelou *et al.* 2008), we found ourselves visiting a wide range of buildings offering services for parents of young children, buildings which we had not visited before. Sometimes these buildings were hard to find and, even when we found them, difficult to get into, if you did not already know the way in. Once inside, the buildings often had a very different feel from each other. Sometimes we felt welcomed and comfortable, at other times we felt unsure of where we were supposed to go and what we were supposed to do in different spaces. And then we thought – if we are struggling with visiting these new buildings, how much more difficult must it be for anxious parents, who might be lacking self-confidence and unsure of what to expect? How would they feel approaching and entering these different buildings? We came back from our visits and exchanged stories about where we had been and how we had felt. This prompted us to consider how these anecdotal accounts of different buildings with different atmospheres might be usefully shared with others in a more principled way.

It became clear to us that we try to 'read' the buildings as we approach and enter, in the same way that we might read a book; hence our adoption of the term 'architexture'. We pick up on cues that we can interpret because of what we have learnt about buildings in the past, particularly buildings offering services for young children. We incorporate these cues into a whole to help us find our way and prepare us for what to expect inside and how we should behave.

We decided to develop a framework to help us understand how people 'read' spaces used for working with children. We started from the position that buildings and their contents communicate information about their use, and that elements of the way buildings appear are often associated with particular discourses. A shop might take on a different styling to appeal to a particular clientele; discourses of private, church or state education can be apparent in the physical features of school buildings, such as choice of font or logo on signs. If a particular discourse is evident in a building, this can shape the possibilities for acting for the people who use it. We noticed that some entrance areas were styled on McDonald's and some on hotel foyers, and these were associated with different kinds of behaviour from parents and children waiting there: one relaxed, dynamic and noisy; the other more restrained, perched on the edge of leather sofas, flicking through magazines with much shushing and glancing around. Physical factors, such as narrow pathways and poor illumination, can also shape behaviour and contribute to the overall feeling about what a visitor can or cannot do in the building.

We started to construct a discourse analytical method of understanding the possibilities and constraints of buildings used for early years services. We turned initially to Lefebvre's (1991) discussions about whether the space occupied by a social group or several social groups can be treated as a message. He argued that buildings, spaces, and identities are mutually constructed: '[s]ocial space contains a great diversity of objects, both natural and social, including networks and pathways which facilitate the exchange of material things and information. Such "objects" are thus not only things but relations' (Lefebvre 1991: 77). To this we would add that things and relations are necessarily, through their dialogical nature, dynamic and fluid. Any reading of spaces and interactions will therefore be relevant to a particular time and place. We added to this Gibson's concept of affordance, developed by Heft, that our perceptual experience includes not only the awareness of the structure of objects and events in the environment, but also an awareness of their functional significance, the opportunities they afford for action (Gibson 1979; Heft 1988).

Developing the framework

Using these ideas and drawing heavily on the work of O'Toole (2004) and his use of Halliday's (2004) lenses of textual, interpersonal and experiential meanings, we developed an analytic frame to produce a model to read the interaction of buildings and space. As part of his theory of language as systems that perform functions, Halliday (2004) identified three metafunctions, each of which is concerned with a different mode of meaning. Experiential metafunctions refer to physical sensations, mental states and functions which can be carried out. The interpersonal metafunction is about the social world, especially the relationship between agent (someone who has made decisions about content) and the receiver (someone who is interpreting or using what the agent has constructed). We interpreted this as referring to social and cultural aspects: what relationships with users are constructed, afforded or constrained, including which discourses are evoked by aspects of the building. The textual metafunction is about coherence and flow. We equated the textual metafunction with spatial and temporal relationships: how elements are placed in relation to each other and 'woven' together. For an extract of our analytical framework, see Table 17.1.

TABLE 17.1 Extract from the 'architexture' analytic frame

Function	Experiential (what happens and how the spaces and contents impact on the senses and emotions)	Interpersonal (social and cultural: what relationships with users are constructed, afforded or constrained)	Textual (spatial and temporal relationships: how elements are placed in relation to each other)
Level: Building	Sensory experience Mental states, e.g. security, comfort Function: • What target user does • What permanent inhabitants (staff) do, etc.	Perspective Ownership/agency Author Discourses used: • Formal/informal • Tone Power relationships Inclusion/exclusion, etc.	Cohesion Flow Reflectivity Geometry Balance (e.g. between dominant and marginal use; natural and man-made materials) Emplacement, etc.

Trying out the 'architexture' frame

We tried out our frame by carrying out analyses of the exterior of four buildings which we felt exemplified the models of building design used in the Sure Start programme, as identified by Ball and Niven (2005). The buildings we analysed differed in their 'designedness', ranging from a purpose-built Sure Start Children's Centre to a converted high-street shop. We presented our analytical frame and case studies at an international conference in San Diego (Boag-Munroe and Georgeson 2008). The analytic frame helped us to communicate some of our thoughts and feelings about these buildings to other people who knew nothing about UK services for children and families. It helped us to tell tales from the field about striking or disconcerting features and events and offered analysis above the level of anecdote. The analytic frame directed our gaze to physical features of buildings and spaces and the way these linked together, and offered a language in which we could begin to conceptualise and articulate recurrent themes and contradictions.

However, when we were talking to delegates about our analytic frame, one of them asked us: 'and what do practitioners think about your analysis? . . . and parents?' We realised that if our work was to have relevance outside academic discussions about analytic frames and techniques, we needed to find out whether our approach had any resonance with people working in or using early years settings. We decided therefore to incorporate the idea of 'architexture' into professional development sessions for early years practitioners. We asked a group of practitioners to exchange photographs and vision statements from their settings. All settings had an explicit focus on welcoming families from all parts of the community, including those who might be less likely to engage with Children's Services. How early years buildings signal who might use them was therefore an important issue. Some settings were sited in generally affluent areas while others were located in pockets of deprivation. The practitioners were then introduced to the 'architexture' frame and explored how the approach to and exterior of each other's settings reflected their vision. This led to animated discussion about the extent to which it was possible to understand what happened in their buildings from the outside and, in two instances, to further investigation of the response of parents to the buildings. These are discussed next.

Setting 1: a new children's centre

Vicki had already shared with the group some of the difficulties which she was encountering in her role as family support worker in a new Sure Start Children's Centre in a relatively affluent area. She and her colleagues were finding that parents were confused about what the centre was for. It was located behind a leisure centre and parents were turning up at the door trying to drop their children off in the Children's Centre while they were attending gym sessions. They thought it was offering crèche facilities. So Vicki carried out an analysis of the exterior and approach, which suggested that the messages provided by the signage and positioning of the centre were creating problems. She asked parents for their comments and these mainly confirmed her analysis:

I got very confused when first visiting as I went through the crèche entrance and walked into a breast feeding group, when I only wanted information . . . Although [the] staff's welcoming, the building was not so friendly at first until you look round.

(Shirley)

If I didn't know the area I would have struggled to find the road as it's not signposted off any of the main roads. When you arrive at the entrance to both Leisure and Children's Centre, the Children's Centre's still not signposted that well. I followed the sign and was directed round the back of the building. It felt a little intimidating at first trying to decide which entrance to use, as I felt other people were looking at me.

(Andrea)

I think that the wording can be misunderstood, because to me 'Crèche Entrance' [the sign above one of the doors] implies that you provide childcare but you don't, only parent and toddler groups, and then you have to walk around the side [to another door] just to get information. Once you have been a few times you know just to head to the crèche entrance where staff always give a warm welcome.

(Natasha)

However, it was not a problem for one of the more confident members of the group: 'It's obvious init, just follow the signs!! Duh!!' (Sophie).

Vicki concluded from her analysis that *experientially* the function of the building was not clear and the signage often made it difficult to access. *Interpersonally* parents voiced their unease about being watched approaching the centre and revealed that they sometimes arrived feeling anxious. This raised concerns for Vicki about whether the approach and exterior might prove too much of a barrier for less confident parents, the very group whom they were trying to reach. Finally, *textually*, the Children's Centre, tucked away at the far corner of the site behind the main building, was positioned as marginal in comparison with the leisure centre, suggesting a lesser role. As a result, an extra sign has now been added to the corner of the leisure centre to direct parents round to the back of the building, but the Children's Centre remains a building that is hard to reach and hard to read.

Setting 2: a day nursery in an established community centre

Michele uploaded photographs of the interior of her day nursery setting for us to share during sessions, and explained that it was located within a community centre. We met up later on site and carried out an analysis of the approach, exterior and interior of the community centre and nursery. This revealed strong textual cohesion through repetition of geometric motifs and an inclusive ethos through attention to the whole experience of access (signage, width of doorways, clear parking for cars and buggies, open access to computers, clear view of reception for wheelchair users). There was also clear identification with community, both as a seaside resort, through sand/sky/sea colour scheme and seaside photographs, and with the local church through the prominent position of the chapel entrance in the central area. We concluded that this was a well-used and popular building that people could 'read' easily.

However, although everything else in the community centre was easy to access, the nursery where Michele worked was hard to spot unless you already knew it was there. It was located at the end of a short, dimly lit corridor with no signs. When visitors arrived on site, the helpful receptionist directed them by pointing to a large mural (which made no reference to the nursery) on the wall of the corridor.

Michele decided to carry out a short survey to find out what parents using the community centre felt about the centre and the day nursery. Parents reported that:

- They liked the facilities, especially the café and opportunities to attend different groups.
- They found the centre 'convenient', 'affordable' and 'non-judgmental'.
- They felt comfortable there; 'people understood'; 'it's OK if children are noisy'.
- Most parents said that they had found out about the nursery by word of mouth.

We concluded therefore that *experientially* the attention to access arrangements and the anticipation of needs of families put people at their ease. The centre functioned well as part of the community. *Textually* the setting was internally coherent and the arrangement of separate spaces round a central communal café area meant it worked well as a meeting place. *Interpersonally* it was easy for parents with young children to meet in the café, and to talk to people who share their interests, anxieties and triumphs, in separate spaces where appropriate. But Michele's day nursery relied on word of mouth to connect it to the life of the centre, so this potentially made it less accessible to parents who, for whatever reason, might not interact.

Response to the 'architexture' analytic frame

We concluded that the analytic frame had encouraged practitioners to look at details that they might have stopped seeing because they knew their buildings so well. The analytic frame oriented them to the interpersonal and textural aspects of the building, as well as to the more obvious experiential elements and encouraged them to consider how the buildings might appear to and be experienced by parents, children and other members of the community.

We discussed with them how useful they found the analytic frame. Some words suggested by O'Toole (2004), like chthonicity (relationship to the earth), had been omitted because they were not words the practitioners (or the researchers!) would use. However, other words we had originally omitted, like 'author' because we thought that practitioners would find this difficult to understand in the context of buildings, had to be reinstated, because of the constant references (not often complimentary!) by practitioners to whomever it was who had designed the buildings.

The practitioners clearly responded to this unknown 'author' (usually assumed to be a male architect with no experience of looking after children) at a personal rather than an abstract level, so 'author' was returned to the list of interpersonal aspects.

Feedback revealed, however, that practitioners would prefer a more user-friendly format with examples, instead of a matrix of nouns. The practitioners who attended the session explained that they had learned more from the way we talked through case studies using the three metafunctions as lenses than from discussing the frame itself. This has been taken into consideration in the design of future sessions.

Some implications for policy

The analysis enabled practitioners to consider the extent to which their buildings were 'hard to read' or 'easy to read'; were they offering clear, consistent messages about whether the space might be somewhere parents would wish to enter and about the kind of things they could do inside? Such an analysis is particularly important when settings are trying to reach parents who might be reluctant or uncertain users of the space, and in particular those parents who might be hard to engage in a genuine partnership in which they feel that their contribution to their children's learning is valued (see Boag-Munroe, Chapter 15). The Children's Centre is a new hybrid kind of building; its identity, purpose and ownership may well be unfamiliar to potential users (whether parents, practitioners, or the general public) and the way in which buildings are presented, or rebranded, is likely to affect how they attract and engage parents. The two settings described here relied on parents being, to a certain extent, 'in the know' about what services they could expect and where they could find them. In both cases, the practitioners who carried out the analyses with us concluded that the way their buildings were presented meant they might still be failing to reach some of the parents who needed their services the most.

When we turned to the literature for guidance on how other people might be constructing understandings about buildings for early years services in the UK, we found limited material. However, a CABE/DCSF (2008) guidance document for those building Sure Start Children's Centres, and the research report from Ball and Niven (2005) offered a valuable starting point for understanding Sure Start Children's Centres and how parents respond to them, though there appear to be contradictions in their positions. The illustrations in the CABE/DCSF guidance (especially pp. 17 and 27) suggest that high-ceilinged, high-windowed open spaces are to be preferred, while Ball and Niven's (2005) research found that parents disliked high atriums as they were echoey and intimidating. The practitioners we spoke to agreed with this assessment of the acoustic problems of high-ceilinged rooms.

Both sources point to the tension between the need for security in and around the buildings, and the need to create the sense of openness and ease of access. The requirement to keep children safe can affect the welcoming aspect of the buildings. The CABE/DCSF guide points to reception areas that have glass windows allowing for clear visibility of offices behind, while Ball and Niven (2005) report that parents find such screens suggest division between 'them' and 'us'; the open dual-height reception desk in setting two, discussed above, was one of the features that made the building feel accessible. Ball and Niven found that families responded to the visual impression of the building and spaces. 'Parents are attracted to buildings which clearly signal the association with young children through design features or decoration: murals, outdoor play equipment, child–friendly garden furniture for example' (Ball and Niven 2005: 4).

These remarks draw attention to the impression that settings might construct, if they position these objects where they can be viewed from outside, and to cues that parents might be using in assessing the suitability of an early years space for them and their children. However, some of the practitioners we spoke to from more affluent areas reported that the exterior (and often the interior) of their shared community buildings had to have all traces of child-presence removed from view. We detected two different cultural motivations for this: (i) the desire to maintain an aesthetically pleasing environment free from clutter that would win the approval of lifestyle gurus; and (ii) the need to hide children away from predatory strangers who would wish them harm. This second discourse of extreme security was called on by staff in Michele's setting to explain why the day nursery was the only facility in the community centre that was not signed. It was the only area where parents left their children for long periods (usually while they worked).

While clear signals about children's presence constitute obvious aspects of buildings to which parents could make explicit reference, there are other less obvious features that might nonetheless also contribute to their enjoyment of the building. For example, parents are likely to be sensitive to the extent to which a building affords ease of access, particularly if they usually push prams, buggies or wheelchairs. According to Gibson (1979), this kind of information in the environment guides behaviour directly without awareness; hence, parents might be unaware of why they find trips to some settings a pleasure (ramps), and others a struggle (steps).

Our aim in exploring 'architexture' was to produce an analytic frame which might assist thinking about the physical, social and cultural aspects of spaces where work with children is carried out, and to show how it might be used to offer a reading of contrasting spaces used in early years work. If parents are unsure about what particular buildings are, how they work and what they are supposed to use them for, this may ultimately affect take-up of services, particularly by parents from marginalised groups.

QUESTIONS FOR THINKING ABOUT POLICY AND PRACTICE

1. Imagine you are a new parent visiting an early years setting. What would help you feel comfortable approaching and entering the building?
2. Many early years settings share their premises with other users. What are the advantages and disadvantages of this?

3. Security concerns prompt some early years settings to 'hide' the fact that children attend. What effects might this have on children, families and staff?

Acknowledgement

Our thanks go to Vicki Axford and Michele Budgen for their enthusiastic collaboration on this project.

References

Ball, M. and Niven. L (2005) *Buildings in Sure Start Local Programmes*, Nottingham: DfES Publications, available online at: www.ness.bbk.ac.uk/implementation/documents/328. pdf (accessed 17 August 2011).

Boag-Munroe, G. and Georgeson, J. (2008) Spatial semiotics of early years settings and the kinds of identity they might construct, Paper to accompany poster presented at the First UK and Ireland ISCAR Conference, Bath, July and ISCAR, San Diego, September.

CABE/DCSF (2008) *Sure Start: Every Building Matters*, London: DCSF, available online at: http://webarchive.nationalarchives.gov.uk/20110118095356 or http:/www.cabe.org.uk/ files/sure-start-every-building-matters.pdf (accessed 17 August 2011).

Children and Young People Now (2010) Early years – Race to the children's centre target, 26 January, available at: www.cypnow.co.uk/news/979402/Early-years–Race-childrens-centre-target (accessed 17 August 2011).

Department for Children, Schools and Families (DCSF) (2007) *Sure Start Children's Centres: Phase 3 Planning and Delivery*, Nottingham: DCSF, available online at: www.education.gov.uk/ publications/eOrderingDownload/DCSF-00665-2007.pdf (accessed 17 August 2011).

Evangelou, M., Sylva, K., Edwards, A. and Smith, T. (2008) *Supporting Parents in Promoting Early Learning: The Evaluation of the Early Learning Partnership Project*, Report No. DCSF-RR039, Nottingham: DCSF, available at www.education.gov.uk/publications/RSG/ EarlyYearseducationandchildcare/Page6/DCSF-RR039 (accessed 6 June 2011).

Garland, C. and White, S. (1980) *Children and Day Nurseries: Management and Practice in Nine London Day Nurseries*, London: Grant McIntyre Ltd.

Gibson, J.J. (1979) *The Ecological Approach to Visual Perception*, Boston: Houghton-Mifflin.

Goldschmeid, R. and Jackson, S. (1994) *People under Three: Young Children in Day Care*, London: Routledge.

Halliday, M. A. K. (2004) *An Introduction to Functional Grammar* (revised by C.M.I.M. Matthiessen), 3rd edn, London: Arnold.

Heft, H. (1988) Affordances of children's environments: A functional approach to environmental description, *Children's Environment Quarterly*, 5(3): 29–37.

Lefebvre, H. (1991) *The Production of Space*, trans. D. Nicholson-Smith, Oxford: Blackwell Publishing.

O'Toole, M. (2004) Opera Ludentes: The Sydney Opera House at work and play, in K. O'Halloran (ed.) *Multimodal Discourse Analysis: Systemic Functional Perspectives*, London: Continuum.

Penn, H. (ed.) (2000) *Early Childhood Services: Theory, Policy and Practice*, Buckingham: Open University Press.

CONCLUSION

Theodora Papatheodorou

It is evident in this volume that early childhood provision now has a central place in policy at international and national level. Research which has demonstrated the accrued value of early childhood provision for children and society has been the cornerstone of policies that set out aspirational outcomes for children and the world they inhabit. In many ways early childhood has become the battleground of many governments to win the war against individual and societal deprivation and poverty. To achieve this, there are calls for setting out standards of quality for early childhood provision and benchmarking for expected outcomes for children (and, in effect, families and communities) through, for example, curricula frameworks, children's assessment and programme evaluation. At the same time, there are concerns that top-down streamlined policies and standardised quality indicators are not the panacea.

As early childhood grabbed the attention and interest of politicians and governments and investment increased, so did the researchers' efforts to interrogate and critique policy and to research practices that derived from such policies. Indeed, during the last two decades, we witnessed a large body of research, conducted by researchers and academics, policy makers and implementers and, most importantly, practitioner-researchers. Children have also become not only the subject of research, but active participants in research processes. It appears that research in the field gradually started to become more democratic, rooted in a strong ethical framework, to reflect multiple perspectives and voices.

It is evident from the range of topics researched and discussed in this volume that the role of the early years workforce is of paramount significance. A well-educated and trained workforce will be able to question and interrogate policies and their own practices to provide enabling pedagogical cultures and encounters, where:

- children's dispositions and learning potential are appreciated and fostered;
- the influence of language and culture on thinking is acknowledged in planning activities and the environment;

- children's educational inclusion and well-being are promoted through functional multi-professional practice;
- families experience fewer barriers to reaching services;
- relational pedagogy is practised to bring about professional, community and inter-generational learning;
- training goes beyond rushed and technocratic approaches to offer time and space for developing a pedagogical base for reflective practice;
- professional barriers are explored and negotiated.

Whilst policy sets outs the general values, principles and requirements for early childhood provision and practice, it is the early years practitioner who is called to interpret and implement policy. This call is an onerous one and requires practitioners who are able to balance the tensions between many policy priorities, personal and professional values, and local cultures, needs and resources, without losing sight of the child.

The chapters in this volume indicate that localised, needs-based and resource-affordable policies and practices are better placed to achieve outcomes that are universally valued and appreciated and to which everyone aspires. Indeed, whilst a lot of policy and practice borrowing is happening, this is not uncritically adopted. To quote Rosenthal (2003: 104), borrowed ideas and concepts are interrogated and scrutinised in the light of the 'cultural scripts' of the borrower. Gradually, a dynamic process of assimilation and accommodation takes place between the 'new' and the 'known' to arrive at 'hybrid' policies and practices that are meaningful and functional in the culture and context of the borrower. Any policy and practice borrowing which remains de-contextualised and irrelevant to users can only alienate and disengage them from the relevant processes.

Moss (2003: 16) reminds us that, 'What we see as "best practice" today may not seem so in another generation, nor will it necessarily be viewed as such from the perspectives of those countries or groups who prefer different approaches or who have different traditions.' The same argument is equally applicable to what might be perceived as 'best' or 'streamlined' policy. This message has been further supported by the contributors to this volume. Their work highlights the importance of understanding the diversity and complexity of experience at different times and in different places, and over time and across places (cultural and historical dimensions of experience) and illustrates the dialectic nature of policy and practice rather than the unidirectional influence of policy on practice. A holistic approach to children's development and learning potential requires a holistic understanding of the field. This involves responsiveness to change and a capacity to negotiate conflicting and competing ideas, in order to inform meaningful policies and practices.

QUESTIONS FOR THINKING ABOUT POLICY AND PRACTICE

1. In which ways would the research discussed in this volume change your practice?
2. Which topics discussed in this volume are pertinent to your context and why?
3. Which issues would you like to be researched further in your own context and why?

References

Moss, P. and Brannen, J. (2003) Concepts, relationships and policies, in J. Brannen and P. Moss (eds) *Rethinking Children's Care*, Buckingham: Open University Press.

Rosenthal, M. (2003) Quality in early childhood education and care, *European Early Childhood Education Research Journal*, 11(2): 101–116.

AUTHOR INDEX

Numbers in bold are references to pictures or diagrams

SUBJECT INDEX

Numbers in bold are references to pictures or diagrams